W9-COP-746

MASCULINITY IN CRISIS

Masculinity in Crisis

Myths, Fantasies and Realities

Roger Horrocks

Consultant Editor
Jo Campling

St. Martin's Press

First published in Great Britain 1994 by
THE MACMILLAN PRESS LTD
Houndmills, Basingstoke, Hampshire RG21 2XS
and London
Companies and representatives
throughout the world

A catalogue record for this book is available
from the British Library.

ISBN 0–333–59322–7 hardcover
ISBN 0–333–59323–5 paperback

Printed in Great Britain by
Antony Rowe Ltd
Chippenham, Wiltshire

First published in the United States of America 1994 by
Scholarly and Reference Division,
ST. MARTIN'S PRESS, INC.,
175 Fifth Avenue,
New York, N.Y. 10010

ISBN 0–312–12020–6 (cloth)
ISBN 0–312–12021–4 (paper)

Library of Congress Cataloging-in-Publication Data
Horrocks, Roger.
Masculinity in crisis : myths, fantasies, and realities / Roger
Horrocks.
p. cm.
Includes bibliographical references and index.
ISBN 0–312–12020–6. — ISBN 0–312–12021–4 (pbk.)
1. Men. 2. Masculinity (Psychology) 3. Sex role. I. Title.
HQ1090.J6 1994
155.3'32—dc20 93-37500
CIP

In memory of my grandfathers
Bob Horrocks and Tommy Nunnington

the old is dying and the new cannot be born.

Antonio Gramsci

Contents

Acknowledgements

Many of the ideas in this book have been discussed with other people, and frequently borrowed from them. In this sense, writing is a social act, and I owe a great debt to many people.

Many professionals in the psychotherapy world have helped me over the last twenty years. In particular I thank Tom Feldberg, John Costello, Sybilla Madigan and Alan Danks.

To my own clients I owe an incalculable debt. Psychological theory has paled into insignificance next to their flesh and blood lives, which have moved me, amazed me, saddened me, angered me, and above all taught me. As Goethe said, theory is grey, but the tree of life is green.

Someone else said that friendship is the bread of life, and my own friends have nourished me hugely – it seems rather understated to thank them for that, but I do: in particular Simon Jackson, Richard Mitchell, Valerie Streater, Victoria Zinovieff, Hilary Horrocks, and the late Norman Farebrother.

A special thanks to Alix Pirani who encouraged me to express my ideas about 'the feminine' four years ago.

I am very grateful to my editor Jo Campling who has been both informative and supportive, and also to Belinda Holdsworth at Macmillan. The anonymous reviewer pointed out many flaws of form and content and has helped make this a much better book: I am indebted to him.

The staff of the Library of University College, London, have been unfailingly helpful.

My biggest thanks go to my parents, and to Rachel and Adam, my own family.

1 Introduction

This book argues that masculinity in Western society is in deep crisis. The masculine gender has all kinds of benefits, but it also acts as a mask, a disguise, and what in psychotherapy is called a 'false self'. But who are we behind the false self?

But more than this, I shall suggest that masculinity *is a crisis* for men today – that the masculine gender is a precarious and dangerous achievement and is highly damaging to men.

For the past two or three decades we have become used to feminism showing the damaging effects of gender inequality on women. It has often been assumed that men, in their positions of dominance, have the most exciting and rewarding careers, feel more powerful in their public and private lives, and are generally favoured over women. While there is clearly some cogency to these arguments, I have found in my work that in fact many men are haunted by feelings of emptiness, impotence and rage. They feel abused, unrecognized by modern society. While manhood offers compensations and prizes, it can also bring with it emotional autism, emptiness and despair.

Many of the ideas in this book come out of my work as a psychotherapist. I work with both men and women, and today I see individuals wrestling with fundamental questions of identity and meaning. But – and in many ways this was the motive for writing this book – I don't see men feeling less confused or less in pain than women.

In the last two decades feminism has obviously been primarily concerned with the subordinate place of women in society, and with the negative ways in which men treat women. There has been a lot of anger, resentment and hurt expressed in the feminist writings, and so the view of men found in them has not been a flattering one. There is no point complaining about that – it is surely right that women have been able to find their voice and express their demands, their resentments, sense of injustice and so on. In fact, feminism has been able to mount a profound critique of patriarchal society as an unjust system.

But men have been relatively silent. There has not been much of a debate or argument about these issues. Some men have agreed with much of the feminist position and have made their own critical analyses of male domination.[1] Gay men have produced their own analysis of sexuality and gender, and have generally been sympathetic to feminism in the sense that they were also concerned to distance themselves from the traditional image of the heterosexual male.[2] And there is some evidence of a backlash against feminism – for example in books like David Thomas's *Not Guilty*.[3] And surely many men have tried to ignore the whole issue, either hoping it will blow over, or that their own life can go on unaffected by it.

But there are signs that gender is becoming an important topic and a crisis for non-gay men as well, and that masculinity itself needs to be critically examined as a whole. Certainly in my work I am reminded daily that being male is not a comfortable or 'natural' position for some men.

Thus the debate must be joined. It is the turn of men to begin to articulate their ideas and feelings about gender, and how the masculine gender acts as a comfort, a prison, a buttress, a poison, or whatever.

It is surely significant that in many bookshops the sections that used to be named 'Women's Studies' are being renamed 'Gender Studies'. I shall assume in this book that gender is a structural phenomenon: that is, the masculine and feminine determine each other, are in a relationship with each other. 'Masculinity' cannot therefore be viewed as an isolated phenomenon.

There are two central concepts that are crucial to my account of masculinity. First, one must distinguish sex identity (the male/female distinction) from gender identity (the masculine/feminine distinction). The first is assigned at birth according to physical characteristics, particularly the external genitals. But gender is a complex set of collective attitudes, roles and fantasies that are assigned in the family in a more unpredictable manner. We might assume that boys are encouraged to be masculine, but some are not, and there are some who are encouraged to be feminine. The interrelations between sex, gender and sexual orientation are complex, confused and not predictable in a one-to-one manner.

The second core idea is the notion of gender as an unconscious formation. I feel that in the study of gender there is a lot of confusion about the nature of the conscious and unconscious parts of the psyche, and the ways in which society itself is – or is not – an unconscious dynamism. Did men create patriarchal society? Do men keep women subjugated? If so, are men more conscious than women? How does a new consciousness of gender arise? How do men become masculine – or, *how do they become men*? If gender is 'socially constructed' or 'invented', then how does this happen? Who does the constructing? These are key questions. If we ignore them, then we fall into the traps of voluntarism (men consciously plot everything) or biologism (men are innately masculine). We also fall into the trap of empiricism – there are plenty of facts around, but how do they cohere?

But the analysis of gender cannot be a purely philosophical or detached activity – I write as a passionate participant, with all the feelings that I have about being a man today: anger, sadness, fear, bewilderment, joy. The critique of gender is therefore part of the struggle against traditional masculine conditioning – for example, the view that feelings properly belong to women, and that men are rational (if violent) creatures.

And the critique of gender must connect with a hope for change. But why should men change? If they are the dominant sex, it would seem in their interest to resist change, and many of them do. Furthermore, moral exhortation and rational demonstrations of the injustice done to women will probably prove of limited value. That is why I feel it is of great importance to demonstrate how much gender divisions hurt men, and in fact how much patriarchy hurts and disempowers men.

What is the origin of gender? Today some fairly sophisticated models of gender have been constructed and tested. For example, social anthropology has produced powerful evidence as to the ways in which different cultures condition their men, so as to carry out certain tasks which are necessary to that society's survival.[4] Feminist sociology has begun to deconstruct 'masculinity' itself, and the term 'masculinities' has been adopted, since there is clearly not a homogeneous monolithic identity possessed by all men in all contexts.[5] Certain social historians are carrying out the invaluable task of investigating the history of gender, in the process demolishing the notion that masculinity (and femininity), and heterosexuality (and homosexuality), are fixed inviolable categories.[6] The psychoanalyst Robert Stoller devoted nearly forty years of work to the study of gender, and produced a body of psychodynamic analysis that is both theoretically coherent and empirically well grounded.[7] Thus the historical and psychological relativity of gender has been well established: there do not seem to be absolute or inviolable gender traits or activities. What is more problematical is the relevance of these theories to each other: are they compatible?

This book concentrates on the psychological analysis of masculinity, but this has followed paths which are relatively separate from gender studies in sociology and feminism (although feminism has certainly been interested in psychoanalysis). I have therefore attempted to construct some kind of 'dialogue' between the two sides. I am not a sociologist, so my inspection of sociological literature and its philosophical underpinning is necessarily limited, but I hope that there is some value in looking at the ways in which words such as 'gender', 'power', 'family', 'mothering' are used in social science and in the psychotherapies.

ORGANIZATION OF THE BOOK

The book falls naturally into two halves. The following four chapters provide some background to the different ways in which gender, and specifically masculinity, have been studied in different disciplines. Thus Chapters 2–5 are more theoretical than the remaining five chapters, which look at some concrete aspects of masculinity.

Chapter 2 gives some of the background to the development of gender studies – how feminism raised it from a relatively unconscious state, and how some sociologists have continued this study. Chapter 3 examines the way in which the concept of power is treated in feminist sociology and psychotherapy, and Chapter 4 considers the value of Marxist and anthropological accounts of gender and patriarchy, and again how they might relate to psychological theories.

Chapter 5 presents a condensed account of psychodynamic theories of gender – how the male infant acquires his sense of himself as a masculine being through his relations with his parents.

Chapters 6 to 10 present more empirical material about masculinity – the various ways in which gender seems to circumscribe and damage men. I have tried to use a variety of sources for this material: from my work as a therapist, but also from literature, film, crime, music, politics and from my own life.

A final point about terminology: the word 'psychology' is ambiguous – it can refer to academic psychology as well as psychotherapeutic psychology, and these are quite distinct disciplines – so I have tended to avoid it, except in phrases such as 'depth psychology', 'Freudian psychology', and so on.

2 Exploring Gender

Manhood is complicated. If we take a particular social setting – say a football game, a wedding, a crowded bar, a family watching TV, a war – how can we describe what the men involved are doing? How can we begin to describe their beliefs, attitudes, feelings? They are all males – the footballers, most of the football fans, the bridegroom at the wedding, the men in the bar, father and son in a family scene, men fighting in war. In fact, we might give up in despair and decide they have nothing in common except the shape of their bodies.

Forty years ago Simone de Beauvoir said this: 'A man would never set out to write a book on the peculiar situation of the human male.'[1] Yet more and more men are sitting down to write such books, and feminists have been trying to understand men for the past three decades. After the enormous surge of feminism, we can see signs that men and masculinity are being brought into the spotlight, are being discussed more, 'problematized'.

And in that trickle of books and articles, the term 'masculinities' has become important. Yet if we look at my brief vignettes we can see why the plural seems necessary. We might not be able to describe a homogeneous masculinity which could encompass the behaviour and attitudes of those boys and men, but we can begin to describe the different contexts they are in, their different personalities, the different tasks they are involved in. The sociologist David Morgan defends the use of the plural word as follows: 'our use of the term "masculinities" is a theoretical and political strategy designed to deconstruct conventional stereotypes which may get in the way of understanding the workings of patriarchy'.[2]

It makes sense to see masculinity as heterogeneous, contextually sensitive, interrelational. It's not something you carry round with you like an identity tag. It's not fixed but fluid. For example, I am a very different person with my female partner, my son, my clients, an intimate male friend, my father, my mother, my dog, at a football match, at a meeting of psychotherapists – furthermore in each situation my behaviour is not fixed. My male identity is protean, fluid, adaptable.

Furthermore, as Morgan points out, masculinity has been a relatively unconscious part of social, political and psychological identity and power. It has been taken for granted throughout the history of patriarchal society as a kind of 'force of nature' – therefore it needs to be broken down and forced into consciousness.

In this chapter I want to give a brief sketch of the background to the study of masculinity. How has it been foregrounded in recent years both as an academically interesting topic and a newsworthy one?

A CONTEMPORARY CRISIS?

It seems a straightforward assumption to make that 'new-wave' feminism, that is, the feminism arising in the sixties and continuing ever since, has produced a crisis of masculinity. This view can be found in a number of writers on men: 'One of the central difficulties in writing about masculinity, is that as a topic, it did not really exist until feminists began to attack the presuppositions of traditional political and social theory.'[3]

Thus masculinity as a 'theorized' and deconstructed topic is new. None the less I think that writers, artists and philosophers have been pondering the problematic nature of manhood for a long time in a more unconscious way. Indeed if we accept that male identity is to a large extent tied up with patriarchy and its rule, then it's likely that the stability and confidence of the male identity has always fluctuated as the patriarchal system itself undergoes shocks, disasters on the one hand, and triumphs on the other hand.

Thus in her book *West of Everything*, Jane Tompkins ascribes the rise of the Hollywood western to a crisis in masculinity, arising from the growing power of women and 'feminine concerns' during the nineteenth century in America. She describes how women introduced a number of social issues into political debate, and campaigned actively for them. There was a whole range of 'feminine literature' of the time which Tompkins sees as championing certain values: a Christian, charitable, sentimental spirit. Her view is that men felt threatened by this, and the western arose as a reassertion of masculine values, to combat the 'suppression of male desire and devaluation of male experience [that] followed from women's occupying the moral high ground of American culture for most of the previous century'.[4]

And long before 1960s feminism we find individual thinkers and writers critically examining male identity: for example, in 1930, D. H. Lawrence launched a blistering critique of the 'modern man':

> Tortured and cynical and unbelieving, he has let all his feelings go out of him, and remains a shell of a man, very nice, very pleasant, in fact the best of modern men. Because nothing really moves him except one thing, a threat against his own safety ... But he feels nothing ... the woman concerned is apt to go a little mad. She gets no more responses.

The fight has suddenly given out. She throws herself against a man, and he is not there, only the sort of glassy image of him receives her shock and feels nothing.[5]

Lawrence was apt to become rather off-balance when he talked about men and women, and increasingly advocated all kinds of bizarre solutions (men should wear red trousers!), and went in search of extreme solutions himself. But his analysis of men is rather similar to the one I shall give in Chapter 7, on Male Autism – he describes the man who does not feel, but only thinks, and finds it hard to relate to others. And Lawrence traces the development of this passionless being back through centuries of European history. In an untitled essay he berates eighteenth-century French culture:

The trouble with the 'good man' is that he's only one part of a man. The eighteenth century, like a vile Shylock, carved a pound of flesh from the human psyche, conjured with it like a cunning alchemist, set it smirking, called it a 'good man' – and lo! we all began to reduce ourselves to this little monstrosity.[6]

And Lawrence sees the great disaster in the eighteenth century as the loss of passion: 'The *homme de bien*, the "good man", performs the robot trick of isolating himself from the great passions. For the passion of life he substitutes the reasonable social virtues.'[7]

In a rather different context, T. S. Eliot made a parallel analysis. Writing of the seventeenth-century Metaphysical poets such as John Donne, he claimed that they were radically different from modern poets, in that they did not separate thought from feeling, and he ascribed this difference to a fracture in the human psyche: 'In the seventeenth century a dissociation of sensibility set in, from which we have never recovered.'[8]

Eliot is not writing specifically about men, but we can link his claim with Lawrence's – the suggestion is that the Renaissance itself (and the Reformation), with its development of reason, science, objectivity, caused a fundamental crisis in human beings: they began to separate thought from feeling, science from religion.[9] One might conjecture that in this division, men tended to be allocated the rational side of life, and women the non-rational.

Thus we might end up with the rather sweeping claim that men and masculinity have been in crisis for at least three hundred years!

It is a rather difficult claim to substantiate, since we have to depend on our own intuitions about the *Zeitgeist* of an age. None the less it is interesting, for example, to speculate about Shakespeare's motives for writing

Macbeth – a play which constantly analyses masculinity, and particularly the hypermasculinity which Macbeth himself adopts. Macbeth is on the make, and to satisfy his ambition has to break all social norms of hospitality and loyalty:

> To beguile the time,
> Look like the time; bear welcome in your eye,
> Your hand, your tongue; look like th'innocent flower
> But be the serpent under't.
>
> (I.v)

In fact, *Macbeth* contains a fascinating debate between Macbeth and Lady Macbeth as to the nature of true manhood, Lady Macbeth constantly stressing that one has to be ruthless and brutal to be a 'real man'.

Many of Shakespeare's plays contain male protagonists who are enmeshed in fierce debates over their own feelings and actions. Think of *Hamlet, Othello, King Lear, Richard III, Henry V* – the nature of the Shakespearean drama, with its long speeches and its soliloquies, produces a detailed psychological examination of male character, ranging from Richard's defiant and seductive 'I am determined to prove a villain' to Othello's agonized self-torture: 'Farewell the tranquil mind! Farewell content!' (III.iii). Here, surely, is a modern self-consciousness, at odds with itself, fractured, split between feeling, thought and action.

Although such artistic reflections on manhood are obviously quite different from a systematic academic study, I think they provide a healthy corrective to the view that would see the 'male crisis' as a recent one. None the less there is something quite distinct about today's enquiry into masculinity: it is much more conscious and systematic, it is able to deconstruct all kinds of beliefs and social structures that to a Lawrence or an Eliot or a Shakespeare were simply given. As Jeff Hearn says: 'No longer is it possible to take for granted maleness or masculinity.'[10] Most importantly, masculinities can now be seen as part of a political power structure, rather than a simple question of 'identity'.

FEMINISM

If we can point to an ongoing crisis for male identity in the whole of the modern (post-Renaissance) era, none the less within it there are periods of maximum crisis, and we seem to be living in one now. I am sure one reason for this is the development of feminism, which since the 1960s has acted like a depth-charge amongst men and amongst those studying gender, sexuality, personality, whether they be sociologists, linguists, anthropologists, literary critics, film critics or psychoanalysts. Many disciplines have been challenged by feminism, both in terms of their theoretical assumptions and in terms of the material they examine. And whilst perhaps many men have tried to ignore feminism, in the long run this has been difficult, because it has penetrated through everyone's defences.

At the risk of considerable simplification it is true to say that feminism has been primarily concerned with the analysis of the male subjugation of women in patriarchal society. From this standpoint, gender has been seen as the ideological expression of male domination: 'Race, class and gender form *synergistic* systems of domination and oppression' (original emphasis).[11] This has meant that generally the analysis of men and masculinities has been subordinate to the overarching themes of female oppression and female liberation. Lynne Segal, in her book *Slow Motion*, one of the best books written about men, says: 'when writing of men, women have done so more to expose the evil of their ways than to explore the riddles of "masculinity"'.[12]

Feminism is politically multifarious – there are left-wing, liberal and 'radical' or apocalyptic strands of feminist thought. The left-wing feminist tends to see the future for women as involving some overall social change to capitalism; the liberal envisages amelioration for women within the existing social order; and the radical movement (particularly in America) sees a future determined by women for women.

Attitudes to men have therefore varied enormously. The left-wing and liberal schools have remained interested in men, since they do not envisage a life without them. Segal is sympathetically critical towards men, or to put it more accurately she is hostile to an out-and-out rejection of men:

> A feminism which emphasises only the dangers to women from men, which insists upon the essential differences between women's and men's inner being, between women's and men's natural urges and experiences of the world, leaves little or no scope for transforming the relations between men and women.

She concludes her best-selling book *Is the Future Female?* with the sober statement: 'the future is not female'.[13]

The liberal voice of feminism clearly would not countenance a rejection of men. Mary Midgley, the British philosopher, addresses these issues in her book written with Judith Hughes: 'righting the injustices which affect women ... takes its place as part of the more general business of righting injustice. In this work many men are allies, and men as such are not conceivably the enemy.'[14] This position is perhaps a traditional one in Britain, and has historical roots in the liberal wing of the suffrage movement, the involvement of women in the Labour Party and in liberal campaigns such as those on abortion and homosexuality in the 1960s. In America it finds its voice in the Democratic Party and in campaigns such as that for the Equal Rights Amendment (ERA).

The radical feminist movement has been strongest in America, and has tended to dissolve all social injustices into the one great oppression of women by men. Rather than seeing gender oppression as a refraction of class oppression in the Marxist manner, it has reversed the equation: male violence or male sexuality are seen as prime sources of social alienation – in Mary Daly's words:

> I am developing the thesis that phallocracy is the most basic, radical, and universal societal manifestation of evil, underlying not only gynocide but genocide, not only rapism, but also racism, not only nuclear and chemical contamination but also spiritual pollution.[15]

In the late seventies and eighties, radical feminism seemed to become more influential, as there was something of a turn away from Marxism amongst feminists. In *Is the Future Female?*, published in 1987, Lynne Segal comments: 'the voice of socialist feminism is now remarkably silent in popular feminist debate'.[16] And in her chapter entitled 'What happened to socialist feminism?' she details the British experience: many splits developing, sectarian groups trying to take over, the rise to power of a right-wing government committed to 'family values', which demoralized some socialist feminists.

The eighties saw long periods of conservative government in America and Britain, which tended to fragment all radical groups. And the break-up of the Soviet Union, although in one sense actually exposing how much Marxism had degenerated into Stalinism, did demoralize some radicals, and suggested that a socialist solution to the problems of gender and the family was impossible, and furthermore that a Marxist analysis of gender was incorrect, or was itself a patriarchal system of thought. The result was pessimism about social change, and a variety of exotic revisions of Marxism, or a complete rejection of it.

The socialist strand of thought is also perhaps more difficult for Americans to adopt – there is less of a left-wing tradition than in Europe and Marxism has had much more fragile roots.

Put in simplistic terms, the left-wing or liberal feminist is concerned to analyse the nature of masculinity because she wants to find out how men can change. It seems impossible to imagine the overall structures of power in the work-place or in the family changing unless men change. For the radical feminist, such hopes of change are illusory, and therefore in a sense, men are no longer interesting. Men and women tend to be opposed as exponents of two quite distinct philosophies and ways of living. Robin Morgan argues that in men we find 'a love of death as the pure, selfless and sole means of expiation for the sin of consciousness. No wonder that woman, the incarnate affirmation of Eros, birth, and life is such a damnable obstacle.'[17]

But as Caroline Ramazanoglu demonstrates in her book *Feminism and the Contradictions of Oppression*, the division of feminism into socialist, liberal and radical is over-simplistic, and there has been considerable overlap and mutual influence – for example, Marxist feminism has been considerably influenced by radical feminism.[18]

The influence of feminism has spread into many disciplines. Sociology, anthropology, linguistics, literary criticism, evolutionary biology – these academic areas along with many others have been challenged by feminism, and have responded in varying degrees by changing both the things they investigate, and the way they do it. A brief example: the study of primates in biology has traditionally focused on male behaviour and made the unwritten assumption that female behaviour was determined by males. However, a group of feminist biologists have shown that in fact female primates have a lot of power in deciding issues to do with territory, foraging, and so on.[19] Such studies have not only changed the material examined by biologists, but more importantly have exposed covert assumptions, for example, that females are inert objects manipulated by males. Thus feminist deconstruction makes such unconscious assumptions conscious. Donna Haraway describes this as an '"anti-aesthetic" of permanently split, problematized, always receding and deferred "objects" of knowledge and practice, including signs, organisms, selves, and cultures'.[20] And central to this deconstructive activity has been the treatment of gender – in the words of Jane Flax: 'the single most important advance in feminist theory is that the existence of gender relations has been problematized. Gender can no longer be treated as a simple natural fact.'[21]

This intellectual revolution which has happened, or is happening, in many different disciplines, has not only changed the way in which females –

whether human or non-human – are investigated, but also how males are seen. To put it simply, men and manhood have been lifted out of a deep unconsciousness by feminism. As David Morgan points out, men have been studied for thousands of years, in the sense that most fields of enquiry have been implicitly about men.[22] But men have not been studied as 'men'. Indeed, disciplines such as theology, literary criticism and anthropology were almost entirely 'androcentric': when they talked about 'humanity' they were really talking about men. In her essay 'Women in Togas', Joan Smith shows how many histories of the Roman Empire are really histories of Roman men.[23] Feminism has exposed this covert masculinism (expressed in the common use of the word 'man' to mean humanity), and has thrown a much greater consciousness upon men and how they are created.

But what of the specific analysis of men made by feminists? As one would expect, it has not been a flattering one: there has been a concentration on male violence, male sexuality (often seen as inherently oppressive), the male use of pornography, the institutionalization of male power in the state and in the professions, the dominance of fathers in families, male homophobia, the concepts of 'manliness' and machismo. Some feminists have made one or two of these ideas central to a whole theory of patriarchy: male sexuality for example has been seen by some as the linchpin.[24] Obviously a great divide in approach has been in terms of change: can feminists look forward to men becoming less violent, less sexually oppressive towards women and gays, more interested in children, less enmeshed in state tyranny?

Some feminists have also noticed that men seem to suffer from the obligations placed on them: there is a price paid for being the male infantry of patriarchy, and this can lead to a feminist optimism that it is in men's interests to resist patriarchy and to work alongside feminists (broadly speaking Lynne Segal's view).

STUDYING MEN

After decades during which the study of men and masculinities was practically non-existent, the eighties and early nineties saw an increase in such work, and it now seems poised to explode. We can see already a considerable variety of approaches, and I shall rather arbitrarily split 'men's studies' into several categories.

1. Sociological/Political

Feminist sociology views gender as an expression of political power. Patriarchy represents political domination by men, and the varieties of masculinity represent the ideological expression of this domination. This approach therefore views the categories 'men' and 'women' not as biological brute facts, but social and political constructions.

By looking at gender relations as power relations, feminist sociologists have been able to demonstrate how male domination is sustained by work practices, by the structure of the family, by heterosexual practice and by the structure of the state itself. It is also able to provide new political perspectives on such areas of life as sport, religion, the academic world itself, in all of which male domination is systematically constructed and consolidated.[25]

A number of writers have attempted to synthesize various approaches to gender, particularly sociological and psychoanalytical. Segal's *Slow Motion*, Connell's *Gender and Power*, Weeks's *Sexuality and its Discontents* all pay attention to the insights of psychoanalysis.

Connell's book is a particularly impressive synthesis of ideas from sociology, psychoanalysis and existential philosophy. He looks for:

A form of social theory that gives some grip on the interweaving of personal life and social structure without collapsing towards voluntarism and pluralism on the one side, or categoricalism and biological determinism on the other.[26]

He offers an astute adaptation of the existential notion of the 'project': 'the power relations of the society become a constitutive principle of personality dynamics through being adopted as personal project, whether acknowledged or not'.[27]

This concept of personal project cuts through the impasse created by determinism ('my personality was moulded by my parents/society, so I'm helpless') and voluntarism ('I can become whatever I want').

It is also a view that accords with the notion of *responsibility* in therapy. Every sane adult has to take responsibility for their life – but responsibility doesn't mean *fault*. For example, I had a client who had had a psychotic mother and a father who committed suicide. This is a terrible background for anyone, and it was tempting for this man to languish in self-pity and enraged martyrdom. But eventually he was able to accept that this was his life, and he had to make a go of it – no one else was going to do it for him.

One of Connell's criticisms of men sits well with a therapeutic sensibility: 'Men can enjoy patriarchal power, but can accept it as if it were given by an external force, by nature or convention or even by women themselves. ... They do not care to take responsibility for the actions that give them their power.'[28]

This is the heart of therapeutic work done with violent men, rapists, child abusers – getting them to see what they actually do, not what they fantasize about. The denial of responsibility for one's own life and actions is one of the key barriers to personal growth.

Gay studies have produced a further deconstruction of the traditional male images, and has particularly been concerned to demolish the idea that the heterosexual nuclear family was somehow 'natural' or inevitable.[29] And homosexuality itself can be shown not to be a fixed transhistorical category – this connects with the anthropological observations that homosexuality has quite different functions around the world.[30]

My chief reservation concerning 'social construction' theorists is that they tend to become rather too Rousseauesque – social construction approaches social contract. Thus towards the end of *Gender and Power*, Connell comments: 'patriarchy, sexism and sexual oppression have never been necessary. Every society has been able to abolish it, whatever the level of technological development; just as class inequality could be abolished at any stage of history.'[31]

But how could class or gender inequality be abolished? By the stroke of an administrative pen? By mass action? But what if the property-owning patriarchs do not want their class/gender supremacy abolished?

There is a rather voluntarist/idealist strain of thought here, which for me ignores the material basis of class and patriarchy – one reason they are hard to abolish is that a lot of people are going to fight to stop you. Thus patriarchy and class society are not produced by people's attitudes, but by economic and social relations which are unconscious.

This brings up the question of social inertia – surely one reason the Soviet Union found it difficult to abolish sexism and gender inequality was the sheer economic and social resistance in a mainly peasant society. The early Soviet leaders never believed that 'socialism' could be built in one country – this was a Stalinist fantasy, now revealed as the tawdry pastiche of Marxism that it was.

I think Connell underestimates how unconscious and compulsive human existence is – most of the time, most of us are driven by powerful covert forces, and to raise these to consciousness is an enormous task. Patriarchy is considerably mystified, but mystification cannot be dispelled easily – witness the large numbers of women who are 'anti-feminist'.

2. Confessional

Writers such as Connell, Hearn and Morgan frequently use autobiographical material to illustrate their arguments. This is a refreshing development – no longer do men feel constrained to be purely rational and 'objective'. And today we also have a growing number of 'confessional' books – men describing their childhoods and their lives as adult men, for example, Sam Keen's *Fire in the Belly*, David Cohen's *Being a Man* and David Jackson's *Unmasking Masculinity*.[32] This is an important breakthrough: it is legitimate to use one's own life, one's own feelings as material for study and analysis. It seems likely that this rupture in the barrier between thought and feeling has been considerably aided by feminism's introduction of personal issues and feelings into discussions of gender and sexuality. Thus, that Renaissance split that I have referred to – Eliot's 'dissociation of sensibility' – can be healed on both sides. Women are able to use logic and argumentation; men are able to be personal and emotional. In fact, both sexes can be simultaneously scholarly and personal.

3. Spiritual

There are signs that both men and women are attempting to deconstruct conventional spirituality and develop a new kind of spirituality. This is a difficult process, since our culture is still saturated with the images of patriarchal religion, organized by male priests and bishops as part of the patriarchal state.

Thus, there have been at least three structural levels in patriarchal religion: the overtly political level, that is, the organization of churches to exclude women from priestly roles, and reinforce the patriarchal order; the symbolic, where the images of Father and Son have exerted a masculine tyranny; and the moral, where the churches have advocated heterosexuality and 'family values'. However, the feminine aspect of spirituality has led an underground but very powerful existence, for example, in the form of the Virgin Mary.

Contemporary attempts to develop a new spirituality have centred around attempts to resurrect the notion of the Goddess. These researches and activities have been very much the province of women, but some men have been involved.[33]

In addition, there are interesting attempts to look into the male 'mystery tradition', and to explore non-Western spiritual methods, for example, Native American initiations, the sweat-lodge, drumming, and so on. Perhaps the most important aspect of these activities is that men come together in a new way, not as macho upholders of male supremacy, but in an attempt to get beneath the stereotypes to a more vulnerable and more primitive male identity.[34]

There are also interesting connections here with the Jungian tradition which has always been interested in myth and ritual, not as luxuries which we toy with once our need for food and shelter is satisfied, but as essential means of connecting human beings with the 'numinous' or the transpersonal. Indeed, Jung argued that the West had fallen into a deep sickness, since it had rationalized out of existence many primitive rituals, and thereby suffered from the backlash of a starved and denied unconscious.[35]

These spiritual researches often seem at odds with the feminist/sociological analysis of patriarchy (although there is a feminist spirituality). In his introduction to *Choirs of the Gods*, John Matthews states: 'Men lack a sense of *inner mythology*, and this leaves them often with a sense of futility and rootlessness which is one of the most basic aspects of male disempowerment' (my emphasis).[36] And Robert Bly comments: 'We have the right to say that there is a deep structure to a man's psyche.'[37] Thus these approaches are anti-empiricist, concerned very much with the inner world, and could be criticized as asocial and apolitical. However, this is not necessarily true – Bly, for example, criticizes the conventional manhood prescribed by patriarchal society as a great barrier for men seeking truth and integrity: 'it is clear to men that the images of adult manhood given by the popular culture are worn out'.[38]

None the less, I see a clear danger in such movements: they can become too 'precious' and too divorced from a political grasp of masculinities. Here we come up against the ancient dichotomy between the individual and society. The New Age movements often ignore the society we live in, and speak in a hyperindividualist voluntarist manner: I can become whatever I want. Not so! This ignores precisely the social construction of identity and relations of power.

4. Popular

The researches I have referred to up to now all show a more or less conscious attempt to deconstruct traditional images of manhood. But we should not neglect the more unconscious study of masculinities that we find in popular art, as here we find those issues that secretly trouble men, their wishes and dreams, their nightmares and darkest fantasies. In fact, popular art doesn't *study* masculinities, but it provides a brilliant mirror in which to view them. I am thinking, for example, of cinema, and its ability to reflect insecurities in the male image, sadistic and masochistic fantasies, problematic relations with women, and attempts to subvert or reinforce traditional machismo (see Chapter 9).[39]

On television, in advertising, in pop music, pop videos, sport and its reporting, we find quite subtle shifts in the way men are shown. For example, at the moment, three of the TV programmes I regularly watch concern male adolescence and its humorous and serious aspects: *Teenage Health Freak* (British), *The Wonder Years* and *Fresh Prince of Bel Air* (both American). These three programmes show fascinating differences and similarities. Both *The Wonder Years* and *Fresh Prince of Bel Air* offer very positive images of male adolescence: for a British palate, there is at times a rather cloying emphasis on love between family members. *The Wonder Years* is about a white boy, with a 'good' father and mother, and with a long-standing girl-friend – not too much challenge here to conventional male stereotypes, although it does have a considerable psychological depth of analysis within those limits. *Fresh Prince of Bel Air* is about a black 'dude' (played by the brilliant Will Smith), who has a crackling line in satirical wit, and observes his rich Bel Air relatives with a certain degree of astringence – but not too much. In the end, everyone loves everyone, rich and poor, white and black, men and women.

Compared with these two programmes, *Teenage Health Freak* is much more disturbing: the central character (Peter) is a mess – inadequate, hopeless with girls. His parents rant and rave around the house – his father, obsessed with cowboy clothes and activities, seems rather demented; his mother is taken into a mental hospital. The British programme is savage compared with the American ones, and the male image is subject to a much fiercer examination, as is the family. Whether these differences reflect a greater degree of self-censorship on American TV, or a greater degree of wish-fulfilment, is hard to say – we could also refer to the deep-going crisis in British post-imperial society, whereby British males see their traditional roles increasingly redundant and demolished. But on the other hand, American TV has produced the excellent *Roseanne*, surely one of the most subversive images of womanhood seen on TV screens.

Of course, a lot of work done on TV or in film is relatively unconscious: it does not set out to examine 'masculinity' and 'manhood'. None the less, it provides a profound insight into the male psyche, and particularly over a period of years we are able to see different images of men waxing and waning.

CONTRIBUTIONS OF PSYCHOTHERAPY

I would like to turn now to psychotherapy: what are its specific contributions to the study of gender? This study is as old as this century – from the beginning, Freud was concerned with the relationships of the infant with its parents and siblings, and how these relationships implanted primitive unconscious patterns that are laid down for life. Furthermore, Freud was primarily interested in the development of masculine identity, and saw women as shadowy images of men. Thus a considerable amount of work has been done in psychoanalysis on the development of the young boy, the conflict in him between heterosexual and homosexual desire, the conflict in identification with mother and father, and the threats which he sees emanating from them.

But these are substantive issues which I shall deal with in Chapter 5. More relevant to this chapter are the basic methodological assumptions made by psychotherapy in the study of sexuality and gender, because these are markedly different from those found in sociology and feminism. I would like to highlight five.

1. First, there is the centrality of fantasy. The analyst or therapist works a lot of the time with fantasies, which are seen as crucial elements in the individual's inner life. But 'fantasy' does not mean day-dreaming or idle reverie: it is one of the building bricks of our sense of reality. Indeed, the analyst Robert Stoller makes the claim that our mental life is built up entirely of fantasy.[40]

This is not the place to consider this claim at length, but gender itself can be seen as a tissue of fantasies about how men and women should act, dress, move, speak, feel and think. But when we say that gender is a fantasy, we do not mean that it is fallacious or wrong or illusory. We might make a useful analogy with our concepts of time – in some ways the past is a fantasy. There is no sensuous tangible past which I can inhabit – only memories, which are themselves present experiences. The fantasy of linear time stretching forwards and back is however one of the key elements in our sense of reality.

The understanding of gender as fantasy has very important implications. First, that fantasies vary from culture to culture, and within cultures, from family to family. An example of cultural fantasy is Mediterranean machismo – a highly complex body of expectations and beliefs about how men should behave.[41] Examples of family fantasies about gender are legion: I had a male client whose parents unconsciously projected the view that men are laughable children; another female client grew up in an ambience which suggested that all men 'wanted to get you in a ditch and get your knickers off'.

A crucial corollary is that since fantasy has been implanted, it can be recovered and dismantled. This does not mean this work is easy – far from it. Such fantasies are often deeply buried, are in a sense so familiar that we often do not realize we possess them. That's just the way reality seems to be. One person expects the universe to be kind, beneficial and nourishing; another expects the universe to be hostile, dangerous and depriving.

A related point is that human beings have an uncanny knack of recreating their fantasies. Thus the client who unconsciously believed men were idiotic constantly found himself in situations where he was made a laughing stock of. The woman who believed men were predators met men like that. The person who believes the universe is kind usually has the experience that it is.

This correspondence of fantasy and external reality poses great problems for many people. Since our fantasies are apparently confirmed by reality, they do not appear to be fantasies, but simple statements of the way things are. Indeed, we unconsciously gravitate towards and create external representations of our fantasies, partly in a quest to understand them and put them right, and also because we are addicted to them.

But therapy is a very powerful tool since it is able to focus on such fantasies as they come into the relationship between therapist and client, and (hopefully) demonstrate their unreality. This is a kind of psychological deconstruction quite distinct from feminist and sociological deconstruction.

Another key aspect of fantasy is that it is psychodynamic. It is a product of relationship. Thus my client who believed men were laughable had himself been treated as laughable by both parents. The woman who saw men as sexual predators had seen her mother treat her father as if he were predatory.

Thus gender fantasies – as with all such deep-rooted fantasies – are not inert descriptions of reality which are given to us like so much prose. They are products of living relationships, images which abbreviate a whole way of living together.

They are learned; therapy believes that to an extent they can be unlearned. Certainly they can be made more conscious – and that is half the battle, since we are then not so much in their grip.

2.   The most important discovery of psychoanalysis is the notion of the unconscious. This is one of the most powerful heuristic tools of twentieth-century knowledge – it has enabled us to explain so much apparently bizarre behaviour. Furthermore, Freud proposed that the unconscious has

its own language and grammar, quite distinct from normal language. The unconscious utilizes contradictions, irrational juxtapositions, blends of images, projections and internalizations in a way that seems quite foreign to rational behaviour but often underlies it.[42]

This 'grammar of the unconscious' is vital in the study of gender. Let me briefly refer to contrasexuality. It is now a truism that males have a female element; females a male element. One of the great contributions of Jung to the study of the psyche was to show the extent to which we are fascinated, horrified, even tormented by the contrasexual, and the lengths we will go to pursue it.[43] For example, many womanizing men are desperately trying to get in touch with their own feminine – but their quest is endless, since the external woman can never satisfy the inner thirst for 'She'. In fact, the womanizer also chases women to avoid his own femininity – as the homophobic man persecutes gays in order to banish and punish his own homosexuality.

Such pieces of analysis are trite and rather clichéd today. But the point behind them is vital: we seek to satisfy our inner deficiencies externally. The amount of mental pain and suffering this causes is incalculable. And so much of the tension and strain that seems to be involved in male rituals and images are bound up with the avoidance of the feminine – dreaded yet yearned for.

3. My third theme is this: therapy works through relationship. The individual does not study reality in some abstract or 'objective' manner, but works in tandem with another person, and often the focus of their joint attention is what is going on between them. This is quite a revolutionary type of enquiry – distinct from the normal scientific methods of observation, hypothesis construction and testing, and so on. It is centred in subjectivity; its aim is the self-discovery of the subject through contact with another. Thus when we work on somebody's gender, we do not do so in a spirit of contemplation or intellectual enquiry, but concretely, focusing on the way that person presents himself in the present. We do not ask the question 'What kind of a man are you in general?' but 'What kind of a man are you being with me now?' If an individual man has problems with aggression, need, grief or spontaneity, we seek solutions in the relationship going on between us. Can you be aggressive with me, or needy of me, or spontaneous with me?

This is the radicalism of therapy: it plunges us into the present moment.

4. The fourth theme I would emphasize is the developmental bias of therapy: it proposes that many of our deepest feelings and attitudes are primitive, that is, go back to early childhood. Along with this goes a notion of re-enactment – that our adult relationships, our work, hobbies, friendships tend to recreate old patterns of relationship. Of course, if you had a loving childhood and you recreate the spirit of that in your adult life, this is fine! Problems arise if you were neglected or emotionally abused in some way – you will tend to find that situation recurring in adult life. In some ways, the repetition is a cry for help.

Thus gender problems for adults are seen as recapitulations of gender problems in childhood.

5. Fifthly, Freud saw sexuality as central to infantile fantasy and development. Some schools of analysis and therapy have diluted this claim, or rejected it outright. But it still stands as a revolutionary and shocking hypothesis, and in the study of gender, it is clearly of great importance. If we find in adult clients memories and recreations of intense love and need, erotic feelings, seductive fantasies, between parent and child, it seems likely that such experiences have profoundly affected gender and sexual orientation.

There is also the danger of child abuse: if we assume that the parent-child relation is naturally sensuous, erotic, seductive even, then parents who have not resolved their own primitive needs will be tempted to turn seductive fantasy into reality. And it seems clear today that such child abuse – particularly emotional, but also physical and sexual – exists on a large scale.[44] Many people who go to therapy are suffering some kind of child abuse.

COLLISION OR CREATIVE TENSION?

This brief discussion of basic therapeutic assumptions and methods reveals the sharp distinction between therapy's approach to gender as opposed to that of feminist sociology. And it often seems that between the social sciences and psychotherapy there is an unbridgeable gulf. Disciplines such as sociology, anthropology and social history, are academic – they are concerned with the formal description and explanation of areas of human existence. Psychotherapy is not academic – it is a practical discipline in which the participants use their own personalities as tools in order to effect change. As we have seen, it is subjective, and its prime focus is subjectivity, or 'intersubjectivity' – that is, the way in which two people relate to each other (or do not relate).

Of course this opposition is not absolute. Therapy has had its great theoreticians – Freud one of the greatest – and the social sciences often carry out practical investigations into the way individuals live – and feminism has permitted a much greater subjectivity. But one cannot teach psychotherapy academically. If you train to be a therapist you will, of course, receive quite an amount of theoretical input – but the main thrust of your training will be your own therapy. Through this, you will learn about your own barriers to intimacy, and the blind spots you have in some areas. For example, if you find it difficult to cry, you will feel tense and uncomfortable if your clients start to cry. Unconsciously you will want to stop them – they will not thank you for that! This illustrates the point that the therapist's chief tool is his/her own personality.

In relation to gender, we see the differences quite sharply. Sociology, anthropology and feminism have tended to look at large-scale patterns – for example, the way gender relations encode dominance and oppression in the work-place, or in the family, or the way gender intersects with class and race. Therapy has made generalizations and has gone in for theory construction in a big way, but it must always come back to the living relationship between two people. That is its *raison d'être*. Thus psychotherapy is very much an outgrowth of the Romantic movement – Freud was prepared to spend years of work with an individual, and this tradition has continued. One only has to think of the great analyst H. F. Searles who spent ten years working with apparently catatonic patients.[45]

At its most extreme, the opposition between radical social science and therapy becomes quite fierce, and amounts to a collision – in Britain there has been a long-standing hostility amongst the Left towards psychotherapy, seen as a kind of 'bourgeois individualism for the rich' that doesn't actually deal with the real problem, that is, social-political oppression. There are signs that this hostility is abating in recent years, but it is not dead. For example, in *Gender and Power*, Bob Connell refers to psychotherapists who 'talk out the tensions of the urban rich and drug or hospitalize the urban poor' (which confuses therapy with psychiatry).[46] And it has been reciprocated – many therapists fight shy of any political statements in their work – understandably, since to bring one's own political views into the therapy session can often seem invasive.

A good example of these contrasting approaches can be seen with the concept of sexism. Many feminist/sociological discussions of sexism would naturally make a critique of it. This would not be a psychotherapeutic approach – a therapist would be interested to find out what feelings lurked beneath the surface of sexist attitudes, and within the safety of the therapy session would hope to bring out these feelings more. For example:

some of my women clients have phases when they hate me passionately, and vilify me as a man. I see this as quite healthy, and it usually unblocks our relationship considerably. Many people hate the opposite sex at times, and in varying degrees. Nearly always one can find good reasons for this in childhood – the hatred is often a projection of a hated parent.

In the therapy ambience, it would be fatal to condemn sexist attitudes – most people have already been overly condemned. I listen to people come out with the most hair-raising sadistic and/or masochistic fantasies. It is a relief for them that I am able to listen and receive their feelings without judgement. From the therapist's point of view it is also a relief when people start to come out with this stuff – it is the repression of it that is dangerous and leads to acting out.

There is also an issue here about perfectibility – some strains of feminism and sociology seem to contain a yearning for a perfect society and perfectly balanced individuals, who do not hate or oppress each other. I suppose therapy is less optimistic – if we can get people to admit how much they do hate each other and want to destroy each other, then they are less likely to do it. A rather modest aim perhaps – but in my experience, surprisingly healing.

Another important example concerns the importance of mothering in early childhood. Whereas many feminists and left-wing sociologists make a critique of child-rearing as part of the stereotyping of women, the therapist often can't afford to do that in the middle of the therapy session. She is confronted with people who were raised by mothers in their early years and has to deal with that concrete fact. It is not up to her, there and then to suggest that child-rearing is dangerously biased towards women – unless the client begins to get interested in that idea. Of course there is a powerful movement amongst some therapists who point out the prevalence of child abuse and the tyranny of the family – Alice Miller is perhaps the best-known example[47] – but one cannot bring this into the actual work, unless the client herself brings it in.

Perhaps the clearest example of the divergence between therapy and social science is the issue of gender inequality itself. For a therapist to make a political analysis of this is pointless, since the client has internalized such values. For example, a woman with low self-esteem cannot change that simply by appreciating how women are devalued in our society – she has to grasp how she devalues herself in many covert ways, and she has to locate the anger that exists against that. The same is true of some gay men – it is their own self-hatred that paralyzes them – and an analysis of society's hatred of homosexuality will not affect the self-hatred. This is why politics and therapy have often been uneasy bedfellows – therapy is looking at the inner world, where political views have been incorporated. The inner values can't be changed by analysing the external world, but by bringing them into consciousness. Of course the political determines the personal (our inner values are incorporated from society's) – but it doesn't follow that we can change our personal self-esteem simply by analysing society. The catastrophe has already happened within the psyche. Indeed we find people who analyse society's oppressions and get angry about them, as an avoidance of their own personal sense of unwantedness.

But let me add something more about the 'collision' between social science and therapy. Conflicts can be destructive or creative, and I see no reason why the clash between these two ways of thinking cannot be very creative. Feminism has found this in its *rapprochement* with psychoanalysis.[48] Each side can supply something that the other one lacks: therapy is rather inept when it comes to talking about historical or social movements; the social sciences may falter before a truly subjective or inner experience. Furthermore it is possible to have a dialogue between the disciplines – as we have seen, there are many concepts that are shared, such as mothering, power, control, dominance and gender itself. It is fascinating to ascertain to what extent such words are being used in the same way, and to what extent in different ways. In the next chapter, I want to look at the notions of 'power' and 'powerlessness', how they are treated in psychotherapy, and how that differs from the view found in feminist sociology.

3 Power and Powerlessness

The main thesis of this book can be expressed as a simple paradox: patriarchal masculinity cripples men. Manhood as we know it in our society requires such a self-destructive identity, a deeply masochistic self-denial, a shrinkage of the self, a turning away from whole areas of life, that the man who obeys the demands of masculinity has become only half-human. Jeff Hearn states this poignantly in his book *The Gender of Oppression*: 'We men are formed and broken by our own power.'[1]

This is the constant threnody I hear from those men who come to see me in therapy: to become the man I was supposed to be, I had to destroy my most vulnerable side, my sensitivity, my femininity, my creativity, and I also had to pretend to be both more powerful and less powerful than I feel. But these men are fortunate – they have gone into a profound crisis, some of them a breakdown, from which they have a good chance of emerging enlarged, more alive, more self-accepting. There are surely many others who struggle on (manfully!), confused, afraid, wondering if there are others who feel the same.

This is the cryptic message of masculinity: don't accept who you are. Conceal your weakness, your tears, your fear of death, your love for others. Conceal your impotence. Conceal your potency. Disparage women, since they remind you too much of your own feminine side. Disparage gay men since that's too near the bone as well. Fake your behaviour. Dominate others, then you can fool everyone, especially yourself, that you feel powerful.

One of the important ways of looking at gender is as a power relationship: men have oppressed women and children and other men for thousands of years by virtue of being men. To be a man has been a qualification in itself for many privileged positions.

But sometimes in feminism we find a rather simplistic syllogism that begins with the empowerment of the male gender and the oppressiveness of the female gender and concludes that women are damaged, and men are exalted, privileged. Lynne Segal describes masculinity as 'the exciting identity, linked with success, power and dominance in every social sphere'.[2]

There is no doubt about male dominance in public areas of life. We look around and see male judges, male policemen, male politicians, male surgeons, male priests. The exception – Margaret Thatcher – proves the rule. We see men consistently earning more than women, employed in better, more skilled jobs. Women are often employed in part-time, non-unionized jobs, where job security and conditions are rock-bottom. Men dominate in areas such as the arts, the media and education.

But I want to make a more complex claim: that men and women have actually demarcated out different zones of influence in life, where one predominates, and where the other is deprived. My thesis is that men are economically and politically powerful, and that women are emotionally powerful. Of course it can be argued that economic power far outstrips emotional power, and is somehow determining, more valuable, more dignified. Interestingly, this is a Marxist idea: that the economic 'base' of society ultimately determines the cultural 'superstructure'.

The point I am making is that the emphasis on male dominance in public areas of life has tended to obscure the emotional poverty of many men's lives.

SONS, HUSBANDS AND LOVERS

Let me move from generalizations to some specific examples. A fictional example: D. H. Lawrence's novel *Sons and Lovers*. There is little doubt that this is an autobiographical novel, and it is psychologically very convincing.

In *Sons and Lovers*, the central family are the Morels. Mr Morel is a miner, and clearly is the one with the money, which he doles out to Mrs Morel, if he is not spending it at the pub. Thus Mrs Morel is dependent on him financially, and is in a weak state in this sense. But emotionally and psychologically the tables are turned. Mr Morel is a shadow of a man, whereas Mrs Morel is an immensely powerful woman. She is so powerful, that she overshadows everyone in the family, and dominates her sons, so much so that their own identity is threatened. The central thread of the novel is Paul's attempt to become free of her, an attempt whose resolution is left in a highly ambivalent stage at the end of the novel.

Here is a typical section in the novel where Mrs Morel turns away from her husband to the children, after he has been ill:

> There was the halt, the wistfulness about the ensuing year, which is like autumn in a man's life. His wife was casting him off, half regretfully, but relentlessly; casting him off and turning now for love and life to the children. Henceforward he was more or less a husk. And he half acquiesced, as so many men do, yielding their place to their children.[3]

Sons and Lovers is a brilliantly realized novel, and I would argue that it represents a common situation in working-class and middle-class families.

There is a division of labour: the man earns the money, and in that sense has economic power and dominance; the woman runs the family, not just in a practical sense, that is, cooking, washing and so on, but emotionally. She is the ringleader of the whole family in the psychological arena. Indeed, in *Sons and Lovers* her power is so great that her sons are castrated and suffocated by her. William is engaged to be married, but cannot endure the conflict between mother and wife-to-be and dies. Paul becomes her surrogate lover and father, and in turn feels incapacitated with women of his own age.

Thus we have the pattern of the father who is emotionally distant, weak and damaged; and the mother who is emotionally powerful, and sometimes too powerful. Working as a psychotherapist I hear this complaint so often: my father was so remote, I never knew him. A therapist colleague of mine has written a book on the subject, *The Absent Father*.[4]

In her book on men, Mary Ingham describes the pattern in her own family:

> It was only after my mother died that I began to realise how much they had functioned as a symbiotic whole, of which my mother was the emotional, demonstratively affectionate half, the one who wrote letters, rang up. A letter from my father always meant that my mother was too ill to write, and he had hardly ever rang me in his life. If financially my mother had always depended on my father, emotionally my father had always existed through her.[5]

That is both an eloquent and a precise description of the reciprocal symbiosis which many marriages become: each partner lives through the other in a certain area of life. We might say that in our culture there is a visible patriarchy – the economic and social dominance of men over women – and an invisible matriarchy, the emotional dominance of women over men.

A very interesting Victorian example is found in a biographical sketch by John Tosh of a nineteenth-century Archbishop of Canterbury, Edward White Benson.[6] Benson's eldest son died at the age of seventeen, and the relation between Benson and his wife changed:

> Mary's role for the remaining eighteen years of the marriage was now set. The memories of the younger sons, Arthur and Fred, were of their father's total reliance on her ability to soothe his irritation and relieve his black depressions. The partnership became more harmonious because Mary was able – like a mother – to intuit her husband's unarticulated emotional needs and to regulate the emotional equilibrium of the household. Benson's dependence on his wife was of course less visible than his

patriarchal authority, not least because it was at variance with the ethos of manly independence. But it was no less real for that, and was surely the underpinning of his public posture of command and self-reliance.[7]

Here is a man who achieved great public office, mixed with prime ministers and other grandees, and yet, in this brilliant little portrait of a marriage, we see Benson as a child, comforted by a wife-mother, who intuits his 'unarticulated emotional needs' – presumably Benson was unconsciously trying to find in his wife something that he was deprived of as a child. The patriarchal outward persona is belied by the child-like dependence on his wife – this might be called the secret underbelly of Victorian masculinity, and surely of twentieth-century masculinity. In a rather pathetic way, the man lives through the woman emotionally, as presumably she lives through his public success.

Another revealing facet to Benson's private life is given in the same essay in the description of his relationship with his sons. Tosh describes how Benson preserved a stiff distance from them, often censorious and cold (whereas in fact he loved them deeply, as is revealed in his diaries). His two sons eventually found a niche in the homosexual sub-culture of the early twentieth century.[8] Thus the 'absence' of fathers has considerable emotional repercussions for their children – in Benson's case, we could argue that his sons were compelled to search for that male love that they didn't get from him. Going back to D. H. Lawrence, we see him throughout his life and in his books also wrestling with an unresolved homosexual love for men – his intense alliance with his mother had required him to cut himself off from his father. The denied homosexual bond between father and son therefore actually intensified, and indeed seems to have tormented him.

My final example in this section is taken from anthropology. The American anthropologist Stanley Brandes studied the men and women in a Spanish town, and found the characteristic Mediterranean divide between public space, dominated by men, and domestic space, which women inhabit.[9] But Brandes also noticed that the men were afraid and in awe of the women:

> The male ideological posture accords considerable superiority to women. It is an ideology that reverses the actual state of affairs that exists in the realm of actual behavior. Women are portrayed as dangerous and potent.[10]

Brandes spends some time describing how this male attitude is expressed, in informal statements, codified folklore, and idiomatic expressions, for example:

Pueden mas dos tetas que cien carretas.
Two breasts can do more than a hundred carts.

And there are a whole range of beliefs that express this male fear of female power, to do with menstruation, the evil eye, female sexuality, the fear of anal penetration, and so on.

But the kernel of Brandes's article is this:

> Why do [the men] portray themselves ideologically as potentially vulnerable and weak, and women as hostile and aggressive? Why do they assume a psychologically defensive position, when their appropriate behavioral role is assertive?[11]

Brandes considers various explanations, ranging from historical factors, psychoanalytic projections, rationalizations of patriarchal oppression (the myth of female power justifies controlling them), but concludes that the 'women really are hostile and powerful'.[12]

This analysis of a Spanish town is rather similar to my own description of the working-class culture I grew up in (see Chapter 10) – the men politically control the women, yet see them as very powerful. And my own intuitions match Brandes' analysis: the women really were powerful. Brandes relates this partly to the importance that sexual honour has in Andalusian culture and the perceived power of female sexuality, but I think he neglects the role women play in family structure, in the expression of emotion, in personal relationship. The public/private divide relates to more than the plaza and the kitchen, or in the culture I grew up in, the pub and the kitchen. The public domain also concerns the outward front that people adopt; the private domain includes the innermost feelings that men and women possess, but which are not publicly revealed. My thesis is that these two great territories of human existence are apportioned to men and women respectively, and this causes great conflict and envy between the sexes in many cultures. Significantly, in Brandes' Andalusian town it is considered unmanly for men to go to church frequently – the affairs of the soul belong to women.

A point here about ethnocentricity: my comments are applicable in the first instance to British culture, which is the one I know best. But I see evidence – such as Brandes' study – that they are true within a wider context, including Europe and America. It would be unwise for me to go further than that, but anthropology does seem to show parallels in other cultures, for example, in Africa, Australia and Native America.[13]

PUBLIC AND PRIVATE

When we look at public life – the great professions such as the law, medicine, politics and education – there is no doubt that men have dominated
for centuries. Only recently have women begun to make any kind of presence felt and it is still the case that although there are more women doctors
and solicitors, the commanding heights of the professions are dominated by
men. Sociologists have shown how work is one of the primary means of
constructing male dominance.[14]

But I would argue that in private life – in the area of relationships –
women are able to relate better, they understand their own feelings better,
and are able to communicate feelings better. How often does one hear this
cry from women: their husbands or partners cannot talk to them about their
own feelings, and do not seem to understand the woman's feelings? How
many marriages and partnerships suffer great strain because the man is
overly intellectual, and finds the woman too emotional?

This suggests that men are, in general, emotionally impotent and inarticulate. Men find emotions dangerous things, they fear them and shun them.
This is what makes them so remote in their families, so that many people
remember their parents in childhood in such contrasting ways: father is a
dim figure who comes home from work and is polite to them, while mother
is the figure who attends to their emotional needs, who *relates to them*. The
feminist Francesca Cancian summarizes a number of studies on working-
class men and women as follows: 'working class wives prefer to talk about
themselves, their close relations with family and friends, and their homes,
while their husbands prefer to talk about cars, sports, work and politics'.[15]

Intimacy is power. That may sound an odd phrase, since we are used to
thinking that power consists of wealth, political leverage, possessions. But
these things do not necessarily give personal power, inner strength. This
comes from the ability to be with people, the ability to listen to them, to
communicate one's own point of view. Think of your own childhood – who
do you remember with greater clarity, greater force?

Thus we live in a schizoid culture divided between public and private
worlds. Women have correctly complained that they have been excluded
from the public world, where lies economic and political power, and they
have begun to make up some of the ground. But have men made an equi-
valent converse gesture? I don't believe they have. They have hung
back, afraid, guilty, feeling condemned, and more and more powerless.

To use an ironic phrase, men now occupy no-man's-land, guilty about their traditional areas of power on the one hand, but afraid to go into new areas, that seem dominated by women. Perhaps there is a sense of injustice, of not being heard or understood. But those still remain the feelings of a little boy, who is unable to speak, unable to act.

Many men that I meet professionally are genuinely confused about what power means. The Victorian notion of the father-tyrant casts a long shadow. That was a tyranny that also covered up fear and powerlessness. Children had to be crushed in the traditional child-rearing practices, since adults dreaded being overwhelmed by their spontaneity and anarchy.

There is a further point to be made about male power. Most men have very little economic power, but are subject to the dictates of other men. The captains of industry, the High Court judge, the chief constable, the army general – these men undoubtedly wield power. But what about the bus conductor, the Ford worker, the ordinary soldier? These men often experience themselves as relatively powerless, which economically they are.

From my work as a therapist, I would conclude that many men are troubled not by feeling overpowerful or dominant, but precisely the opposite. Sexual impotence is a very common problem with men, but it symbolizes a deeper sense of powerlessness. When I see young men stealing cars, vandalizing property, burglarizing, and so on, they don't strike me as domineering tyrants but as helpless children.[16] They are bewildered at the scant attention society pays to them, the way they are devalued in dead-end jobs. From one perspective their masculinity seems rampant or over the top – but from another it is fragile, precarious. In the words of Winnicott, the Freudian analyst: 'When there is an anti-social tendency, there has been a true deprivation.'[17]

The same is true of violent men – men who beat up their wives and girlfriends, who carry out violent robberies and muggings, rapists – these are not men who are comfortable with their masculinity and their relations with other men, and with women and children. Frequently we find that such men have deep feelings of inadequacy, impotence and unwantedness.[18] The violent male often secretly fears he is not a man, and sees no other way of proving he is than the method demonstrated to him by his society – violence and oppression. Patriarchy recruits and trains violent males as its shock-troops, but the cost to them as individuals is enormous.

The clearest example of public power shrinking personal power is seen in military training. National armies are the supreme expression of patriarchal state power, used externally against other states and internally against strikers and other dissidents. But what about the individuals in those armies? Military training sets out methodically to reduce their individuality, to take away their power of choice, in a word, to dehumanize them. The soldier, who is the embodiment of public state power, learns to obey, and to suppress his own individual conscience. But is not this inverse relation between public and private power an extreme version of patriarchal power as a whole? Men are recruited as its agents, and in the process have to reduce themselves. We can see this in the 'company man', who has to shrink his emotional existence in favour of loyalty to his company and his product.[19]

The duality to tough masculinity can be seen clearly in film imagery: on the one hand, there is the image of the avenger, the High Plains Drifter, remorseless, without compassion; but on the other hand, there is the sense that he is mad, maddened, in despair – see Robert de Niro in *Taxi-Driver*, or Micky Rourke in *Angel Heart*.

One might argue that all these examples are of deviant men, criminals, people on the margins of society. But I find in many of my male clients a deep feeling of hurt, a sense of profound damage that has been done to them. Again, one might try to marginalize such men, and argue that they are unrepresentative or pathological. But who is the normal man? Where is the man without wounds?

I believe that many men are in fact overawed and threatened by the ability of women to experience and communicate feelings. They tend to flee from the domestic world, they tend to hide away from relationships, they dread intimacy. They also have enormous envy of women's abilities in relating, women's fertility and their ability to create life. I shall suggest later in this book that the famous penis envy attributed to women by Freud can be matched by an unconscious breast and womb envy in men and a desire to be feminine and female that must be denied at all costs. The macho man has to protest constantly that he is not feminine – does he not protest too much?

There is considerable evidence from anthropological studies of cultures around the world that many male rituals reveal a profound envy and fear of women. *Women are perceived as extremely powerful by men.* This might contradict the socio-economic analysis of patriarchy, but it is psychologically undeniable. For example, in the many taboos concerning menstruation and the defloration of the virgin woman, in the male *couvade* which mimics pregnancy, the nose-bleeding ceremonies which seem to echo menstruation, pseudocopulation, homosexual rituals – all of these point to that 'dread of woman' that Karen Horney wrote about.[20]

This brief discussion of male attitudes illustrates quite well the difference between the approaches of social science and psychotherapy. Whereas feminism and sociology can point to male violence as an expression of 'hegemonic masculinity', one of the ways in which women are controlled in patriarchal society, psychotherapy can point to the violent male as a brutalized, damaged figure. This contradiction is not a terminological or metatheoretical one: it reflects a contradiction within patriarchal masculinity, which must dehumanize its agents, whilst also promising them power and glamour. Thus the prominent images of machismo in our culture – Rambo, the Terminator, the Man with No Name – are simultaneously images of glamorized brutality and of deranged autism.

The psychological and sociological analyses of gender appear to clash, for each takes as its subject matter a different 'gender'. As Donna Haraway says in *Primate Visions*, science is a form of story-telling and the stories told by different disciplines are quite distinct, even when the words they use appear identical.[21]

The different stances of the two approaches to gender are revealed terminologically in the use of the terms 'masculinity'/'masculinities'. In feminism and feminist sociology the use of the singular term is now heavily criticized on the grounds that there is no such unitary monolithic phenomenon as 'masculinity'. The use of the plural term deconstructs the notion of masculinity, and subjects it to a political critique.

But within psychotherapy there is a valid argument for the continuing use of the singular term: masculinity in men does have a unitary function. All shades of masculine identity, ranging from macho to the effeminate, have this in common: they convey the message: 'I am not a woman'.

The heavy anxiety that surrounds masculinity in our culture, and prob-ably in other cultures, flows from this defensive quality. The male has to distance himself from femaleness and feminity, in order to prove that he is a male. The way this is done varies from culture to culture, and from sub-culture to sub-culture. There are rituals of masculine initiation, there are clothes, hair-styles, jewellery styles, there are occupations, ways of speak-ing, hobbies, sports, there are special segregated dwellings and spaces – but in all these variegated expressions of masculinity we see one driving force – the need to prove that a man is not a woman.

'Masculinity' in this sense is defined in opposition to 'feminity'. The masculine is the negation of the feminine, and this opposition varies in con-tent from culture to culture. Thus in one culture long hair in men can denote masculinity; in other cultures, femininity. What counts is not so much the content but the structural opposition between the two genders.

POWER: PERSONAL AND POLITICAL

We can see that there is a split between personal power and political power. When I was an academic, the people who enjoyed the most political power in the academic hierarchy – usually men, of course – didn't excite much envy in me or my friends. But that is too sweeping – I did envy their power, but not their personalities! They often seemed rather dead people, devoted to their little empire, or sometimes rather manic. Happy? Fulfilled? The janitor in my block of flats looks a much happier man to me.

Indeed my circle of friends pitied the top brass in the academic world – I am not talking about the top researchers or the great teachers, but those who were administratively powerful. They struck us as rather pathetic – wedded to the job, submerging their own individuality so as to achieve a corporate identity.

Of course, this in itself provides a powerful double-edged critique of the structures of power and oppression in our culture. The people at the bottom are treated like dirt – but the people at the top are like drug-addicts. They get their fix of power and privilege – but they have to keep on taking the fix endlessly. They disappear into what they are, they become what they do.

In some ways psychotherapy has taken a rather Buddhist position to these issues. Zen teaches this:

> Is there any dividing line between rich and poor? It's only a matter of comparison. Only when you give up such a comparison will you be able to settle in your true self, any time, any place. People may compare you with others, and call you either rich or poor, but that is only applying a label which has nothing to do with the real you. As you return to the reality of your life, to your true self, and become manifest as such, that is when 'blue things are blue and red things are red' which is called Paradise.[22]

I don't think that is too dissimilar from the spirit in which many therapists work. It is a teaching also found in Christianity: 'Consider the lilies of the field, they toil not neither do they spin' (Matthew 6:25), although clearly the Christian churches have not been able to expound that teaching, and have indeed rejected it in favour of the work ethic and the guilt ethic.

Of course, we all know that finding 'your true self' in our culture is not easy. There are so many practical problems – paying the bills being one of them – and there are so many restrictions put on people and their creativity. After all, most people end up in dead-end jobs, and have to try to express themselves outside work.

None the less therapy embodies the hope and promise that despite all the material and social difficulties it is possible to realize the true self, and manifest it. This is what I mean by personal power – being centred, rooted in the self, and being able to speak and act from that centre. I have seen too many people achieve that state – usually with a great deal of pain and anguish – to be able to deny it.

Who is the happiest person you ever met? I think for me it was a woman who ran a bed and breakfast guest house in Somerset. She just radiated contentment, happiness. She was in contact with her environment – with people, with the plants in her garden, with animals – and she was in contact with herself. I didn't get to know her well enough to find out the details of her life, but I would bet that as a child she was loved and accepted – it shone in her eyes.

Most of us are not like my guest house landlady. We don't have that natural sunniness. But it is possible to get closer to it, usually by first working through the darkness, the hurt and anger left over from childhood.

My observation is that many people who try to achieve great power and privilege do so because they feel so deprived and unwanted. They have to make a splash in the world, otherwise they feel so desperate. Of course this isn't true of all powerful people – there are some whose inner truth is expressed in their work, and I think you can usually tell this.

But men have been particularly sucked into the spiral of power and privilege that is disconnected from personal power. They chase external power as a compensation for their inner emotional poverty.

One of the greatest days of my life was the day I gave up being an academic. I was a Senior Lecturer, with a Ph.D., two research assistants. I'd been a real power junkie, but it burned me out and I stopped. Of course I also felt very peculiar for a period. I felt empty, deprived, I missed my regular fix. But that emptiness, which lasted two or three years, eventually filled up with something else that was more creative, more spontaneous, more to do with me. My role as an academic had been a kind of image, a mask, and for many years I was in love with that mask. It gave me a massive buzz. But it burned out, as such things do (if we are lucky!).

I became powerless in one sense. And many of my friends were aghast at what I had done – thrown away a career, future promotion, research, publications, and so on. I seemed to have given up my life. And yet all that academic power had made me feel powerless, and I had to leave in order to find myself.

This is my story – I am not saying that other academics feel the same at all. I had been seduced into academia because it seemed to offer power, privilege and status. It did. But as I got older I realized I wanted something else – myself.

This is the true radicalism of psychotherapy – that it searches for and celebrates the self, not the outer trappings.

However, it would be wrong to construct some kind of dichotomy between finding your true self, and being in the world, taking part in society, having a job and so on. In the Zen quotation above, the crucial section is this: 'As you return to the reality of your life, to your true self, and *become manifest as such*' (my emphasis). Finding out who you really are is not some eso-teric or other-worldly activity divorced from concrete reality – the two go together. My argument is that many men have found an external position in the world that may provide power, privilege and status, without providing a deep internal satisfaction. The split between work and home goes deeper than that – into the male psyche itself, where there is a split between outer and inner, between doing and being, between the mask outside the man, and the heart inside the man. It is this split that psychotherapy aims to heal.

THE PERSONAL IS POLITICAL: THE POLITICAL IS PERSONAL

It seems clear that when sociology and psychotherapy talk about gender, they are referring to different concepts. Social and political studies are con-cerned primarily with the public world[23] – gender is seen very much in terms of structures of power and oppression, as a political relation, whereas for therapists, gender is more to do with personality traits, attitudes towards life, fantasies about how men and women 'should' behave. For the feminist sociologist, gender derives from or determines the political structures of patriarchy; for the psychotherapist, gender derives from the primitive ex-periences one had as an infant, and the way in which the male infant was trained to be male.

This is a sharp divergence. One emphasizes the political; the other the personal. One looks at the public world; the other at a private inner world. The first might argue that the personal is political, the second that the political is personal.

That last sentence needs amplification. Sociology and feminism have argued that 'private' issues are actually individual manifestations of polit-ical issues. In his book *Discovering Men*, David Morgan states: 'masculin-ity is best seen not simply as some kind of quality that is attached to individuals, but a kind of cultural resource, of a set of potentialities which may be realized and shaped in particular contexts'.[24] Notice here the words 'cultural', 'realized and shaped in contexts' – the focus is very much on gender as cultural information which is socially determined. The personal reflects the political.

Feminism has amplified this idea, and has therefore criticized many forms of therapy, psychoanalysis and psychiatry as being too individualist and apolitical (and oppressive) in their treatment of 'personal' problems. In her 'Letter to Her Psychiatrist', Nadine Miller castigates 'the psychological' in no uncertain terms:

> The whole psychological thing is based on the premise that there are individual problems rather than a social problem which is political. I have reached the point where I know there is only one solution for me as a woman – unity with other women and ultimately a revolution.[25]

In this view, personal problems such as depression, being withdrawn or unable to relate to people, can only be explained and mitigated satisfactorily when seen as by-products of an oppressive society and its gendered institutions.

But we can reverse the direction of explanation: depth psychology has tended to take political and social positions and take them back to personal roots. An example: a client has been very upset about environmental pollution, angry, weeping about it. It is worth investigating the possibility that she feels personally polluted, for example, she has been emotionally or sexually abused in some way. Another client is obsessed with Ireland, constantly explaining to me the way in which it was divided up in 1922, and suggesting ways in which it could be unified. It does not really stretch the imagination to suggest that he feels divided himself, and yearns for a greater feeling of harmony. Such feelings and opinions can be seen as concealed messages, concealed as much from that individual as from others. They conceal (yet also reveal) the unbearable. Politics expresses the personal. Therapy is an autobiographical journey.

Another way of illustrating the divergence between the two disciplines is to look at the way books and articles are written about gender. *Discovering Men* by the sociologist David Morgan, includes the following topics: men at work, unemployment, upsets at the work-place, the suffrage movement. Those social contexts and events are seen as consolidating or challenging masculinity and male dominance.

Take by way of contrast the psychoanalyst Robert Stoller's book *Presentations of Gender.* Here are some of the key topics in his book: core gender identity, marked femininity in boys, a child fetishist, origins of male transvestism, sex-change treatment and its evaluation. Here we have a very different picture, very much based in the family, in infancy, so that gender is seen as having a very primitive origin: 'for masculinity to develop each

infant boy must erect intrapsychic barriers that ward off the desire to main-
tain the blissful sense of being one with mother'.[26]

What a marked difference between the two approaches! Different in the
terrain which each describes, and the way the description is carried out.
One could imagine a fine and mighty argument between proponents of
these two notions of gender. It is always tempting to prove one approach
right, and one wrong.

But let me propose something else: that both conceptions of gender are
equally valid ways of looking at gender, and furthermore that they can shed
light on each other. For example, if we take Stoller's description of the
infant boy lolling blissfully in his mother's arms: one doesn't have to be a
sociologist to see that this scenario is a 'political' one. Why is he so at one
with his mother? Where is his father? Is this an inevitable scenario, or is it
part of his society's gendered method of child-rearing?

We can carry out the reverse procedure. Take Morgan's topics – they can
be psychoanalysed without too much difficulty. For example, his theme of
'upsets at the work-place' – he describes previously male occupations
which are 'invaded' by women, for example, clerical work. The idea of
men being alarmed and angered by women 'invading' them could be taken
from a psychotherapy textbook: many male infants sense their mothers as
too invasive, abusive, unable to separate from them, and this feeling is
taken forward into adult life. One can apply psychological analysis to many
social phenomena: feminism itself contains certain conflicts, for example,
over nurturance and independence, that can be related to the mother–
daughter relation.[27]

We can look through the telescope two ways: from the personal to the
political, and vice versa. Naturally, most people seem to prefer one way or
the other – I prefer the latter. But both are valid, and it is likely that they
can enrich each other, as well as come into conflict. They have different
purposes, different origins and different results.

In this light we could argue that therapy has been too apolitical, and has
simply taken the family as an inviolable and eternal category. Left-wing
sociologists and feminists can argue with some justness that therapy
appears to accept uncritically many aspects of social life – sexuality, child-
rearing, work – that can be deconstructed and shown to encode powerful
political beliefs and power structures.

However, there is a straightforward reply to that: it is not the business of
a therapist to make a critique of anything initially. That is the client's work:
therapy is client-centred. When therapy or analysis makes explicit judge-
ments – for example, take the way in which psychoanalysis has often

condemned homosexuality and seen it as something to be 'cured' – then it has become untherapeutic.

Therapy is able to examine any aspect of a client's life, whether it be emotional, sexual, political or whatever. But *the client sets the agenda* – otherwise we are merely reproducing the authoritarian atmosphere that many people have experienced in their family and at school. Nothing is taboo in therapy – but nothing is prescribed (or proscribed).

This 'conversation' between therapy and sociology is a fruitful one and a difficult one. It is bound to be full of conflict – but then conflict is necessary to creativity. At the deepest level, the two disputants reflect two different ways of looking at reality – macro and micro, public and private, external and internal. Psychologically, we could say that we are confronted here with one of the primary splits in the human mind – but it is a split which has probably been essential for intellectual enquiry and discovery. Not all splits are malignant!

PUBLIC MEN

Sociology and feminism are concerned with power relations in the 'real world', if I can call it that. Their intellectual stance is one of realism, or scientific objectivity. This stance is also a materialist one: it presupposes that there is an objective material world independent of human consciousness.

Rather than discuss in abstract terms the social-political analysis of men in patriarchy, I would like to consider briefly Jeff Hearn's book *Men in the Public Eye*. This book describes very convincingly and in great detail the consolidation of male power over women in the public domain, particularly in Britain between 1870–1920. Hearn gives a wealth of material concerning the way men grew in dominance, not so much in the great professions such as medicine, the law and education, but in other areas of employment such as the Post Office and the Civil Service, in the beginnings of the welfare state in the nineteenth century, in the control of sexuality, for example, through laws on divorce and prostitution, in the growth of the police, and in many other areas. This is a dense and rich document, but Hearn is not simply making a list. He argues the publicness of men *qua* men: 'men are constructed through public visibility'.[28] He devotes much attention to the divide between 'public' and 'private', arguing that this divide is in itself problematic, and represents a patriarchal fracturing of life, that enables men to control both areas:

> *I see public patriarchies as materially founded on men's power and*
> *dominance in and over the private domains,* particularly around *bio-*
> *logical reproduction, domestic work, sexuality, nurture and violence.*
> (original emphasis)[29]

In one sense it is difficult to make a critique of one man's book about
men, since it is *his story*. Jeff Hearn makes this clear: 'The motivation for
writing this, and for publication, has been intensely personal.' And later he
writes of his sense of 'spilling the beans on my gender class – which I feel
so antagonistic to, yet love so much'.[30]

These are moving words, which no doubt conceal more than they reveal.
One of my responses is to say 'But it's not my story', but then I might fall
silent as well, since the difference in our stories is real and genuine, and
neither invalidates the other. But I don't share Hearn's antagonism towards
men or fathers, and I haven't been so struck by the 'enormity of men's
material powers' as he has. As I mentioned earlier, my childhood experience was like the Andalusian town described by the anthropologist
Brandes: women were very powerful in certain areas of life, and for children, particularly so. Furthermore, as a psychotherapist I don't simply see
men as public men. What strikes me is that many men, when they are out
of the public realm, are incoherent, emotionally autistic and unable to be
intimate.

Let me be more specific. Over a period of fifteen years I have worked
with a number of violent men, in group and individual therapy. They had
different histories – street-fighting, burglarizing, prison or drugs. From the
social/political point of view, these are the shock-troops of patriarchy. I
could not disagree with that. Most of them were misogynists, and at the
same time very fearful of women.

But one overwhelming impression left by those men is that they could
not sit with me and be with me. They were incapable, in the beginning, of
being intimate. In a quiet room, sitting in armchairs, they were like helpless
babies.

I'm not out to construct a sob-story about them, or say 'it's not their
fault'. Some of them frightened me a lot. But my point is that in that context *they felt powerless* – in fact, that's what made them so dangerous.
Indeed a great part of the therapy consisted of helping them experience
their own sense of impotence and begin to recover some sense of self.

This kind of analysis simply doesn't fit into the public–private division.
You could argue that these men didn't function well in 'private space' – but
psychologically one has to say more. They had no *inner space*. They had
no internal relationships with the elements of their own psyche. They were

gripped by powerful unconscious forces. Their life consisted of one blind acting-out after another.

Social studies or sociology or political studies cannot describe these men in such terms. This is not through any fault of those disciplines – it is not their aim.

Thus my critique of Jeff Hearn's book cannot be in terms of the analysis he has provided – it is convincing and amply backed-up. But it's what it leaves out that troubles me. He does refer to contradictions within patriarchy, and to the complexity of oppression – men oppress other men, sometimes women oppress some men – all within the overarching theme: 'men's structural location within patriarchies as members of the oppressor class'.[31] But curiously enough the concept of 'public men' itself – a concept which dominates *Men in the Public Eye* – is monolithic and demands a psychological deconstruction. Let me point again to Edward Benson, who I discussed earlier. Here was a 'public man' if ever there was one. Yet our analysis of him reveals the power of his wife in regulating the 'emotional equilibrium of the household'. Who dominated who in the Benson household? There is no obvious answer to that question.

THE DIALECTICS OF POWER

In therapy, we are concerned both with the external world and with the world of the unconscious, from where other kinds of information are transmitted, particularly fantasies, dreams, feelings, moods, and so on. This produces a sense of paradox in therapy – for every statement the opposite may be true. Within one person, there are different levels of feeling and perception, which may contradict each other. Let me give some examples to illustrate this idea: three examples from the analysis of culture, and two from therapy itself.

1. Pornographic images can be seen straightforwardly as male fantasies about women. They can be interpreted as 'men possessing women', the subtitle of Andrea Dworkin's book on pornography.[32] The images of women vary – from the sexually submissive and available woman to mild sado-masochistic fantasies, on to very violent fantasies: death, dismemberment, torture.

Here is a classic case where therapy might intuit other meanings, in particular the sense that such images represent the contrasexual in men: the 'inner woman'. In Jungian psychology in particular, there has been a keen interest in contrasexuality, and Jung himself devoted much research to it. For example, he argued that Rider Haggard's book, *She* ('She-who-must-be-obeyed') described such an 'anima' figure, an image of the man's own feminine that fascinates him because it is so elusive.[33] Indeed, Jung argued that many relationships are bedevilled by this mutual fascination: each partner is trying to find part of themselves in the other one.

This approach is a valuable one in literary criticism, and other forms of art criticism. For example, it is perhaps rather obvious to argue that male novelists have heroines who represent their own feminine side, and female novelists have heroes who represent their own masculinity. Clear examples are Flaubert's Madame Bovary and Emily Brontë's Heathcliff.

Thus, in the pornographic image the man unconsciously sees himself as a woman – available, body exposed, yet also unavailable, frozen in a photograph, beyond reach. In fact, pornography is much more complex than that, recapitulating infantile experiences (the eroticized mother), homosexual desire (the viewer becomes the woman inviting the male embrace), spiritual experience (the Goddess). The point I am making is that we cannot uniquely interpret such overdetermined images. Analysis of them must be multivalent, dialectical. Thus, so far from seeing the male viewer as exerting power over the inert female figure, I would tend to reverse this: porn reveals the powerlessness of the viewer, paralysed by his own traumatic fantasies.

2. The iconography of the western is one of the key myths of masculinity in twentieth-century culture. At first glance we might argue that here we have an extreme version of 'men without women': the western hero dispenses justice, patronizes women and children, eradicates Indians and rides off unscathed. However, the western is much more complex than this. Let me confine myself to two observations.

First, the western hero is a very mutilated human being. He is often cut off from society, certainly from family, from women. One of his chief duties is to suffer stoically without complaining. He is also emotionally severely restricted – as Jane Tompkins says in her study *West of Everything*:

> The ethic of self-denial – denial of the needs of the flesh for warmth and comfort, succor, ease and pleasure; and denial of the needs of the spirit for companionship, affection, love, dependency, exchange – turns the hero to stone in the end. He becomes desert butte.[34]

This is an essential attribute of masculinity: the ability to suffer and remain cut off from human feeling. Male hegemony has a very dark shadow side: masochism, self-destruction, self-denial.

As I mentioned in the last chapter, Tompkins also argues that the rise of the western novel and film at the beginning of this century is a response and a refutation of 'the dominance of woman's culture in the nineteenth century and to women's invasion of the public sphere between 1880 and 1920'.[35] She argues that the western stresses male values, male companionship because these things had been so devalued.

It is interesting in this light to consider the development of the western in the last two decades. Many critics agree that in the 1970s, the western lost its way: there were spoof westerns, black humour westerns – and some undoubted fine films: *Pat Garrett and Billy the Kid, Monte Walsh, The Missouri Breaks* – but it seemed as if Hollywood had lost the sense of the 'classic western'.[36] In the eighties, the western nearly disappeared, and it really looked as if this was the 'end of the trail'. But then at the beginning of the nineties, American TV started to make westerns again – for example, *Lonesome Dove, Son of the Morning Star* – and the cinema saw the release of *Dances with Wolves, The Last of the Mohicans* and Clint Eastwood's *Unforgiven*. These three films are not apologies for westerns; they are expansive, confident, and Eastwood's in particular is an extraordinarily resonant film, showing the director's deep knowledge and love of the genre.[37]

Is it fanciful to suppose that the resurrection of the western (if it is that) is an answer to feminism? Just as Tompkins sees the western hero riding out of the feminine nineteenth century, perhaps we are about to see a renewed image of him riding out of the seventies and eighties? Tompkins refers to 'literary gender war', and sees the western not as a triumphant assertion of male hegemony but as part of a struggle to win back lost territory. The western largely excludes women from its generic icons (except for the saloon girl and the homely wife) not out of a sense of triumphant conquest, but out of a defiant refusal to submit to female power.

3. Let me give a third and brief example from religion. Who are the key symbolic figures in Christianity? Theologically, dogmatically, they are the Father and the Son, as befits one of the world's important patriarchal religions.

But at another level – emotional, intuitive, soulful – the key figure is the Virgin Mary. Go into one of the great centres of Roman Catholicism, such as Chartres Cathedral, and the statue of Mary is the focal point. But this is true in many ordinary Catholic churches – the candles burn in front of Mary, not Christ or God; the flowers are brought for Mary, people pray in front of her.

Why is this? There are many complex things to be said about Mary,[38] but fundamentally Mary is perceived as human, as approachable – she is the aspect of the divine that ordinary people can grasp. She is also of course a patriarchal image of femininity – desexualized, idealized as the perfect Mother, the obverse of the dark witch. But whereas Father and Son are perceived as abstractions, theological constructs, Mary is flesh and blood. Therefore, paradoxically Mary is the emotional powerhouse of Catholicism, and one of the crucial acts of the Reformation in its demolition of Catholicism was the excision of Mary. Destroy her and you destroy folk Catholicism – destroy folk Catholicism and you destroy Catholicism.

4.   Let me turn to therapy itself and its dialectical understanding of relationships. One common theme in therapy is that 'the victim has undisclosed power; the aggressor has hidden weakness'. I am referring here to victim/aggressor relationships which are ongoing.

A brief example from my own work. For years, James[39] has been insisting that I overwhelm him, I wreck every small step of progress he makes – many sessions end with his poignant cry that another session has been wasted. However, this poignancy becomes irritating! Here is an important clue – suggesting that James is secretly enraged with me. I suggest to him that his masochism, his self-presentation as victim conceals the message: 'You are a lousy therapist. Even the little things that I've gained from you are ruined by your stupidity and clumsiness. I hate you.' James starts to grin, and the more he grins, the better I feel, as he begins to release the hidden sadism. His role as the victim has been his greatest triumph, but he was also desperate for me to call his bluff, and to penetrate beneath his victimhood to a deeper level where he persecuted me, and indeed needs to persecute me. In his family, public demonstrations of hostility were taboo – what a relief for him to hate me openly.

5.   We can see why the issue of control is a very subtle and complex one in therapy – quite often we are not quite sure who is trying to control who. The American analyst Robert Stoller had a very fine grasp of such complexities. In his book, *Sexual Excitement*, he describes one of his patients who showed strong sado-masochistic and exhibitionist tendencies in her sexual fantasies. In the introduction to the book, Stoller discusses male exhibitionists, who on the surface want to frighten women with their genitals. But Stoller argues that this 'power trip' conceals something else:

> This idea that he is powerful, a dominating male who causes fear as he subdues a woman by the mere sight of his genitals, is, then, an illusion he has brought into the real world. He seems to be running great risks: he may be caught and arrested, his family and job put in jeopardy.

But the true danger that perversion is to protect him from – that he is insignificant, unmanly – is not out there on the street but within him and therefore inescapable.[40]

This analysis contains some characteristic elements of therapeutic work, although expressed with Stoller's customary elegance: for the exhibitionist, one idea (he is powerful) conceals its opposite (he is insignificant). The apparent triumphant act of exhibiting his genitals conceals and attempts to contravene the deeper trauma – he is unmanly.

Later in the same book, Stoller applies the same kind of 'split-level' analysis to his female patient:

The other person is always the brute, she is always the victim; but at the level where the action really is, she is secretly the victor. She has demonstrated the alleged attacker's cruel inhumanity. The double bind – 'no matter what you do to me or for me, it's wrong' – is the masochist's device for keeping supplies of masochism and sadism flowing.[41]

I have discussed this book with a number of feminists, and some of them were annoyed by it. They saw it as yet another male therapist's refusal to understand a woman, and an attempt to turn her complaints about men (and about him) into female 'masochism' concealing triumph. In methodological terms, Stoller's statement about 'where the action is' shows the vulnerability of descriptions of what goes on in therapy: how does he know that's where the action is? However, one must reply that therapists have intuitions about such matters, but these intuitions are valueless without the client's assent. And it is not just a matter of formal assent: such an interpretation could only be considered correct if it released the client from such behaviour, in other words if it had a liberating effect ultimately.

I could go on multiplying examples of paradoxical therapy and cultural analysis, but I hope that these five examples have shown how therapy is interested in that which lies beneath the surface of events: it is interested in contradiction, negation.

The point I am making is this: social science and therapy are using words such as 'power' and 'gender' in very different ways, and within totally different methodologies and epistemologies. Therefore, when I look at certain statements made in sociology and feminism – 'men dominate women', 'men control women' and so on – I tend to see them in the same light as a client's statements, and immediately ask: 'but how do women control men?' Or I think: 'male power must be partly a response to female power'. This kind of approach does tend to either infuriate or perplex some sociologists or feminists – it just doesn't fit into their way of thinking. The description of masculinity as 'hegemonic' (Connell) is from the psychological point of view monolithic, and makes one raise one's antennae, on the look-out for contradictions to it.

It is clear that masculinity itself is not monolithic, but is the relation between men and women? Is it one-way traffic in terms of power? Psychologically, this is very counter-intuitive: for example, in most families that have an obvious tyrant figure, it is surprising how much power the victims covertly exert. And anthropology certainly seems to confirm that men in many cultures have seen women as powerful beings, who must be kept at bay, denigrated, segregated – not because they are perceived as weak, but as strong. For example, there are many taboos on menstruation – some tribes believe that a man who touches a menstruating woman may die, such is the aura of power and magic surrounding women.[42]

In her article 'Femininity and its Discontents', Jacqueline Rose makes a similar comparison between sociology and psychoanalysis far more succinctly than I have. She makes the point that the notion of the unconscious in psychoanalysis makes all ideas of stable identity impossible to sustain:

> What distinguishes psychoanalysis from sociological accounts of gender ... is that whereas for the latter, the internalization of norms is roughly assumed to work, the basic premise and indeed starting point of psychoanalysis is that it does not.[43]

Thus psychoanalysis and the therapies it has spawned are *anti-empiricist*: they refuse to accept the surface of events or our beliefs about events as 'reality', but suggest that there are other realities that lurk beneath. As I said earlier, the sociological notions of the 'public domain' and the 'private domain' leave out a major component of personal identity: the inner world. Take for example sexuality: there is a public world of sexuality (controlled by legislation, morality and so on); there is a private world (where people meet, go to bed, and so on) which can still be said to be regulated by the public domain; and there is an inner world (of sexual fantasy). The relation between these three sexual zones is fearsomely complex, and often quite contradictory, as many people find to their embarrassment – what we do in our dreams and beds may be quite at odds with our social/political beliefs, but no less important. And the inner world is itself divided into different compartments, often warring with each other.

But there is an overarching issue here: how do we evaluate these different areas of human existence? Which carries most weight? Here we find, surely, a great division between feminism and its associated studies, and psychotherapy. For the former, patriarchy is defined as the 'global dominance of men over women'.[44] But I want to argue that much of human life goes on in private and inner space, and here female power is considerable.

Let me use pornography as an example again. In my view in pornography women are simultaneously objectified ('consumed') – and *deified*. Many pornographic images of women strike me as images of the Goddess, erotic, available yet totally unavailable, loved and hated. Whether one derives these images from the infantile idealization/hatred of mother (Freud/Klein) or from an archetypal Great Mother template (Jung) is irrelevant to this argument. I connect porn with ancient fertility art and erotic art, some of the oldest forms of human representation, as in the prehistoric Venus figurines.[45]

I am not arguing that male power and female power are equal. In the first place, I don't know how they can be measured, since they are so different. But secondly, the masculinization of existence is pretty advanced – the Renaissance and Reformation produced a kind of hyperpatriarchal culture, in which both women and 'the feminine' have been considerably devalued. But thirdly, I am arguing that there is a power *struggle* between the sexes. Connell has a section in *Gender and Power* entitled 'Working Class Feminism' in which he details the ways in which working-class women have fought for their own areas of power. 'Patriarchal authority has been rolled back some way', Connell comments.[46] The way I look at it is that working-class patriarchs and matriarchs slug it out in a ferocious power battle. Working-class men have the preponderance – they have the backing of the patriarchal state and culture – but working-class matriarchal power is considerable. When people start talking about their genealogy, how often is some grandmother or great grandmother still remembered with awe as pivot and centre of the whole family?

But this brings up a crucial question: how do we ascertain the truth? Is Connell right or am I? Furthermore, how would we go about comparing our respective statements? Connell can cite impressive statistics about employment, education and violence against women.[47] But such arguments tell us only about the public world and certain aspects of the private world. In this chapter, I have presented some evidence that men are emotionally and relationally disadvantaged compared with women. But how does one compare such arguments, grounded as they are in different premises and employing different kinds of selectivity?

In the end we are left with subjective truth, which is notoriously flawed. But from this point of view I would argue that Connell and I are both correct, since our arguments are fundamentally personal, autobiographical ones.

My deconstruction of notions such as 'power' and 'dominance' is akin to feminism's, which pointed out that many aspects of life that were considered just 'common sense' or unalterable, were in fact social constructions, for example, heterosexuality, childcare, language. Rose comments: 'Feminism's affinity with psychoanalysis rests above all, I would argue, with this recognition that there is a resistance to identity which lies at the very heart of psychic life.'[48]

This is precisely the way I see male identity: it is contradictory, ambivalent. It constantly wrestles with the feminine, absorbs it and then expels it; it purports to be tough, and then reveals its fragility; it seeks to hide neediness and intense feeling – and privately clings to others. We might use Hegelian language and call male power a thesis which makes us immediately seek for antithesis.

4 Gender and Patriarchy

If psychotherapy can make a critique of sociology, then sociology can return the compliment: a purely psychological approach to gender in isolation is inadequate. So long as we see the separation of boys and girls as a family drama – admittedly one of great intensity and importance for the individual's identity – it remains a mystery. Why should so much importance be placed in our infancy on the acquisition of the masculine and feminine traits? Why should there be such fierce taboos on transgressions of gender rules? Why have recent years seen an increasing desire to deconstruct gender and play around with its categories and boundaries?

In this respect psychoanalysis has a less than distinguished record in examining cultural formations such as gender. It has tended to see them simply as expressions of the Oedipal drama, or the pre-Oedipal drama. Within this model, concepts such as penis envy and the castration complex have dominated. This is all very well and good (apart from its phallocentrism) but it leaves gender stranded, isolated within the family. The psychotherapist Margot Waddell makes the point in an essay on gender studies: 'the terms "masculinity" and "femininity" largely denote sociological categories rather than psychological'.[1]

This is a vital premise in the psychological study of gender: that gender itself, although of tremendous importance psychologically, is not an intrinsic property of the psyche or the body, but is a cultural formation. Gender is a highly complex focal point of biological, economic, social, cultural and psychological values and ascriptions that are mediated through the family, but do not simply arise within it.

Space forbids a lengthy examination of these different functions of gender. In this chapter, I shall concentrate on the economic and social meanings that it has.

PRE-PATRIARCHY

All animals are driven by the need to obtain food and produce offspring. Human society has constructed very complex cultural systems around these two activities, and patriarchy could be loosely defined as the social system in which men control both. Thus in hunter-gatherer societies, men obtain food through hunting, and tightly regulate women's sexuality and reproductive powers. Since property became established among human beings this male control has been expressed as the ownership of women, or the treatment of them as property.

But what are the origins of patriarchy? Considerable confusion and speculation has surrounded this question. If the division of labour between men and women simply reflects biological differences, then patriarchy seems destined to last for ever.[2]

In his book *The Origin of the Family, Private Property and the State*, Engels speculated about a pre-existing matriarchal system which had property in common – and therefore the overcoming of patriarchy would mean the return to an ancient communist system.[3]

Engels's arguments for an ancient matriarchal culture now seem rather romantic and based on dubious anthropological data.[4] But none the less, during the 1980s various kinds of research were undertaken into pre-patriarchal society.

For example, feminist biology and sociobiology have looked at the female power exercised in primate society, and concluded that traditional primate studies had underestimated this.[5] Primatology had made the patriarchal assumption that female baboons, for example, were simply controlled by the males. There is plenty of evidence in fact that female primates control many aspects of their life, and that the males have to fit in with them. This has led to speculation that early human society had a similar kind of gender solidarity: 'centering females'/women's extended foraging, sharing, and sexual and reproductive self-determinations constituted a reconstruction of the potent, foundational, originary moments of what it means to be human'.[6]

In an entirely different field – mythology – scholars have long pointed to many ancient myths that describe female power.[7] Certainly patriarchal religions seem to have been preceded by matriarchal ones, in which goddesses were seen as givers of fertility to both the earth and to women. Various speculations have arisen from such mythological studies – and also from archaeological evidence – that the myths are a dim echo of ancient matriarchal societies.[8]

Anthropology, which has traditionally had a masculinist bias, has begun to find evidence for female authority in ancient cultures. For example, anthropologists have studied menstruation myths and rituals and find evidence that menstruating women were (and are) not only seen as polluting but as very powerful.[9] Chris Knight, in his book *Blood Relations*, has constructed a very challenging thesis, involving the alternation of hunting and menstruation, and the exchange of food and sex between men and women. Certainly, in many remaining tribal societies the interconnection of female fertility with hunting is a strong one. For example, the ban on pre-hunting intercourse is widespread, as is the taboo on menstrual women preparing food. Knight ties this in with Levi-Strauss's distinction between the raw and the cooked in a very ingenious way.[10]

What seems less clear in Knight's thesis is the basis for the evolution of patriarchy. If women used to exert power through their control of reproduction, and (uniquely among the primates) forced men to bring food for them and their offspring (no food, no sex), then how have men been able to take over subsequently? And many aboriginal myths do seem to reflect a male take-over – for example, there are many rites of 'male menstruation', where men cause blood to flow from the penis or the nose, as if men have stolen the female blood flow, symbol of fertility and life itself.[11]

Of course these activities can be seen as expressions of 'castration anxiety' or vaginal envy, but we are still no wiser as to why the control of reproduction shifted towards men. In particular, the material basis for this does not seem clear – did food become scarcer or technology more complex? What seems difficult to explain is why female solidarity (expressed according to Knight through menstrual synchrony and concealed ovulation) weakens, and male solidarity strengthens, so that in patriarchy, women themselves become the objects of exchange. If the arguments for an ancient female power have any credence – and they are highly speculative – it is clear that at some point in hominid evolution a catastrophe occurred for women.

The arguments about pre-patriarchal female power have a fascinating corollary today – that feminism itself may represent its reassertion, whereby women are beginning to take back control over reproduction – seen in the use of contraception and abortion. The increase in one-parent families (mainly women) could be interpreted as a 'sex strike'. Women can now conceive without men – this gives them a new weapon in the struggle between the sexes.

The whole argument is complex and confused – but one thing that stands out is the notion of gender solidarity and gender conflict. Human culture itself is seen as arising from the exchange of food and sex between men and women, each of whom band together in order to compel the other sex to deliver its part of the bargain. No food, no children, and no children, no food.

These studies therefore tend to demolish the inviolability of the mono-gamous nuclear family floating around in an individualist culture. Most human cultures have witnessed a complex struggle and negotiation between the sexes, who are only permitted intimate contact under very restricted conditions – and such relations between men and women are still seen in hunter-gatherer societies. The privatization of sexuality and reproduction and the isolation of the nuclear family as seen in Western culture today are bizarre phenomena when we take the long view of human history.

MARX AND BEYOND MARX

The Marxist theory of patriarchy is materialist: it claims that it is a reflection of economic production and property relations. Or to put it more simply, patriarchy is a means of organizing production. Thus Engels argued that matriarchy gave way to patriarchy because of the division of labour between men and women:

> According to the division of labour within the family at the time, it was the man's part to obtain food and the instruments of labour necessary for that purpose. He therefore also owned the instruments of labour ... the man was also the owner of the new source of subsistence, the cattle, and later of the new instruments of labour, the slaves.[12]

But considerable confusion surrounds the relation between gender and class, or between patriarchy and class society. Engels seems to suggest that the domination of men over women arises because of private property and the development of classes. Thus speaking of the wealth acquired from agriculture and cattle, he says: 'this wealth dealt a severe blow to the society founded on pairing marriage and the matriarchal gens'.[13] Engels argues that private property led to male inheritance, overall male domination and social classes.

However, anthropological research suggests that a pre-class patriarchal form of society has existed, in which production is organized *by means of kinship* not class (and kinship is clearly structured around gender). For example, Native American societies do not have stratification by means of class, but by gender.[14] This suggests that patriarchal gender relations (male domination) pre-date class society. Class society therefore builds on the established patriarchal relations of production. Thus a class society such as capitalism, organizes production through class and gender (and race).

Let me simplify considerably: at some point in human development, property emerges as an economic surplus, and the split between property-ownership and those without property is reproduced in the family, as it is reproduced in all areas of society and culture: man is the property owner, woman the property-less (proletariat), *and the property*. The woman's primary value as property and exchange commodity is as the means both of reproducing life, through bearing children, and ensuring the male inheritance of wealth, through her premarital virginity and postmarital fidelity. Monogamy can therefore be seen as a form of marriage designed to ensure paternity: 'the sole exclusive aims of monogamous marriage were to make the man supreme in the family, and to propagate, as the future heirs to his wealth, children indisputably his own'.[15]

But these patriarchal attitudes and roles themselves become reified and mystified, are seen as divinely ordained, as absolutes and not as relative phases in human social development. They seem to have a life of their own, divorced from the social and economic foundations that gave rise to them. Woman is absolutely reified as divine mother, eternal virgin – and as chattel and whore. And the feminine side of male identity must also be fiercely repressed – 'the outer woman and inner woman both represent danger to patriarchal masculinities.

The Engels analysis of the patriarchal family was recognized as authoritative within Marxism, and, for example, in the Soviet Union was seen as something of a blueprint for the emancipation of women. Thus we find Alexandra Kollontai, the first Minister of Social Welfare in the Soviet Union, stating as a matter of course: 'family and marriage are historical categories, phenomena which develop in accordance with the economic relations which exist at the given level of production'.[16] In her early writings she also projects an optimism about the reform of relations between men and women that now seems rather premature in terms of the subsequent Stalinization: 'In the place of the individual and egoistic family, a great universal family of workers will develop, in which all the workers, men and women, will above all be comrades.'[17]

But the Engels analysis has also been challenged: for example, the notion that men were the primary producers of food has been criticized – it has been claimed that women controlled food gathering. Certainly in horticultural societies there are many male activities – for example, homosexual rituals, pseudo-pregnancies and pseudo-childbirth – that suggest a defiance of a female economic power.[18]

But modern feminism has made more serious criticisms of the orthodox Marxist analysis. Jeff Hearn, for example, gives reproduction an importance that goes beyond the Marxist view: 'a materialism based on reproduction is a more basic and fundamental account than the "traditional" materialism, focusing on production'. And Hearn goes on to define two great classes – of men and women, who are involved in the 'class struggles of reproduction'.[19] This analysis obviously has connections with the anthropological ideas discussed earlier about an ancient female solidarity concerning reproduction versus a male solidarity over food.

Feminists have also argued that Marxism (as a patriarchal body of thought itself) has ignored the centrality of male power in social oppression. Thus whereas gender is seen in classical Marxism as arising from economic relationships – the male supremacy in gender arose from his economic supremacy – for some feminists, gender supremacy is the linchpin of patriarchy. In Robin Morgan's words: 'the key to male terrorism undoubtedly lies hidden somewhere in man's complex sexual nature'.[20] And perhaps less extremely, Bob Connell argues in *Gender and Power*, that 'gender divisions are not an ideological addendum to a class-structured mode of production. They are a deep-seated feature of production itself'.[21]

Here we can point to a possible ambiguity in Marxism: Engels does seem to accord gender relations great importance – his famous reference to the 'world historical defeat of the female sex' sees male domination as a key socio-economic development.[22] But subsequent Marxists often saw female oppression as a side-issue. For example, one of the greatest women Marxists, Rosa Luxemburg, devoted very little attention to women's issues, and was very scathing about 'bourgeois women' who she said 'will always fanatically defend the exploitation and enslavement of the working people by which they indirectly receive the means for their socially useless existence'.[23]

Marxism is completely rejected by feminists such as Andrea Dworkin, who argues that male power is self-existent. It just exists like God without cause:

> The power of men is first a metaphysical assertion of self, an *I am* that exists *a priori*, bedrock, absolute, no embellishment or apology required, indifferent to denial or challenge. It expresses intrinsic authority. It never ceases to exist no matter how or on what grounds it is attacked; and some assert that it survives physical death.[24]

Of course, if gender oppression is related to an inherent male violence, or male rapacity, we have passed beyond economic materialism into a different kind of explanation, either biological (men are innately more aggressive) or idealist (men are just like that).

One very important corollary to all theories of gender is their historical or evolutionary dimension: is gender seen as fixed or changing, as self-existent or having other causes? Clearly the Marxist view is that gender oppression can be changed only through social revolution – the underlying economic order must be broken up. Jeff Hearn posits something quite different: 'a radical restructuring of the social order imagined and derived from greater consciousness, no doubt feminist-inspired, around reproduction'.[25] One could argue that this is already happening – the campaigns during this century over contraception, abortion, and now the new technology enabling women to conceive without sexual intercourse – all point to a radical restructuring of reproductive relations in our culture.

For the non-Marxist, gender oppression can be ended through women's own efforts:

> She finds herself dazzled by the discovery of her own indestructible shape. She knows how to flock with other women – and how to separate but remain connected, how to combine yet retain her integrity. The model for what she is and what she can do is everywhere around her, one energy, evincing itself in multiple forms, omnipresent, erotic: the model is herself and her selves.[26]

In Robin Morgan's view, women can change history by opposing male power, and realizing their own power.

But the adherents of innate male rapacity also tend to project a sense of pessimism: how do we change biological or otherwise inherent traits? Thus Dworkin's apocalyptic vision seems without limit: 'For men, the right to abuse women is elemental, the first principle, with no beginning unless one is willing to trace origins back to God, and with *no end plausibly in sight*' (my emphasis).[27]

One of the great problems with notions of 'reproductive revolution' or gender solidarity is how these dovetail in with existing political struggles. What about concrete struggles against unemployment, cuts in services, racism, and so on? For example, in the British coal-miners' struggles of 1984–5 and 1992–3 against pit-closures, the women from the pit villages were very prominent politically, agitating and organizing all over the country.[28] It would be a brave soul to argue that these women should organize *as women* against male power – what about their solidarity with their husbands/boy-friends/fathers/sons? Thus a radical feminist theory could prove very divisive in actual grass-roots struggles. The same is true in anti-racist campaigns: should black women not solidarize with the black men around them against persecution, police harassment, and so on? Or if the workers in a factory are fighting against closure, wage-cuts or worse conditions, can the women workers afford to separate off from the male workers?[29]

One of the interesting results of the miners' struggles mentioned above is that some marriages in pit villages seem to have changed, as the men accorded the women a new respect.[30] This suggests, surely, that the struggle of women against oppression by men can go on *alongside and within* campaigns in which they fight with men. It also suggests that all political and social theories can only really be tested out in struggle: as contemplative exercises some of them may seem attractive, but 'theory is grey' compared with the actual grass-roots fight for jobs and services. But the 1980s, which saw such right-wing governments and ideologies in both America and Britain, tended to produce doubts that a linked feminist and anticapitalist struggle was possible.

MASCULINITY IN PATRIARCHY

What is the relation between the masculine gender and patriarchy? The anthropologist David Gilmore relates gender to the material conditions that exist at the time – as he puts it:

> The data show a strong connection between the social organization of production and the intensity of the male image. That is, manhood ideologies are adaptations to social environments, not simply autonomous mental projections or psychic fantasies writ large.[31]

He concludes that it is the harshness of the environment, the scarcity of food and other resources, that impels the male to take a 'masculine' and dominating role. The earliest primitive division of labour has often been assumed to consist of men doing the hunting, fishing and carrying out warlike activities, and women looking after children, cooking, and taking care of the home. And indeed this division still exists in those preindustrial societies that survive today: 'Men are always given the tasks of procuring animal protein, fending off predators and fighting wars.'[32]

Gilmore makes the profound point that men do not take easily to such a life, and therefore have to be conditioned by means of all kinds of rituals and social expectations to show valour. In this sense male aggression and courage is 'unnatural' and highly culturized. An example of this from our own culture occurred in the First World War, when a massive propaganda exercise was conducted to recruit men to go seek honour and glory, and when women went round pinning white feathers on men in civilian clothes, hoping to shame them into joining up. The Vietnam War is significant in this respect since the state propaganda machine began to break down, as more and more men were prepared to reject the expectation that they should go and fight and die (and kill) for their country. The cultural norm of masculinity itself began to disintegrate.

Anthropologists such as Gilmore are therefore not content to envisage patriarchy purely as a question of male attitudes and feelings or fantasies, isolated from the social context as some kind of absolute or 'essentialist' phenomenon. For one thing, that leaves unexplained those cultures, such as Tahiti, in which men are much less masculine, and where there is little expectation as to how men should behave, and there is a greater equality between the sexes.[33] If patriarchy is purely an 'autonomous mental projection' or an expression of male biological drives, then we are at a loss to explain societies where these projections and drives do not seem so strong. Gilmore indicates that in Tahiti there is little pressure on men to provide for families, since the environment is relatively benign:

> Few demands are made on Tahitian men. They do not hunt. ... There is no warfare or feuding. ... The local lagoon provides plentiful fishing. ... Arable land is also plentiful. ... Domesticated animals are plentiful. ... The economy, rather than fostering competitiveness amongst men, fosters an unusual degree of cooperation.[34]

There are also indications that in cultures where women have economic importance, their social value also increases, for example, in Iroquois society and parts of West Africa.[35] And in many pre-industrial cultures still existing, the relations between men and women seem to correlate with the complexity and intensity of production – in his analysis of New Guinea societies, D. K. Feil comments: 'it is in societies of relatively low production, those in the eastern highlands, which compared to those in the western highlands, have more recently intensified agriculture and pig husbandry, that we find the most antagonistic and exploitative male-female relations'.[36]

Patriarchy is in this view an economic organization of society, that propelled men into economically dominant positions in the external world, and propelled women into the home. But where conditions permit, this harsh division need not occur – there can be greater cooperation, and less stereotypy of gender. This relaxation of gender can be seen going on in our own society: there are men who do not go along with the macho woman-demeaning male image. How can we explain this if patriarchal attitudes are inherent in men? Masculinity and machismo are shown to be clinal not absolute categories, and correlate with the degree of social hardship and deprivation. Furthermore, misogyny correlates with the denial of the feminine aspect of male identity, which in many cultures is considered suspect and indeed catastrophic.

CAPITALISM

Capitalism might seem to contradict Gilmore's 'harsh environment' thesis, since it is very affluent. None the less, it is a ferociously competitive and anarchic culture. For many people, there is the permanent danger of falling into poverty, becoming unemployed, going bankrupt. Thus the work ethic has evolved, which translates these material conditions into a psychology of abstinence, hard work, thrift and guilt (and blame). There is also a super-abundance of military aggression between nations, and fierce class tension.

Capitalism is therefore a culture of conflict and great inequality – a kind of jungle. We could argue that in this wilderness men still emerge as providers, protectors and economic tyrants of their families, and still bound by the ferocious requirements of masculinity.

But Gilmore's notion of the harsh environment has to be modified to include not just material or economic harshness but emotional and spiritual deprivation. Our culture must be the most affluent that has ever existed: it is possibly one of the most negative in terms of how nurturing it is to people. Child abuse – which appears to be a massive iceberg in our culture – is testament to that, and is not confined to working-class families. An example of non-economic deprivation is seen in the British boarding school system, where boys from mainly affluent families were traditionally put through a harsh, even cruel regime, that bred fierce ideologies of masculinity ('don't blub for your mother').

Thus the purely materialist analysis of masculinity – that there is 'a strong connection between the social organization of production and the intensity of the male image' (Gilmore) – is inadequate, since it fails to take into account psychological factors. We might argue that in our culture one reason young males are so angry and destructive is not so much that they haven't got any money, but that as persons they are devalued. They are seen purely as units of production. This fails to nourish the heart and the soul, and many men in our culture – including affluent ones – feel soulless and heartless. Their creativity is suffocated in dead-end jobs; their imaginations are curtailed by our blinkered education system. At least the hunter-warrior males in tribal societies have an authentic contact with nature, they experience the flow of energy in their own bodies, and they have a deep contact with myth and ritual. What do we have in comparison? Quiz-shows on TV, the occasional football match, drinking in the pub. Our culture is impoverished to an astonishing degree: it has been disembowelled, emptied out. The triumph of commodities, and the dominance of machines, has torn out the heart and soul of men.

Capitalism seems to pose great dangers for all human beings, for it is in its essence anti-social, atomistic. Whereas tribal and other pre-industrial societies are characterized by their various stabilizing solidarities (gender, clan, tribe, and so on); in capitalist culture nothing is stable. No sooner have a community of people established themselves than the material basis for their community is destroyed by the ever-restless technological and commercial drive. This is clearly seen in the external colonialism that has gone on – for example the destruction of the aboriginal peoples of North America – but there is an internal colonialism as well. Thus in Britain many of the great working-class conurbations that came into being as a result of the Industrial Revolution are being torn apart by unemployment and poverty – the same is true in America.

Thus when Margaret Thatcher proclaimed 'there is no such thing as society', she expressed a profound truth about the capitalist order. It cannot recognize society as a community, since it is based on the commodity. Fetishism and alienation have assumed monumental proportions – but in the process, people are naturally plunged into despair, rage and meaninglessness. They become cultureless.

The nub of this argument is that it's not men who create harsh and conflict-torn cultures, but those cultures which create the cult of masculinity, and propel men, *whether they like it or not*, into the traditional male roles. Thus the famous Mediterranean machismo can surely be related to the harsh rural lives that the peoples of that region endure – southern Spain and Italy, Greece, Turkey, Morocco, Algeria and Tunisia. In all of these cultures there is a pronounced macho culture, where a man is expected to father many children, provide for his family economically, usually by working extremely hard, and also protect his family against bandits, feuds with other families, and other dangers.[37] In the more urban and more affluent north of Europe, these pressures are reduced. Such macho cultures also tend to be extremely homophobic, and feminine men are intensely feared and disliked.

Counter-examples shown by Gilmore (e.g., Tahiti, or the Semai people of Malaysia), prove that men are not innately aggressive and harsh, or indeed innately 'masculine'. Masculinity has been demanded of men in many cultures in order to economically preserve the tribe and the family. But in cultures where there is no external danger, and where food is plentiful, and there is a cooperative economy, it seems that men do not have to become 'masculine'. They are quite happy to cook, visit the village homosexual for sex, and run away from fights. Gilmore reports that in Tahiti: 'Macho types are regarded as foreign and unsavoury.'[38] There is clearly a danger of idealizing such cultures, and wishing or supposing somehow that ours could be the same – but this cannot be achieved simply by good intentions. That ignores the underpinning social conditions that permit or forbid men to be nonmacho. How are these conditions to be changed? Can they be changed?

At any rate, there is plenty of evidence that things are not unalterable. Masculinity is no more unchanging than society itself, with which it is indissolubly linked.

WAR

Another way of describing the need for tough masculinity is that in conditions of great danger, such as war or famine, men are dispensable, whereas mother and baby are not, if the family/tribe/clan are to survive. Thus it makes sound biological sense that men go out and face the dangers, apart from the obvious point about the greater physical strength of the male. There have not been many women warriors, and it is rare to find women hunters.

Again I am suggesting that it is not male aggro that produces fighting, feuds and wars, but those social conflicts that require the production of male aggression and warlikeness. Conflict is not hormonal but social. We would therefore expect to find societies which are not aggressive and do not practise war, and anthropology has become very interested in such cultures, for example the Semai, and the Xingu of Brazil. Thomas Gregor comments about the latter:

> there is no tradition of violence among the Xingu communities. In fact, the value systems of these communities are 'anti-violent' in nature. Supernatural sanctions inhibit the expression of aggression, prestige is awarded to men who avoid conflict, and methods of socializing children discourage displays of anger.[39]

Thus facing environmental dangers is not innately given to men: they have to be 'hyped up' to do it. Gilmore makes a telling point about warfare:

'Numerous studies have shown that the average soldier is extremely timo-
rous in battle-field situations and that he "regresses" and reacts "passively"
under enemy fire.' He goes on: 'as it often includes a military obligation,
the male role often requires a certain kind of discipline or indoctrination to
put reluctant youths in the proper frame of mind'.[40] The key phrase here is
'reluctant youth' – killing people is not at all a natural male activity – men
have to be browbeaten and brainwashed into it, and taunted with accusa-
tions of cowardice if they object. Indeed, Lynne Segal has made the very
profound point that soldiering, so far from being an aggressive activity, is
primarily masochistic:[41]

> Theirs not to reason why,
> Theirs but to do and die.
> (Tennyson)[42]

I am also reminded here of Hemingway: supreme macho masochist! (see
Chapter 6).

I remember when National Service ended in Britain, one of the arguments against ending it was that it helped boys 'become men'. It 'made a
man of you'. Speaking for myself and my friends at the time, we were
heartily glad to miss that pleasure!

Peter Lewis, in an article in the collection *Male Assertions*, describes
wonderfully the uninterrupted passage he made from boarding school into
the army and then to Oxford. What was common to them all was the excision of femininity. He discusses the violence of language used in the army,
not just in the form of swear-words, but the use of sexual imagery to
describe the operation of guns:

> It points up with clarity the logic of a masculinity that uses women
> instrumentally. Under that regime women stood for emotions and feel-
> ings that might, unless they were outlawed, impede discipline. In the
> end, a trigger had to be pulled, a button pressed, and it took 'men' to do
> it, because only men were capable of surrendering all compassion.[43]

I think the last comment is incorrect – women have often demonstrated
their ability to be ruthless, but his descriptions of school, army and university demonstrate vividly the *socialization* of males that goes on in our
culture. This socialization is designed precisely to construct the artifice of
the man without feelings or compassion, the man who 'gets things done',
the man who makes five hundred people redundant, the man who fires the
Cruise missile into an Iraqui city. But such men are not born, but made.

They are the creations of our own culture, and our own unconscious violence and hatred.

At the end of Lewis's essay, he comments ruefully on the emotional damage all of this did to him, leading to a chain of broken relationships. And the damage caused by the training of men is incalculable: every week I see it in my consulting room – men broken, weeping, enraged, isolated, virtually autistic, men asking what can they do to heal these terrible wounds.

THE END OF PATRIARCHY?

I have argued that the creation and cult of masculinity goes on unconsciously – the male in Sumbaru society in East Africa, who is about to undergo the agonizing ritual of circumcision, in order to prove that he is man enough to embark on cattle-rustling,[44] cannot be expected to refuse the ritual on the grounds that it is a cultural artifice! It is normally impossible to stand outside the process, or refuse to take part in it, or even become conscious of it as a cultural construct. We cannot just leave the culture we were born into, or reject its fantasies – where would we go? In a stable culture, gender assignment is a very stable process. Clearly it is not an arbitrary or meaningless artifice – different cultures need differing kinds of men, but generally there has been a need for men to carry out dangerous and difficult tasks. Hunting, fishing, defence against other tribes, propagating many children – being a man has been an awesome and hazardous responsibility.

What is remarkable about our own culture is that more and more people, both women and men, are beginning to challenge the erstwhile sacrosanct rituals, attributes and roles appointed to men and women. This suggests surely that our own gender system is going through an immense crisis and change, reflecting an even deeper crisis in the bowels of society. The rise of feminism, the rise of ecology, the peace movements, the increasing self-awareness of gay men and women, and other 'soft' political movements point to this. Does this not suggest that the unconscious symbol system that holds patriarchy together, and the social and economic relations that underpin that symbol system, are in fact, disintegrating?

I ask that question in a tone of genuine curiosity. For myself, I hope the answer is yes. I hope that men can begin to let go of some of this baggage which they have had to carry around for thousands of years. Just as feminist women are tired of being wives, mothers and housewives, I feel many

men are becoming fed up with being traditional husbands, fathers and providers, protectors and soldiers.

But the fact that some of us are fed up with it doesn't mean it's at an end.
For one thing, there are probably many men who don't want their traditional roles and attitudes to be 'deconstructed' at all, who want to stay as
traditional men. My own background is abnormal (but not uncommon),
having been raised in the working class and moving up to the middle class.
This gives me a kind of bird's-eye view of the whole thing, and tends to
detach me from the pigeon-holes into which many men are slotted.

But there is plenty of evidence that traditional masculine roles are still
expected of men – look at all the wars and conflicts in the world. As I was
writing this chapter, I read in the newspaper that four IRA men were killed
yesterday by the British Army in Ireland. Their ages were around 20. Here,
there is no sign of a slackening off in that male role of patriotic defender of
the motherland, however misguided we may feel they are. And in many
parts of the world we see men being very masculine, for example, in the
Islamic world.

The 'harsh environment' thesis leads to a rather gloomy scenario, since
most of the world today can safely be assumed to provide harsh environ-
ments, one way or another. Does this mean that men are still required in
those cultures to be hunters and warriors? Are the gangs on the streets of
New York and Los Angeles merely twentieth-century versions of an
ancient tradition? Are men irrevocably trapped in such roles?

As against that argument, one can point out that in Western culture there
are also clear signs of disintegration of both genders. Even the androgyny
that we find in pop music may be a sign or a harbinger. And for the whole
of the twentieth century, women have been demanding that they be allowed
to compete in the public world, for professional careers, for a public political voice, for choice over issues such as contraception and abortion, for the
recognition of women's sexuality as something in its own right. There is a
clear shift going on: the division between the male world of work (and
earning money) and the female world of home (and relating to people), is
being eroded.

To my mind it is impossible that one sex begins to do this job of criticism and dismantling, while the other sex looks on unchanged. Each
gender determines the other one – gender is a structural relation between
opposing categories that define one another. This suggests that the rise of
feminism is in fact part of a larger shift in the balance of gender roles and
values. If women have demanded a right to the public world, then men can
begin to demand a right to the world of feeling, intuition, relationship, the
private and inner world.

Let me ask a pointed question: what would make men stop oppressing women? It is doubtful if moral exhortation works, as many utopian socialists since Robert Owen have found to their cost. Two things seem to be required: first a profound crisis in patriarchal capitalism, so that both men and women become aware that it exists and that it is oppressive; secondly, a realization amongst men that patriarchy damages them. These two conditions are clearly connected, and it could be argued that they exist today in an embryonic form.

Patriarchy may be ending, not so much because we wish it to, but because the unconscious economic and social relations which give rise to it are ending. That particular form of property ownership and production, that form of human alienation, is disintegrating – we can see this for example reflected in the decay of religion, the 'holy form of human self-estrangement' (Marx). The actual symbolisms of patriarchy are breaking up – this is remarkable, since such symbols tend to be very long lasting, and appear to be permanent. Shifts are happening both in the archetypal systems of the unconscious, and in the deep-rooted social structures underpinning the culture.

The family, sexual relations, child-rearing – all of those hitherto taken for granted aspects of modern society are under scrutiny. People are increasingly dissatisfied with the old forms – marriages that were hollow, child abuse that was sanctified by custom, sexuality that was degraded and suppressed. This rotten core of modern civilization now disgusts us and has become intolerable. We see that many of today's youth are in profound despair, and are full of rage and hatred that they have been dehumanized in such a manner. Of course their despair is largely unconscious and inarticulate – but perhaps their violence expresses our own despair vicariously?

MARX AND FREUD

Are Marx and Freud compatible? Freud basically pointed to the ways in which human infants are deeply affected by their first relationships with their families, and how this early upbringing gives us deep-rooted attitudes and feelings for the rest of our lives. But Freud accepted the bourgeois patriarchal family as a given. It has been the task of Marxism, sociology and feminism to demonstrate the relativity of the bourgeois family and the patriarchal bias shown in Freud's own thought.

Thus, Freud tended to see the Oedipal relations in the family as eternal and unchangeable. This is not particularly surprising – Freud was a man of his time, a bourgeois scientist living in Vienna. Furthermore, psychoanalysis is after all confronted by people in great suffering who are not looking for social/political explanations or solutions, but want some relief from their neuroses.

At the same time, Freud tore away the hypocritical veil which had enshrined family relations like a halo of sanctity – he demonstrated the ferocious power struggles and the primitive erotic needs which are constantly present in the lives of young children, and which furthermore unconsciously dominate and undermine our adult relationships. Thus he dethroned the god of rationality and showed us what irrational primitive creatures we really are.

If we say, therefore, that Freud was a political conservative but a psychological revolutionary, we could argue that Marxism (and Marx) have been the reverse of this. Marxism has projected a social solution to the problem of the family, and has understandably been less interested in the individual's struggle with his own feelings, fantasies and inner conflicts. At its crudest this attitude has suggested: 'There is no personal solution to your personal problems.' This is palpably untrue – people do find a better way of living through doing therapy.

However, the political view of the family, sexuality and gender does give us a horizon much wider than Freud's. Whereas Freud suggests that 'ordinary unhappiness' is the best that human beings can hope for (although many analysts and therapists have disagreed), the radical critics of society have been more optimistic than this, and have seen Freud's pessimism as a political *rapprochement* with the bourgeois state.[45]

Despite these profound differences, we can see Marx and Freud as comparable pioneers, both investigating the unconscious well-springs of society, and laying bare the less than palatable truths about how and why we relate to each other in the ways that we do. It is significant that for both Freud and Marx the notion of fetishism was important, since it is a concept that is needed to explain so much of our social and psychological existence. Our material existence is fetishized, so that money has become our true god and our society is driven by the relentless and inane need to produce more and more consumer goods; our emotional and spiritual existence, and our relations to each other are also ossified and 'estranged'.

Both Marx and Freud pointed to an alienated power standing over us – for Marx, the economic relations we are involved in ('men inevitably enter into definite relations, which are independent of their will'[46]); for Freud, the unconscious itself (coupled with the superego – the inner critic) is the force that debilitates us ('[the] ego is no longer able to fulfil the task set it by the external world'[47]). And both point to a means of liberation – the unconscious can become conscious. The working class can grasp its revolutionary capacity to change the productive relations; the ego can extend its self-knowledge and become less paralysed by the unconscious.

It's surely not an accident that two such monumental bodies of knowledge should arise within fifty years of each other in the nineteenth century. Both of them tackle the issue of human impotence and the possibility of transforming that impotence into empowerment, one at the social, the other at the individual level. Both offer *practical* solutions to human problems: 'the reform of consciousness consists entirely in making the world aware of its own consciousness, in arousing it from its dream of itself, in explaining its own actions to it'.[48] Both of them bring to fruition the modern task of emancipating the human being from all forms of mental and physical servility and bad faith.

On the subject of the relations between men and women Marx said this:

> The immediate, natural, necessary relation of human being to human being is the relationship of man to woman ... this relationship reveals in a sensuous form, reduced to an observable fact, the extent to which the human essence has become nature for man ... it is possible to judge from this relationship the entire level of development of mankind.[49]

In this sense, patriarchy has represented not only the dehumanization of women, but also of men. Women are transformed into objects, a form of property. But the property owner in this relationship is thereby himself rendered inert, machine-like. If he cannot see woman as subject, but only as object, then his own subjectivity is ruined, shattered. If he cannot *relate to* woman, then he cannot be related to. This is the fundamental loneliness of man, and the desolation of militant masculinity.

He has become a man without a woman, a man without men, a man without himself, turned against himself. Patriarchy has turned him inside out, has dismembered him, castrated him, made his heart into a desert. He is no longer a man, and only half human. But from this desolation new life can be created. From our lingering death, we can be reborn – as men, and as human beings.

5 The First Woman

I have spent the last three chapters examining some of the background to the study of male identity, particularly the way gender is approached in feminism, sociology, anthropology and Marxism, as well as in psychotherapy. In this chapter I want to devote more attention to the psychodynamic approach to human personality, particularly in relation to gender and sexuality.

PROJECTION

One of the fascinating processes that goes on in psychotherapy is that clients start to treat their therapist as if they were someone else – a parent, lover, child, sibling, servant, god, worm, or an element in their own psyche. And these projections are unconscious and automatic – we have no control over them, and usually the client has no idea at first that it is happening. From this we can infer that projections of this kind go on all the time between people.

This phenomenon has had a most dynamic effect on the theory and practice of therapy. From it sprang the idea that many adult neuroses have childhood origins: that we unconsciously repeat old patterns of relationship and behaviour.

Let me give a typical example. Bob treats me with an unusual degree of deference and politeness. At first I make no comment about this, but gradually we are able to discuss it, especially when Bob himself starts to notice it.

From the beginning, I have been curious as to what his deference concealed, because experience teaches that excessive deference often conceals its opposite – some kind of negative feeling. And after several years' work (these processes take time and trust) Bob starts to show a scorn and hatred for me that is as fierce as the deference was placatory.

Here is a conundrum: Bob hates me, and probably hated me from the beginning, yet covered this up with politeness. He begins to connect these complex feelings with many aspects of his family – who were very polite and reasonable to each other on the surface. But Bob also begins to remember also how much covert back-biting went on, and how his mother and father tried to undermine each other in quite subtle ways. Thus his family was quite hateful beneath the surface.

Matters are more complex than this – for example, Bob also hates me because he needs me, and neediness in itself was considered unreasonable in his family. But we can leave the example at this point, for it suffices to illustrate the idea that our attitudes and feelings to others have origins in childhood relations. Bob has brought his emotional history into our relationship – not voluntarily but in a compulsive manner. The unconscious commands us and we may not say no.

The role of parents as early emotional influences is clearly crucial for most people, since for several years after birth they are the key people in our lives. Thus we arrive at this key principle in many forms of therapy: the present recapitulates the past.

Freud realized that many adult sexual and emotional problems stem from sexual and emotional conflicts in childhood – issues to do with desire, seduction, prohibition, which he brought together in the Oedipus complex. A simple example concerns the split between love and sexuality in many men – Freud related this to the intense love felt by many boys for their mother, coupled with the incest taboo which forces them to drive underground their intense erotic interest in her. This split continues in adulthood – in Freud's words: 'where they love they do not desire, and where they desire they cannot love. They seek objects which they do not need to love, in order to keep their sensuality away from the objects they love.'[1] Thus the erotic unavailability of mother haunts some men throughout their adult life.

FREUD, POST-FREUD

Freud's thought was imbued with patriarchal and biological notions: he was unable or unwilling to see that women's second-class status was socially determined. He saw women as castrated men, forever mourning their inferiority. He could not relativize gender inequality but saw it as eternal and unchanging. A school of orthodox analysts has continued to this day to assert that women are biologically doomed to live in the shadow of the penis – as Freud said, both boys and girls 'start off from the premise of the universal presence of the penis'. This has the important corollary that little girls are seen as having a masculine sexuality, and have to make the hazardous shift towards femininity at puberty.[2]

But feminism has been able to take up Freud's insights and show them to be, not universal biological structures, but the psychological reflection of patriarchal gender inequality. Juliet Mitchell's book *Psychoanalysis and Feminism* was instrumental in turning attention back to Freud, who exposed the fundamental oppressions of patriarchy: 'psychoanalysis is not a recommendation *for* a patriarchal society, but an analysis *of* one' (original emphasis).[3] She also criticizes those feminists who had presented a debased and popularized form of Freudian thought as Freud's genuine psychology. However, her own view of Freud strikes me as rather rosy – there is considerable evidence from his own writings that he saw female inferiority not as a consequence of patriarchy, but a cause of it.[4]

But within psychoanalysis itself a considerable movement has developed that turns away from the 'rule of the father' towards an investigation of the mother–infant relationship. Post-Freudian psychology has shifted the emphasis of empirical investigation towards very early infancy. For both boys and girls, the mother looms large in the first year or two of life: she gives birth to the baby, feeds it, usually deals with excretion, cleaning, bathing, comforts the baby physically, talks to it, listens to its babbling, and so on.

What effect does this early dominance of the mother have on children and on later life? In her book *The Rocking of the Cradle and the Ruling of the World*, Dorothy Dinnerstein asserts that it has a most crucial consequence:

> At her breast, it is not just a small furnace being stoked: it is a human being discovering its first great joy, handling its first major social encounter, facing its first meeting with a separate being enormously more powerful than itself, living out its first awareness of wanting something for which it must depend on someone else, someone who is imperfectly benevolent and imperfectly reliable because she is (although the infant of course has no way of knowing that she is) also a human being. This tie is the prototype of the tie to life. The pain in it, and the fear of being cut off from it, are prototypes of the pain of life and the fear of death.[5]

These are large claims: that this first relationship with another human being, with the first woman, is in many ways determining of the way in which one will come to regard life, the way in which one deals with dependence, feelings of helplessness, abandonment, and the need to be met and held, seen and heard. Are such claims purely hypothetical?

One must argue here that a massive amount of empirical research has been done on the very early relations between infant and mother, and the effect of this relation on later attitudes. Important figures such as Bowlby, Winnicott, Klein, based all of their work on intensive clinical work.

In one of his essays Winnicott emphasizes the empirical basis for his approach:

There are three main sources of information: studies by direct observation of infants and small children; studies based on the investigation of early histories of those who are ill; and follow-up studies of groups of deprived children in various categories.[6]

In the same essay, he cites Bowlby's explicit claim about the importance of mothering:

What is believed to be essential to mental health is that the infant and the young child should experience a warm, intimate and continuous relationship with the mother (or permanent mother-substitute) in which both find satisfaction and enjoyment.[7]

One might argue at this point that 'mother' need not be a woman, and that patriarchal culture has imprisoned women in that role. Is there any evidence that babies actually need a woman to look after them? With the obvious exception of breast-feeding, I am not aware of any – although we should not ignore the fact that many mothers want to look after their babies. Thus we have to distinguish between describing what actually happens in our culture, and its desirability or inevitability.

PSYCHOLOGICAL BIRTH

In the beginning, the infant defines itself in relation to a woman.[8] Its early primitive feelings of need, love, hate, fear, anger are in relation to her. Its sense of physical well-being and its sensual, even erotic, needs are catered for by her body.

Then it begins to emerge as an individual – in our culture, with its bias towards maternal care, this means that the mother carries a great responsibility in helping the infant deal with all the confusion and fear that surround this. Every baby is a solipsist. It sees the world as revolving around itself, or more accurately, there is no distinction between self and world: the Freudian analyst Margaret Little calls this 'primary total undifferentiatedness'.[9] This is a position of great omnipotence, and eventually, if the child is to establish a sense of self separate from the world, it has to be disillusioned of its omnipotence, and shown how relative its own importance and power are, and how other people have to be taken into account. But the way this is done is crucial. If the mother does it harshly, punitively, the infant will forever associate separation with punishment, or it will experience its own separateness as a kind of abandonment. On the other hand, it is equally dangerous if a woman needs the symbiosis with her baby as a prop for herself, and therefore refuses to let the child become separate from her.[10] So a kind of loving disillusionment is required.

The way in which one's mother handled these vital stages of symbiosis and separation will affect the child's view of women – and indeed of people in general, and the whole of reality – for the rest of its life. Did your mother refuse to let you be separate, and wanted you to remain fused with her for her own gratification? Did she force you to separate too soon, and wanted you to be a little grown-up, and look after her? Was she able to respect both your need to be separate from her, and your need to be close to her at times?

These issues of being an independent person, while acknowledging one's dependence on others, and being able to trust both those aspects of life, make or mar one's later life. Many people find as adults that their relations with others are bedevilled with some difficulty that goes back to those first weeks and months. We find people who daren't get close to others, in case they are swallowed up; people who want to swallow others up; people who can't bear not to be close all the time; people who feel permanently rejected; people who retain an infantile omnipotence towards other people – such problems are quite common in adult life, and wreck many marriages and other relationships.

DESIRE AND IDENTIFICATION

But in addition to these issues of fusion and separation, the infant is immersed in networks of desire and identification with both parents that are awesomely complex, and beyond the scope of this book to summarize adequately.[11] Crudely put, the child is involved in relations of love, need and desire with both mother and father, that is, it finds itself the object of their love and desire, and comes to desire them. At the same time, it yearns to be like its parents and also looks for an image of itself in them.

We can set out an idealized paradigm for heterosexual development – the heterosexual male infant is involved in a relationship with mother that is both loving and seductive: she treats their relationship as one between gendered opposites, and through this he learns that for her he is a desirable other. And for him, she becomes the prototype of the sexually desirable other. He also discovers that his father also desires his mother – he has a rival and a model. The boy admires, envies, and wants to usurp his father's

position as his mother's lover, but if these conflicts in the boy are successfully contained by his parents, he will be able to let go of his mother, and
compete with his father in other symbolic ways, identify with him – and
eventually find his own woman.

This question of 'containment' of the boy's Oedipal desires is a most
delicate issue. On the one hand, the boy needs to realize eventually that he
is not his mother's lover and that that is his father's prerogative; on the
other hand, he needs to feel that his incestuous desires for her are understood and not condemned out of hand, and indeed are to a degree reciprocated by his mother. It is a question of accepting the feelings, but not their
being acted out. If you like, the boy must be allowed to want to replace his
father (and seduce his mother), but not allowed to do it. Within that male
rivalry and identification lies the seed of the masculine development of the
boy.

We can see how the masculine gender is closely tied up with four great
developments in the heterosexual male infant: he separates from the female
symbiosis; he perceives himself as an opposite to his mother (and someone
who is loved and desired by her); mother is seen as the first desirable
woman in his life; and father is perceived as a rival/model. But these developments – separation, desire and rivalry – are linked. That first separation
gives boys a yearning for mother, a sense of deprivation which sexuality
promises to redeem. This blend of loss and recovery is not in itself pathological – damage arises when the balance swings too much one way or
another, towards incest or abandonment.

Thus we find men who have been damaged by being allowed too much
sexual contact with their mother – the infantile symbiosis is perpetuated
and overly eroticized; and men who have been damaged by not being
allowed to have any sexual feelings towards her or from her – then their
guilt and rage and fear about their own and women's sexual longings can
be overwhelming. *There can be too much incest between mother and son,
but there can also be too little.* I have clients who are still in a state of erotic
fascination about their mothers, and therefore find it very difficult to relate
to other women; but I also have clients who are completely baffled by
women, since their mothers were emotionally and erotically deadened
towards them. Thus the incest taboo is a relative one: there is what the
Jungian analyst Andrew Samuels calls an 'optimally erotic relation'
between parents and children.[12]

Earlier, I used the phrase 'idealized paradigm' to describe the above
account of heterosexual development. It is schematic and theoretical and
ignores many other factors. In particular, the reverse paradigm also applies:
the male infant loves and desires his father (and is desired by him) and

yearns to take the place of his mother as his father's lover. The clash of the two paradigms is partly affected by the wishes of the parents themselves (in turn reflecting society's requirements): many parents expect their sons to become heterosexual, and no doubt many do so in filial obedience, thereby repressing the obverse homosexual paradigm: 'As a rule the father prefers his daughter and a mother her son; the child reacts to this by wishing, if he is a son, to take his father's place.'[13]

This partly explains the homophobia found in men – they fear and punish their own homosexual desires which were forbidden to them. For many heterosexual men, love for other men remains a sore area, one that they either avoid totally, or express in symbolic ways, for example, in physical contact sports, or heavy drinking with the boys, and so on.

Parental influence obviously counts for a lot: the psychiatrist Richard Green in his research found that very feminine boys had often found parental approval for cross-gender behaviour, for example, dressing in girls' clothes, playing with dolls, and so on.[14] These were boys who had not been allowed to separate from the maternal symbiosis, and had identified with mother (and mother's body) very strongly.

Green also found that feminine boys tended to become homosexual or bisexual, suggesting that there is a connection between gender and sexuality. None the less, it is not an invariable connection: many gay men are not feminine – indeed there are macho gay men, for example, gay skinheads. And there are many feminine heterosexual men. Thus the link between gender and sexuality is not an absolute one – we cannot predict one from the other with certainty. The psychological stereotype that in boys, identification with the father leads to a masculine heterosexuality, and with the mother to a feminine homosexuality, is not necessarily true. One meets many heterosexual men who have a very powerful connection with mother and a weak one with father. D. H. Lawrence is a classic example – of course, he had an unresolved homosexual identity, but then which Western heterosexual man doesn't?

We also have to be careful about our ethnocentricity here: in some tribal societies homosexual activity often seems to go hand in hand with aggressive masculinity. D. K. Feil describes lowlands societies in New Guinea where male homosexual behaviour is widespread, and where 'warfare was widespread, head-hunting an occasional concomitant, and male aggressiveness was highly valued'.[15] In horticultural societies homosexuality has often been prevalent as an expression of anti-feminism, since women have been the main food producers in such societies (and men felt devalued).[16] And David Gilmore quotes Ian Buruma's discussion of the Japanese samurai warrior, among whom homosexuality was viewed positively: 'Good lovers make good soldiers.'[17] Not a slogan to be found on the notice-boards of Sandhurst or West Point! The accumulation of anthropological evidence shows clearly that homosexual activity has very different functions in different cultures.[18]

Thus we have to distinguish between three types of identity: sex identity, normally assigned according to the external genitals at birth; gender identity, usually but not necessarily linked with sex identity (that is, most boys are encouraged to be masculine); and sexual orientation – whether one is heterosexual, homosexual, bisexual. Clearly the relations between these three categories of identity is much more complex than popular mythology ('males are masculine and heterosexual') would have it.

None the less, the connection between gender and parental influence can be painted in broad brush-strokes: boys who have close relationships with their fathers will tend to adopt a variety of masculine gender; boys who are closer to their mother will tend to be more feminine. And the same is true for girls: girls with distant mothers and who become close to their father tend to become more masculine than girls who are closer to their mothers.[19] But this research also demonstrates that Freud's suggestion that little boys and girls are both masculine is wrong. Indeed, one might invert this idea, and say that both little girls and boys are bound into the feminine symbiosis – but boys have to break from this in order to become not-women.[20]

FEMALE POWER

One can assume that generally femaleness, in the concrete form of mother, comes to take on different meanings for boys and girls: the girl learns to incorporate her into her own identity; the boy, whilst unavoidably taking her into himself as part of his own feminine make-up, must also distinguish himself from her: 'the boy must achieve an inner detachment from the incestuous links to his mother, though these will remain the foundation and model for later love'.[21]

That quotation from Melanie Klein encapsulates two very important points: that men need to have separated from their mother if they are to form satisfactory relations with other women; but that those later relationships will to a degree re-enact that first relationship. This is obviously quite a delicate balancing act – to have good relations with women, a man needs to have had good relations with his mother, but not too good! Otherwise he will never want to be with another woman (and he might become a transsexual). On the other hand if his relationship to mother wasn't so good, that will also tend to get repeated in adult life.

But there are wider consequences. It can be argued that female power is so awesome in early infancy, and often so unrelieved by a masculine presence, that males must strive to contradict it, and spend their whole lives taking refuge in structures of power, male preserves, in order to get away from that deep primordial memory of being dominated by a woman. Women are feared, yearned for, hated, adored, needed, despised – some of the intensity of that early relationship with mother survives in all relationships with women. Adult sexual experience recalls to some degree that early physical dependence, when he sucked the breast of, slept in the arms of the first woman. Sexual intercourse itself recapitulates the original symbiosis, but that symbiosis is also intensely feared. In many cultures, intercourse is surrounded with many taboos – for example, that hunters do not have sex before hunting.

Thus, there is a deep conflict at the heart of men's relations with women: there is the wish to be intimate with a woman, to become one with her, and also the dread of being enveloped again.

Women also have very ambivalent and powerful feelings towards women and towards themselves as a woman, as a result of their relationship with their mother, and their need to separate from her. But there is a fundamental identity between daughter and mother: the girl is able to become that which her mother is; but the boy must become that which she is not. Thus he must turn to his father for an image of maleness, in order to find out what he must become. Here lies a potential danger: that that first massive influence of the mother may be so great, and possibly not sufficiently corrected by the aggressive potency of the male presence, that the boy is unable to separate from his mother, and unable to establish a non-female identity for himself. R. J. Stoller gives a succinct summary of these ideas in his psychoanalytic study of gender:

> To be a male, one must guard against being [like] a female in one's physical features, movements, emotions, erotism and so on. This task can become a frantic preoccupation (for example machismo) in sexually polarized cultures where boys in early life are close to their mothers and have aloof fathers.[22]

In such cases, the adult man will be full of contradictory feelings towards women. He may unconsciously want to be a woman like his mother – for she was powerful, she was alive, she was nourishing, she represented life itself. He wants to be like her, and to be close to her, inside her. He wants the symbiosis to go on for ever. But then he is faced with an enormous conflict: he also needs to get away from her, to emerge from within her, and be born again. He envies her, but alongside the envy is a wish to destroy her, and reduce her power over him, and his need for her. If he gives in to the pull towards her, he tends to feel powerless (castrated); if he moves away from her, he feels abandoned.

This produces that push–pull relation towards women that is so common in men. They want a woman, until she gets closer; then they want her at a distance, but then they want her close again. This drives women mad, as unconsciously it is often meant to. The sexual desire for a woman is often overly confused with the longing for the ancient symbiosis – the man's penis becomes the baby crawling back into the woman to find again the only safe place he has ever been. And women detect this sexual subterfuge – they find it creepy, disgusting, or just peculiar.

Let me make the point that I am not shifting blame from men to women. I am not arguing that the problem for men is simply that their mothers are too powerful, and that the mother is to blame. That may be what individual men feel, and they have to work through their own feelings of anger and need towards their mother. But as an overall psychosocial explanation, it is fatuous. There was a tendency in the sixties to posit the 'schizophreno-genic' mother as responsible for driving her son or daughter mad. For example, H. F. Searles defines the relationship between mother and child as crucial in the establishment of schizophrenia: 'deeply denied positive feel-ings are the most powerful determinants of the relationship between the schizophrenic and his mother, and of the development and maintenance of the patient's illness'.[23]

This clinical observation can be used in isolation to make women the cause of madness in their sons and daughters: it's all mother's fault, (this is not Searles's position). Then it becomes an historical untruth, ignoring as it does the relation of the family to society. It becomes a kind of mirror-image of those feminists who say that it's all men's fault.

The question is: why is child-rearing so skewed towards female care of the child? Why do so many people get too much mother, and not enough father? Is this an innate disposition in men and women – that (like many male animals) men are indifferent to children, women are programmed to care for them? Or is it a culturally conditioned division of labour – men go out to work, women stay at home; men switch off from feelings, nurturing, and babies in general, while women are devoted to them? If it's the first, then it can't be changed, but possibly ameliorated. If it's the second, then it can be changed. The feminist Janet Jacobs provides an excellent summary of an object relations approach to these issues:

Child development, as it is understood within a feminist framework of object relations, is not based on the adequacies or inadequacies of the mother, but on a structural arrangement of family relations that locates the mother in a central position with regard to the affective realm of personality development.[24]

And anthropology provides evidence that in some cultures the mother–relation is not given the high profile it is in ours – for example, in Polynesia, infanticide, fostering and wet-nursing are widely practised, since 'mothers and children do not (much to the chagrin of Western observers …) appear to be strongly committed to each other'. And Sherry Ortner provides evidence that parenting itself is not given great value in Polynesia – children bond with a wide range of kin.[25]

In Western society there are signs that men are taking more interest in child-rearing, and that the rigid division of labour between work and home is crumbling. This is not the only requirement that will help male children to find their own identity – they need older males who will initiate them into a recognizable male world. They need men who are not functional robots in a mechanistic society.

FATHERING

Thus the role of fathering in the crisis of maleness is crucial – or rather the lack of fathering. In Chapter 3, I described the split between work and home, whereby men have disappeared from the home into the remote world of factory or office. For many children, Dad becomes a sepulchral figure who returns from work late in the evening just before they go to bed.

But for boys, this separation from father is critical for the development of their male identity. One of the father's key roles (and 'father' need not be the biological father) is to initiate the boy into manhood, into the world of men, where he can assume his identity as a man. Paradoxically, if he does not do this, he will find it very difficult to relate to women – he will either feel too merged with them, and/or he will have to keep a million miles away from them.

The father is needed to rescue the boy from the female world, so that he can identify himself as male. In many cultures this transition is marked as a solemn, highly-charged ritual. Vestiges of such rituals have remained in our culture – the Jewish barmitzvah, apprenticeship to a trade, and so on.

But it is pitifully weak – most boys are left floundering, unsure what it means to be a man, desperately short of male wisdom, male support, and so on.

Robert Bly makes the point that industrialism has caused this great wound, by splitting up the family: 'the love unit most damaged by the Industrial Revolution is the father–son bond'.[26] Whereas in the pre-industrial era, boys would see their fathers working at their trade or in the fields, and would join them at an early age, now boys have little experience of their fathers in this way.

Bly's nostalgia for an ancient state of intimacy between father and son may be overly romantic or just plain wrong – some tribal cultures have ferocious initiation rites for boys precisely because they have been so soaked in female life for years. Stoller describes the fathers in some New Guinea tribes implanting masculine values with brutality, not love:

> Cut off from their mothers, the boys are harangued, beaten, radically resocialized, and threatened with terrible physical dangers, including death. The initiations demonstrate overwhelmingly the fathers' powers to punish, and whatever incestuous yearnings the boys have for their mothers are shockingly thwarted in the rituals.[27]

Anthropologists have accumulated much evidence concerning the place of ritual in many societies in rescuing the youth from the world of women, and inducting him, often with such drastic measures, into the world of men.

Edward Tejirian, in his book on bisexuality in men, describes Melanesian cultures where homosexual rituals are used to help young boys make this dangerous transition. He highlights the symbolic importance of the erect penis in this culture as an image of manhood:

> It is because the phallus symbolizes male power that it can be credited as the means through which power, strength and maleness are transmitted to still-weak and powerless boys, *newly wrenched from the feminizing influence of their mothers*. (my emphasis)[28]

In *Iron John*, Robert Bly makes many references to initiation practices among Native Americans:

> Among the Hopis ... the old men take the boy away at the age of twelve and bring him down into the all-male area of the kiva. He stays down there for six weeks, and does not see his mother again for a year and a half.

The boy between eight and twelve years of age, having been taken away from the mother, passes into the hands of the old men guides who cover his face and sometimes his whole body with ashes to make him the colour of dead people and to remind him of the inner death to come.[29]

Such ceremonies are found throughout the world in pre-industrial societies, but as Bly insists, they have disappeared from our culture. In fact, for most boys, their father is the one who disappears every day on his journey to work.

Thus within our patriarchal society there is a hidden matriarchy – and this hidden culture is much concerned with feelings, with relationships, with raising children, with concrete living. If a boy grows up within this matriarchy, and sees his father as an ambassador of a grey emotionless world, to do with rationality, work of a rather disembodied nature, shallow relationships with other people, what is he to do?

Some men are still able to make a successful transition to male identity, because their father was able to bond with them, and share with them some of the creative aspects of his own world. Other men successfully become male, but inherit the emotional deadness, the inability to relate, of their father. Some men remain in the female world, and adopt its values, and come to despise or hate men, who they see as insensitive and coarse. Paul Morel, in *Sons and Lovers*, has some traces of this attitude in him. And there must be many men who hover between the two worlds, trying to take from both, live in both.

A boy needs his father both to protect him from the danger that his mother represents for him, and to protect her from the danger that he represents for her. What I mean is that the mother-son relationship, if isolated, can become too intense, too incestuous, too seductive, too destructive. *The third party* is required to intervene to protect both mother and son from these dangers. The boy's fantasies of seducing or destroying his mother, or her seducing or destroying him, can become unbounded and terrifying unless he sees concretely that his father is there as his mother's partner, and that his father and mother can confront each other, can be angry with each other, hate each other, love each other, without destroying themselves.

He sees father and mother seduce each other – that is a great disappointment (the Oedipal 'defeat'), but a necessary one, that leaves him free to pursue his own sexual fantasies without guilt or fear. What a relief that he does not actually have to become mother's lover! Ideally, he also finds that his hatred for his father is OK – it does not actually castrate his father, nor does it preclude them having a warm relationship. Indeed, the rivalry is part of the father–son bonding, and his hatred is a necessary part of establishing his own masculine identity. In addition, a homosexual love develops between father and son, – expressed in horse-play, wrestling, and such displaced activities in our culture. This is a vital ingredient in the boy's acceptance of the masculine role.

Perhaps this is the most crucial role of the father for the son: the father can rescue the boy from his archaic visions of a reactive primitive masculinity that feels desperately threatened by the woman and his need for her. Father demonstrates concretely that primitive masculinity is not the solution, and that one can learn to live with a woman without mutual destruction. Of course, in families where the parents themselves are locked in a primitive rudimentary relationship, this civilizing influence may be lacking, and the boy may grow up as a primitive in his relations to women, and adopt his father's violent misogyny.

The unfathered male is left holding his fantasies – that he can be destroyed or absorbed by the breast, the vagina, the female presence, or that he can destroy them, and in the process destroy his father. Women come to seem too dangerous, and he too dangerous to them. Love and sex become terrifying battle-fields, swamps, to which he is irresistibly drawn, but from which he must flee periodically to ensure the safety of himself and the woman he is involved with. He must remain remote and isolated, but within that isolation is tormented by feelings of yearning, desolation, despair. He can try to cut himself off from women, in the hope that that will make him a masculine being, but that simply reveals his deep fear of women. He can become a womanizer, but that is only another way of avoiding women and, often, one's hatred of them. He is left with his deep yearning for his father and his body – how is he to express this in his life? There is a poignant line in *Macbeth* which summarizes what I am saying:

> Fathered he is, and yet he's fatherless.
>
> (IV. ii)

He feels deeply abused and damaged, and tends to relate to others in an abusing way, since he knows no other way. Such is the condition of many modern men.

BREAST ENVY

The breast is both maternal and sexual; it nourishes and stimulates; it enfolds and penetrates. It is quintessentially feminine, yet may also be phallic, erect, shoved into orifices. Thus it is a most complex symbol, not only for men, but for women as well. This can provoke confusion and guilt around sexuality, since many men, under the guise of an adult sexual act, covertly refind their mother's breast. It's all a question of degree: an element of infantile gratification and 'perversity' can be assumed to be benignly present in all sexual activity by men and women. But if a man is acting out his desire to attack the breast, take it as his own, devour it, destroy it, or whatever, then his woman partner can start to feel abused. Needless to say, women have the same covert feelings about the penis (and indeed the breast).

But men are prone to breast envy. This was one of the lacunae in Freud's distinctions between the sexes: he perceived and described penis envy in women – which can be described both as an actual desire to have a penis, and as a more symbolic wish to replace men, or do men's traditional occupations, hobbies, and so on – but failed to notice that many men have very strong feelings of envy for the breast, the womb, the vagina. But then Freud was the idealized son of a Jewish mother: it was inconceivable to him that his penis should not be revered and envied!

The concept of penis envy is central to a patriarchal psychology, since it defines women and women's psychology in terms of men. The woman is a castrated man – both sexes are defined by their relationship to the penis: 'Freud believed that maleness and masculinity are the primary and more natural states, and that both males and females consider femaleness and femininity less valuable.'[30]

It is interesting that in Lacanian psychoanalysis this centrality of the penis is maintained. Or rather it is the phallus as a signifier which comes to define both sexes: 'By its presence or absence the penis becomes the defining characteristic of both sexes.'[31]

Basing himself upon a biological psychology ('Anatomy is destiny') Freud was not able to relativize or question the phallic bias of his culture. Penis envy has therefore been seen by orthodox analysis as an irreducible anatomical fact – this is indicated by the title of Freud's 1925 article: 'Some Psychical Consequences of the Anatomical Distinction Between the Sexes'.[32] Women are seen as castrated, not psychologically or socially, but biologically. The clitoris is a second-class penis, and the vagina is a complete blank ('is virtually non-existent') until puberty.[33]

But later analysts have begun to analyse penis envy itself, and discovered that it reflects not an immutable sense of biological inferiority, but a denial of sexual and personal potency in oneself, stemming from some failure in the little girl's relations with her parents, and frequently her early relation with her mother.[34] Put simplistically, penis envy asserts 'I wish to be male since I am not allowed to be female (I am not allowed to love my clitoris/vagina).' But in actual therapy or analysis, these unconscious attitudes can be broken down, dissolved and transcended, and a new sense of being female recovered. Furthermore, many little girls do adopt 'feminine' traits at an early age, and have no desire to be 'masculine' – they have accomplished a good enough identification with mother. Of course, that feminine identity includes the veiled message, imparted by patriarchy, that women are second class and that femininity exists *for men*.[35] Hence clitoridectomy is practised in some cultures as a physical sign of female mutilation and the denial of female sexuality.

One might also suggest that orthodox psychoanalysis, in its treatment of women as castrated men, itself perpetuates a profound and unconscious denial of female identity: its masculinization of girls reflects the 'dread of woman' that Karen Horney emphasized.[36]

Analysts such as Horney have suggested that for the very young infant the breast is the most important bodily organ, and the most important symbol of relationship, and this importance is retained unconsciously by adult men. For example, over sixty years ago Karen Horney described her discovery of men's envy of women:

> When one begins, as I did, to analyze men only after a fairly long experience of analyzing women, one receives a most surprising impression of the intensity of this envy of pregnancy, childbirth, and motherhood, as well as of the breasts and of the act of suckling.[37]

Melanie Klein posited that both male and female infants have very intense feelings towards the breast, including envy, the wish to destroy, as well as adoration and the wish to incorporate the breast into oneself:

> In phantasy the child sucks the breast into himself, chews it up and swallows it; thus he feels that he has actually got it there, that he possesses the mother's breast within himself, in both its good and its bad aspects.[38]

The earliest experience ideally is that the breast is the source of nourishment and comfort. We might say that for a time in early infancy it represents life, love itself.

Thus a woman's body can become suffused with mythological and mysterious qualities. It becomes far more than flesh. It is temple, home and source of life. It provides food. The womb is the place where we all began our fleshly existence. The vagina is the gateway to the womb, which men can periodically re-enter. Men yearn to get inside this body again, to feed from it again, to go back to their point of origin. There is also the strong feeling of loss in many men: the breast has been lost for ever. This is a proto-castration, perhaps the first and most traumatic of all separations.

Secretly, men yearn to have such a body, to be such a fountain of life, a source of nourishment, to inspire desire in other men. In many non-Western cultures the *couvade* – men having a pseudo-pregnancy and a pseudo-labour when their wives are pregnant – is common,[39] and we could argue that in our culture still exists in a considerably camouflaged form, or is sublimated in male creativity, exploration, and so on. In pre-industrial societies anthropologists have found very complex male rituals which seem designed to mystify female reproductive power: 'we find in Aboriginal initiations vomiting, blood-letting, phallic symbolism, simulated coitus and "envy" of female reproduction, all of which ... allot to men priority in fertility and reproduction'.[40] Here is a denial of female reproductive power that is not simply a patriarchal suppression, but also a product of envy.[41]

Klein has also described the darker side of infantile perceptions of the breast: that it is bad; that it will consume the child; that it will be destroyed by the child's anger:

> In the earliest reality of the child it is no exaggeration to say that the world is a breast and a belly which is filled with dangerous objects, dangerous because of the child's own impulse to attack them.[42]

As an adult, later in life, one can, in fantasy, repeatedly go back to this breast, to punish it, to check that it hasn't been destroyed by one's own ferocity, or that it will not destroy oneself. One can conquer it, play with it, disdain it, feed from it, adore it. Thus for some men, the breast remains reified, dehumanized, as a storage house of all the feelings that were not worked through in infancy.

Infantile fantasies – yes, but these fantasies remain as a dark hinterland in the unconscious, and become entangled with sexual desire, sexual fantasy. As fantasies, they have the inestimable value for many men in converting women into objects, and thus avoiding the dangers of intimacy. The breast replaces the woman, or perhaps the woman has never replaced the breast – women have never been perceived as persons.

In addition, in the earliest period of life, the breast is both self and other. If we assume that the new-born infant is in a state of undividedness, whereby subject and object are not distinguished, then it is likely that men yearn for the breast as a symbol of that time, when all things were one, before the lonely and separate ego made its entrance upon the stage. The breast represents oneself in a state of paradise.

We might also point to a homosexual element in breast envy: the man wishes for breasts, so that other men (originally his father) would desire him. In this sense he wishes to supplant his mother.

The breast fetish prevalent in our culture (seen clearly in pornography, fashion and cinema) shows that we are dealing with a very early period of relating. If you like, the yearning for the breast (and the woman) has remained intact, since it was not satisfied in some way or another, or possibly was satisfied too much. It is a kind of frozen archaeological layer in the psyche.

MATERNAL PSYCHOLOGY

I began this chapter by referring to certain important developments in post-Freudian psychology. Indeed the shift towards the study of early infancy and the mother–baby relation has been a sea-change. The phallocentrism of psychoanalysis has been overturned, as the vital role of the mother has been increasingly emphasized. Indeed it is possible this has gone too far, and the role of the father is now being underestimated – as we have seen he has a vital role in mediating the mother-son relationship, and as it were giving shape to the boy's inchoate masculine identity. The father is also needed by daughters, who need to be extricated from the maternal symbiosis.[43]

We might argue that this shift in the discipline of psychology reflects a deep unconscious shift towards the feminine in our culture. But many feminists are critical of 'maternal psychology' since it carries with it the danger of focusing entirely on the mother–infant relation and ignoring public male domination in patriarchy.[44]

There is also a danger of identifying women as mothers: from the observation that babies seem to need a very close relationship with their mother in the first few months, it may be a short step to arguing that women are obliged to fulfil that role – *Kinder, Kirche, Küche* again. However, if we accept that babies need close contact with an adult human being, who is able to offer them reliable 'mothering' – it may well turn out that, with the exception of breast-feeding, men are able to carry this out equally well. On the other hand, one should not underestimate the intensity of the bond that often develops between mother and baby – when something has been part of your body for nine months, it is not surprising that one has intense feelings about it after birth. Many women who are uncertain about their feelings about having a baby are surprised by the intensity of the love (and hate) they feel for it. Perhaps also we should not underestimate the psychological importance of breast-feeding for the baby.

The other reason that feminism has been critical of pre-Oedipal psychology is because of the importance it gives to the mother in the development of masculinity. Some feminists would much prefer to see fathers as the central figures – for then the inheritance of 'male violence' is clearly seen as passing down the male line (father to son). But suppose that male violence is partly a result of over-symbiotic mothers (and absent fathers), and a *lack* of masculine identity?

We shall see very clearly in the case of Peter Sutcliffe (see Chapter 8) that some feminists would dearly love to blame his father for his hatred of women, and feel uncomfortable with the idea that Sutcliffe was over-feminized by his intense involvement with his mother. Thus feminism tends to utilize classical Freudian theory – where the father rules, and is the main castrating figure. In fact, it is quite probable that Freud had a massive blind spot towards the mother-son relationship and, for example, in the Little Hans case ignored considerable evidence in his own case-notes that Hans fears castration not by his father – but by his mother.[45]

The deepening study of the unconscious psyche has revealed the great importance of the feminine and the female for all human beings. Whereas in external society we see so many signs of male power, in the repressed psyche we find evidence of a primordial female power. Dorothy Dinnerstein has put this rather extremely:

> Female will is embedded in female power, which is under present conditions the earliest and profoundest prototype of absolute power. ...

> The essential fact about paternal authority, the fact that makes both sexes accept it as a model for the ruling of the world, is that it is under prevailing conditions a sanctuary from maternal authority. It is a sanctuary passionately cherished by the essential part of a person's self that wants to come up (like Andersen's mermaid) out of the drowning sweetness of early childhood into the bright dry light of open day, the light of the adult realm.[46]

This position argues that the visible signs of male domination that are everywhere around us in society are in fact a protection against a deeper, more unconscious, less visible, female domination.

I think Dinnerstein has gone too far out on a limb – surely paternal authority is not simply a refuge from mother? Did patriarchy evolve purely as an antidote to matriarchy? This argument ignores the economic and social reasons for the development of patriarchy. It also tends to fall into circularity, since one can argue that maternal authority is itself part of the division of labour brought about by patriarchy. Feminists can argue with some cogency that the identification of women as wives and mothers is a symptom not a cause of patriarchal structures.

Lynne Segal makes the following objection to maternal psychology:

> Despite the insights of this approach into men's fear of intimacy and of female power, it cannot, however, carry the weight of explaining male domination. ... Nor can such an approach fully account for the nature, power and privilege of masculinity.[47]

I agree with this. To say as Dinnerstein does that masculinity – and patriarchy itself – is purely a defence against maternal symbiosis leaves out of account the non-psychological functions of gender. Masculinity has biological, economic, social and other functions which go far beyond 'the rocking of the cradle'. In a sense, Dinnerstein reduces the whole of modern history and human socio-economic development to the mother–child relationship. This is surely over-reductionist and overly psychological. Throughout the history of psychoanalysis there has been this grandiose temptation to explain phenomena such as war, sexuality, and creativity purely in terms of Oedipal or pre-Oedipal conflicts. This approach transforms psychology into a theology rather than an empirical discipline.

None the less, maternal psychology has been a necessary corrective to Freud, for it has demonstrated that for many people, mother, not father, is the significant other. She is not just the first woman, but the first person, the first environment, and presents us with the first shock of the not-me. For the male infant, this presents him with fundamental questions about his own identity and his difference from mother, questions that without doubt help to explain many aspects of masculinity as a compensatory force.

VAGINAL PSYCHOLOGY?

Semi-jokingly, one might suggest that since classical psychoanalysis – as the psychological ideology of phallic rule – is a massive cover-up and denial of female power, that a new vaginal psychology must be promoted. This would argue that, in fact, boys are terrified of women, envious of the breast and the vagina, see the penis as a pathetic 'widdler',[48] and desperately begin to construct defences against these fears. Everything can be reversed. Whereas classical psychoanalysis states that the boy (and the girl) is appalled to realize women do not possess a penis, and infers that his could be removed, we argue that he is appalled to realize he does not possess a woman's body, will never bear children or breast-feed them. He therefore idealizes his penis in a desperate attempt to recover something from an overwhelming sense of impotence and loss. His penis is not something that might be removed, but visible evidence that he has already lost something: he is only half or less of a woman. Castration is not a catastrophe waiting to happen, but one that has already happened: he has lost the breast that he believed was his by right. His penis marks him out not as supreme ruler but as an ignoble periphery. Secretly, he fears that the penis is not the pivot of the world, but an addendum. His most primitive wish is to be a woman like his mother – but this wish gives him enormous anxiety.

But he is also relieved to discover that adult men have already constructed ideologies that relieve his anxiety – misogyny, machismo, and so on. The external world of men offers some relief from the archaic perception of woman as goddess, and there are many male rituals designed to lessen the fear and envy of women. Men imitate pregnancy and menstruation, have homosexual rituals, go off into the men's hut, or down to the bar, and denigrate women. However, he can never entirely lose sight of that primordial fear – women are bearers of life, and he is not.

But vaginal psychology is uncomfortable not only for classical psychoanalysts – but for some feminists! Those analysts such as Karen Horney who had the temerity to point out certain facts staring them in the face – for example, that boys have a strong wish to be women, that little girls are aware of their vaginas and so on[49] – are dismissed both by the ultraorthodox analysts and the radical feminists. Strange bedfellows! Neither of them can accept the proposition of a deep-rooted female power.

STRIVING FOR WHOLENESS

The term 'penis envy' often has a perjorative connotation. But in my view, such intersex envy is not simply regressive or destructive – it also represents a striving towards wholeness.[50] Patriarchal gender mutilates human bisexuality, and forces each sex to adopt 'masculine' and 'feminine' traits and behaviours and suppress the contrasexual. Therefore, men and women yearn for the missing component.

Thus when female clients of mine have dreams or fantasies of penises, they often see such dreams as indicative of their need to be more potent, more penetrative in their lives. In this sense, penis envy is a positive sign, if we can unlock the feelings and needs within it.

In terms of sexuality itself, studies of female sexual inhibition have noted that there is frequently a fear of aggressive feelings towards the man's penis. Female orgasm is considerably aided and intensified by permitting a sadistic component to sexuality.[51] But it is precisely this healthy sadistic component that patriarchal society has tried to forbid women.

This, for me, highlights the erroneous thinking in the common assertion: 'all men are potential rapists/killers'. My rejoinder to that is: 'are all women potential rapists/killers? And if not, why not?' The point I am making is that sadistic feelings are not the prerogative of men – but men and women are socialized through patriarchal gender to adopt sadistic and masochistic positions respectively – unless that is, one believes that men are inherently sadistic. This takes us into biologism, which presumably also indicates that women are inherently demure.

But feminism itself contradicts such a gloomy view. The revolutionary quality in feminism consists in breaking through gender prescriptions, thus demolishing biologism at one fell stroke.

Therefore, I conclude that women could be just as violent as men, if society so ordained, and men could be just as 'feminine' as women.

Envy is based on lack; each sex lacks the contrasexual element, and therefore seeks it in the other sex. But this is not an inviolable state of affairs, laid down by biology or innate psychic archetypes. It is a socially constructed lack, and therefore can be changed, both through individual development (as in therapy) and collective political change.

6 The Fragile Male

Up to now, I have argued that boys are impelled towards some kind of masculine identity by great social and psychological forces. Many cultures demand it as an economic necessity: males are needed for hunting, war, the propagation of children, the protection of the tribe and the family. Thus there is a strong pressure on boys to separate from their mother, to break the 'proto-feminine' identity they have initially formed. Patriarchal society requires its infantry and its officers, who will regulate the exploitations essential to its survival, and in particular will keep women oppressed.

Many cultures also reveal a great male fear and envy of women: men tend to distance themselves from women by means of ritual and segregation and denigration.

Gender as power and gender as difference interlock. To exert power as males, men must be distinguished from women.[1]

There are probably other factors at work in the production of masculinities, which this book cannot explore – for example, it is possible that biological reproduction itself is facilitated by exaggerated sex differentiation – we see this clearly in the animal kingdom. The whole area of evolutionary biology – one of the most exciting areas of research into gender and sexuality – has to be omitted from a book of this nature.

Another area I have to bypass reluctantly is the concept of gender as the source of aesthetics and pleasure. Sometimes one gets so engrossed in the seriousness of the subject that one forgets that men and women do have fun together!

But in this chapter I want to look at the soft under belly of masculinity – there is a strange paradox at its heart: the more it is trumpeted, exaggerated, as in the bizarre displays of machismo, the more it easily appears to be threatened. Many varieties of masculinity are fragile through and through, and men seem perennially worried about not being masculine. This shows itself in many ways in our culture.

For example, cross-dressing is much more taboo for men than women. For women to wear trousers, jackets, ties, boots, is perfectly acceptable, and often fashionable. For a man to wear a skirt or a blouse is highly taboo – boys who persist in doing so are often referred to a child psychologist.[2] The same is true of cosmetics. Indeed male clothing is conservative, less brightly coloured than women's, and for many men, virtually a uniform: 'the suit and tie facilitate the sublimation of individual needs and desires to bureaucratic procedures and loyalties'.[3]

Homophobia appears commoner amongst men than women. Boys become terrified at school of being thought sissies, or being seen crying. In male institutions such as schools, the army, factories, there are many jokes about 'queers', 'shirt-lifters', and so on. But many people have commented that along with the homophobia goes a fascination with homosexuality – perhaps we should say that the homophobia reveals and conceals the fascination.

Men seem to have to constantly reassure themselves that they are men, not women. This goes along with the contempt and hatred that many men feel and express towards women, and towards gay men.

In his book *Presentations of Gender*, Stoller describes how many boys construct a kind of defensive armour against femininity:

He therefore creates a protective shield – 'symbiosis anxiety' – inside himself, in the form of fantasies that, if successful, endure, that is, become character structure. The behavior that societies define as appropriately masculine is filled with the forms of this defensive maneuver: fear of female anatomy; envy and resulting derision of women; fear of entering their bodies; fear of intimacy (of entering – even more than bodies – into women's inner selves); fear of manifesting and thereby revealing that one possesses 'feminine' attributes, in many cultures categorized in such qualities as tenderness, affection, uninhibited expressions of feelings. ... Therefore be tough, loud, belligerent; abuse and fetishize women; find friendship only with men but also hate homosexuals; talk dirty; disparage women's occupation. The first order of business in being a man is: don't be a woman.[4]

That is an excellent and comprehensive summary of the traits of machismo. In simple terms, the macho man protests too much. He has to go round telling and showing everyone what a man he is, because there is such a strong internal pressure the other way, towards the feminine. But even men who are not overly macho retain some of the features described by Stoller. Thus, misogyny – hatred of women – connects with a hatred of the inner feminine in men – both must be crushed for men to be 'men'.

This fragility in masculinity is not restricted to Anglo -Saxon or Western culture: Gilmore, in his anthropological survey of manhood stresses that in many cultures it is seen as problematic and not easily attained:

Amongst most of the people that anthropologists are familiar with, true manhood is a precious and elusive status beyond mere maleness, a hortatory image that men and boys aspire to and that their culture demands of them. ... Its vindication is doubtful, resting on rigid codes of decisive action in many spheres of life: as husband, father, lover, provider, warrior. A restricted status, there are always men who fail the test.[5]

Elsewhere, he states that 'men are made not born'.[6] Thus, complex rituals in many cultures emphasize to the adolescent male the awesome journey he must make in leaving the embrace of his mother in order to enter the sterner male world, where he will be required to carry out the arduous tasks allotted to men.

One thing is clear – maleness and masculinity must be distinguished. Maleness is nearly always incontrovertible. One can be the most camp queen on the block, but one is still male. Only transsexuals actually want to convert femininity into femaleness. Most feminine men do not.

It is the masculinities that are cultural artifices, constructs, and each culture produces the masculinities that it needs. Thus, there appears to be a spectrum of masculine roles and attitudes: from the highly macho to the relatively relaxed and anxiety-free. The macho image is always an anxious one, since it is not inherent in the male – one is always liable to find oneself doing or saying something that doesn't fit. Hence macho subcultures are often highly homophobic: I can remember football crowds mercilessly baiting footballers who were thought to be gay. The gay man is a threat to the macho man, since he reveals explicitly that which the macho man must suppress as deeply as possibly: his need for the love of other men, and the possibility of taking the feminine role.

It is significant that Gilmore reports anxiety-free homosexual activity in certain cultures, where masculinity is relatively stress-free.[7] We can tentatively conclude that hypermasculinity in men is 'unnatural' and has to be forced. Both men and women contain both masculine and feminine elements: but men are constantly vigilant about and repressive towards their own femininity.

POOR OLD HEM THE FRAGILE ONE

In Western culture, machismo is often turned into a myth, lived out by certain mythical figures such as Ernest Hemingway. This myth of masculinity is even more of a burden, a stressful role that is performed to a greedy audience. I was recently reading through some of Hemingway's writings, and I kept feeling exhausted. There is something relentless and strained about him, for example, in *Death in the Afternoon* – a kind of solemnity, a reverence for stoicism and death, a humourlessness, that eventually palls. I want to shout out: 'for heaven's sake, so some men like killing bulls, why do we have to go on and on about it!' Indeed I find Hemingway nasty, in his obsession on violence. It's as if he's saying: 'to be a real man, you have to watch the horses die (notice their guts trail on the floor), and the bulls die, and maybe watch the man die'. Then you are a man.

At one point in *Death in the Afternoon*, Hemingway lies awake in bed while something nags at him. Then he remembers it: one of the matadors was gored in that evening's bullfight, and 'when he stood up, his face white and dirty and the silk of his breeches opened from waist to knee, it was the dirtiness of the rented breeches, the dirtiness of his slit underwear and the clean, clean, unbearably clean whiteness of the thigh bone that I had seen, and it was that which was important'.[8]

Typically elegant Hemingway prose, but there is also something nastily erotic here: nasty because it delights in undressing a man and observing his wound. Is it fanciful to see the goring by the bull as the ultimate deflowering of the man, and the killing of the bull as the ultimate penetration by the man? Penetrate or be penetrated: this is Hemingway's horrified and thrilling fantasy-wish, which he repeatedly had to exorcize by seeing it performed by others, or by doing it to other men and animals in warfare and hunting.

It is clear from his writings that his great unconscious desire was to take the feminine role, whether emotionally or sexually, and also that this desire filled him with terror. Those of his fictional women who are rather submissive and passive – for example, Maria in *For Whom the Bell Tolls* – might lead one to conjecture that this is Hemingway's sexist view of women. But this argument posits a very rigid one-to-one identification between male author (or reader or viewer) and male characters. I would argue that Maria is in fact part of Hemingway himself – a feminine part of him that he dreaded being exposed, but that relentlessly pressed towards expression and consciousness. Robert Jordan expresses another part of Hemingway: heroic, courageous, ultimately doomed, masochistic.

It's only in his posthumously published novel, *The Garden of Eden*, that Hemingway's fascination with bisexuality and gender confusion comes out into the open – Catherine cuts her hair short, pretends to be a boy, and begins to address her husband as 'Catherine', and makes love to him in a rather undefined (presumably anal) manner: ' "You are changing," she said. "Oh you are. You are. Yes you are and you're my girl Catherine. Will you change and be my girl and let me take you?" '[9]

In his remarkable biography, Kenneth Lynn demonstrates again and again how in his stories and novels Hemingway devotes great attention to the woman's point of view. Of the short story 'Up in Michigan', Lynn says: 'Hemingway kept strictly within the consciousness of the half-resistant half-yielding, thoroughly frightened young woman lying on her back'.[10] Lynn also shows how the theme of lesbianism is not only recurrent in his fiction, but in his life – he knew many lesbians, and obviously enjoyed their company. Lynn comments: 'it was surely his firsthand experience of knowing how it felt to look like a girl but feel like a boy that was the fountainhead of his fascination with the ambiguities of feminine identity'.[11] Lynn is referring to Hemingway's odd upbringing, not only dressed as a girl until he was three or four, but treated as his sister's twin, dressed in her clothes, and so on. There is also the point that his mother had lesbian tendencies.

As against this strong unconscious pressure to be female and feminine, Hemingway therefore needed to constantly create his own rituals for manhood. This bipolarity also has its roots in his childhood: his parents not only treated him as a girl, but demanded of him that he be a virile boy – for example, go hunting with his father, use guns, hide his fears. Hemingway in turn had very high expectations about his father's masculinity: he is very dismissive about his father's suicide, seeing it as cowardice. One of his biographers speaks of 'the hated flaw of cowardice in the once-adored man who had sired him'.[12]

Hemingway's self-imposed test of manhood is so extraordinarily fierce and unrelenting that one suspects that he felt exhausted by it, and must have yearned to give it up. It is significant that he was a very heavy drinker, since alcohol allows one some relaxation, some refuge from all that self-flagellatory homoeroticism. It is of course an eroticism that is denied and suppressed, and this produces that sense of strain and tension that for me spoils some of his writing.

It seems odd perhaps to describe Hemingway's masculinity as 'fragile', but one is continually struck in his books by the role or persona that Hemingway puts on, or that his male characters put on. They are playing a part, a part that demands honour, courage, the ability to kill, 'grace under pressure'. Behind this mask lurks the traitor, the coward, the more feminine part, who wants to run away from war, who feels terribly needy and dependent on other people, who misses his wife desperately when she goes away, (and hates her for that), who doesn't want to take the male role, who wants to be made love to, who wants the penis inside himself. That side of him has to be suppressed, and if he (she?) gets too demanding, killed.

In one of his letters in which he is exhaustively (and exhaustingly) narrating one of his mammoth fishing trips, ('99 days in the sun on the gulf stream, 54 swordfish. Seven in one day. A 468-pounder in 65 minutes, alone, with no help'), Hemingway makes the presumably sarcastic comment, 'Poor old Hem the fragile one,' and repeats it a line later: 'Poor fragile old Hem posing as a fisherman again'.[13] Yet what tragic irony lies in those words – does it show in fact that Hemingway had some awareness of the discrepancy between his inner fragility and the outer macho pose?

Hemingway literally blew his brains out because of the competing pressures of femininity and masculinity within him. The masculine myth he lived by told him that non-masculine feelings and attitudes were lethal – and must be suppressed. But they were feelings that would not go away, indeed they were very important feelings to do with need, caring, love. He therefore suffered all his life from tremendous tension, depression and a manic escape into activity, and finally, death.

It is dangerous to generalize on the evidence of one man. But in Hemingway, we see something that is startling and paradoxical, and that makes us ponder the implications for all men. The machismo that Hemingway flaunted is profoundly masochistic – being a man for him involves risking being gored by bulls, shot at in wartime, and poisoned by alcohol. To prove that he was not a woman Hemingway had to submit himself to a wearying round of ritualistic contests with danger and death.

I have noticed this association in clients of mine: bravura masculinity involves a self-disregard, a 'taboo on tenderness', an erotic flirtation with danger, that is deeply masochistic. Of course, along with the masochism we find in some men all kinds of sadistic displays, rages, thuggishness, and so on. That is the conventional image of masculinity, much favoured by the radical feminists. The masochism is less obvious, but I would argue, goes deeper. I have already referred to war as a masochistic holocaust for men (see Chapter 4) – machismo as a whole points to a profound male self-destructiveness demanded by society. The 'real man', the tough guy, the Man with No Name, the Clint Eastwood character in spaghetti westerns – in real life he would be actually very sick, suicidal, stoical, doomed. He flirts with death because he wants to die, for he has never lived. That is too dangerous, for it will reveal aspects of himself that are taboo. He has never been allowed to live fully, and has now taken over the task of censoring and punishing himself.[14]

An astonishing example of male brutality and masochism is Gary Gilmore, who in 1976 killed two men in Utah and demanded to be executed by firing squad. Gilmore had a very disturbed childhood, was ignored, bullied and hated by his father, and took to a life of crime from his teens. At a crucial point in his life, he was given parole from prison and offered a place at art college, to further his considerable artistic talents. He stood at a crossroads in his life – and immediately took the path of self-destruction, carried out an armed robbery, and subsequently the two murders.[15] I would suggest that Gilmore wanted to be punished, could not grasp the opportunity to develop his talent, since unconsciously he felt he was too bad to live, since his father had not loved him. In men such as Gilmore, we see the truth in the psychological cliché that profound guilt and self-hate turn some men to crime in the unconscious hope of being punished.

LANCASHIRE

Hemingway and Gilmore may seem extreme examples of the masculine myth, but I remember my own fierce anxiety about being male when I was an adolescent in a Lancashire town, and went around in a gang of lads to pubs, dances and parties. We had a strict code of behaviour, and watched each other like hawks to make sure that we all followed it. Any divergence was usually instantly spotted and ridiculed. For example, the fact that I stayed at school until I was eighteen was treated with great suspicion: it wasn't 'manly'. So I did my best to hide the fact, particularly at dances or parties, when girls would say: 'What do you do?' How I used to wish I was something heavy and masculine like a plumber's mate, like one of my gang, or mended cars. But to be in the sixth form at school, studying for A levels – I was deeply ashamed.

Not only that, I was specializing in English – reading poems, plays, novels, a traditional 'girl's occupation'. So I couldn't even console myself with the thought I was doing something virile like physics or maths. And even at university I found the same code – the engineering students definitely thought I was a bit odd to be doing English with all the girls. I used to go in the bar with the engineers and the rugby players and manfully down pint after pint, determined to prove I was no less a man even though I liked Keats and Emily Brontë. Of course this suggests that somewhere I agreed that I wasn't 'manful' enough.

So many aspects of life infringed the strict code of masculine behaviour. The writer Sid Chaplin, who originally worked down coal mines, describes how writing itself was seen as unmasculine:

> I never thought in terms of becoming a professional writer. In the first place it was somehow feminine, that's why it had to be a secret occupation with me. It wasn't until I got my first postal order for half a crown that my mother found out, and then the whole family. I wrote completely under pseudonyms the whole three years until I came out of my apprenticeship, so nobody ever knew excepting the immediate family. That was the feeling you got in a mining village, a man found his place through his muscular strength and ability, or agility. Same whether it was the big

hewer, or a good footballer, or a breeder of pigeons, or a leekman. These were masculine things, and writing was very effeminate, so I said nothing about it.[16]

My own memory from adolescence isn't just that writing wasn't masculine – it wasn't 'proper work', it wasn't a decent way to earn a living. The power of these shibboleths is huge – it took me until my late thirties before I could begin writing seriously, so strong was the taboo. Thus we internalize these injunctions, we carry them around with us all the time. Big Brother is watching you from inside your own head. And the code reached out to all the tiny details of life – what kind of glass did you drink your beer from? (Even now I get a twinge of anxiety when I have a half, not a full pint.) If someone offers you a drink you musn't turn it down, (I can remember pub fights that blew up because someone turned down an offered drink). When I worked as a barman in Bristol, I learned that there are 'ladies' glasses', and these must *never* be offered to a man.

I remember that classical music was considered a bit 'off' for a man – my father used to play it, but I bet he didn't talk at work about it. Which newspaper you read, the haircut you had, the way you talked to your wife, what you did in your spare time, what tie you wore, what kind of underwear you wore, how you danced, how you walked, what records you liked – nothing was exempt from the eagle eye of 'masculinism'. If I go into a working-class pub now I can still detect the stirrings of anxiety in me – will they think I'm effete? How do you behave in this pub so as to pass muster as a man? Here is that profound masochism again – I mustn't be myself if I'm to be a man.

We can imagine how much talent gets smothered by these codes of behaviour. How many men never express their writing talent, or acting talent, or dancing talent? How many men have hidden their emotional delicacy and responsiveness, their deep feelings of love for their wives and children, and their friends? How many men have never touched someone, or allowed themselves to be touched?

Of course, one can also see the strength and richness of communities such as the one Sid Chaplin grew up in. A whole generation of British novelists began to describe it – Alan Sillitoe, David Storey, Barry Hines – and before them Lawrence had shown the warmth and companionship. But Lawrence also knew how crippling it could be, how much it made a man split himself into pieces, some of which had to be hidden from others, and from oneself.

I am not arguing that these strict codes are unique to working-class culture – one only has to read accounts of life at public school to see that an equal ferocity of censorship operated there. Peter Lewis begins his article about his experiences at boarding school by quoting *Tom Brown's Schooldays*: 'Don't you ever talk about home, or your mothers and sisters ... or they'll call you homesick or mama's darling'.[17] Lewis talks about the weekends when his parents would visit him at school, and the conflicting feelings this would arouse: 'The only thing to do with one's affectionate feelings was to store them deep in some tuckbox of the heart'.[18] Thus a boy would end up at war with himself: his masculine identity conflicted so much with natural feelings and interests, and it was these that had to be suppressed.

Indeed, I identify with both Sid Chaplin and with Peter Lewis, since I went from a working-class background to Manchester Grammar School, which is a quasi-public school. This was a shattering experience. I felt bombarded from all sides by different versions of the cult of masculinity. With my working-class friends, I felt apologetic that I went to such a bizarre place, completely outside their culture and knowledge. At school, I was anxious about being working class – how did this measure up to all these posh kids? My first week at this school was devastating – my teacher told me that my Oldham accent simply wasn't on, it would have to be improved. I still get a rush of fear and hatred when I remember that incident.

Thus class and gender intertwined: it wasn't just a question of finding the correct masculine identity, and maintaining it successfully, but different masculine identities were required in the different social levels in which I lived. With my mates in the pub, having a posh accent was not recommended – yet at school, it was being demanded of me. I had to live like an actor, remembering which costume, which identity to put on, depending on which setting I was in. I had to compartmentalize myself – the things I talked about, how I talked about them, how I swore, the things I did – were divided into two categories.

Of course, the interesting thing about all these fierce injunctions is how much fear they must conceal. That is, men as a whole cannot feel relaxed or at ease about being masculine – otherwise we wouldn't have such prohibitions, such an inflexible control mechanism. The core question is why? Why should masculinity be so fragile, filled with so much tension, requiring so much vigilance? Anthropology tells us that it is something demanded by culture, and not a spontaneous development at all. Psychology tells us that boys find it very difficult to tear themselves away from their mothers, with whom they are identified, and find it very difficult to disguise or suppress their other feminine side. Marxism tells us that gender itself has become another alienation, a fetishism, that rules over us and conquers us, annihilates us.

We can conclude that for all these reasons, genderization itself has gone wrong, has become a perversion. The 'masculine' and 'feminine' areas of life have been divided up in too black and white a way, and identified too closely with male and female. People are not born in such strait-jackets, but have to be forced into them. Men have to be so on guard, so vigilant about their own and other men's masculine image, because unconsciously they want to express the feminine, they want to be more than masculine. To put it simply, we all want to be whole, but our culture chops us into bits, and demands that we identify with the fragments.

IMPOTENCE

One of the great fears of the macho man – and many Western men are infected with machismo – is that he will be revealed as impotent, either literally or symbolically. I've described how my protracted schooldays were seen by my working-class friends as somehow effete, less than potent. Studying books and so on was seen to be a diminution of my masculine power.

In my work as a psychotherapist, about a quarter of the heterosexual male clients I have seen over the past fifteen years have suffered periods of sexual impotence; about ten per cent have never had a sexual relation with a woman, yet consider themselves to be heterosexual; about eighty per cent overall describe considerable difficulties in relating to women. And therapist colleagues report the same kind of picture.

Sexual impotence has often been seen in behaviourist, mechanistic terms. All kinds of surgical and medical solutions are attempted – Hemingway received electric shock for depression and found that his sexual potency returned; doctors give injections, drugs; psychiatrists recommend going to see a prostitute (this has happened to a number of my clients); there are all manner of devices for sale to ensure an erection, or a long-lasting erection.

Undoubtedly in some cases medical attention is needed, when impotence results from a specific disease. But in many men the root of the impotence is not physiological but emotional. There is a block on certain feelings, and the emotional block prevents sexual arousal.

For example, quite a number of impotent men have a great fear of being assertive, aggressive, penetrative. They have learned at an early age that such qualities in men are not desirable. Furthermore, they often have a terror and guilt about their rage at women – they fear lest their pent-up aggression would explode uncontrollably if let out. They fear that their penis is a loaded bomb, which will explode inside a woman causing massive damage.

Most impotent men haven't let themselves experience their true feelings – both of helplessness and powerlessness, and of rage and hatred towards women. They have denied these feelings, and the feelings have taken a bodily form, have been somatized into sexual impotence.

Thus the solution for them, paradoxically, is to go further into their feelings of being powerless, which often involves feelings of humiliation, shame and ridicule, and at the same time explore the rage.

We might generalize on this condition and say that for many men their fear of women is highly complex: both a fear of being overpowered, (the penis will get lost inside the vagina, or will be cut off), but also a fear of the damage they could do to women if they let loose. Impotent men often have fantasies that their penis is a dangerous weapon which must be kept hidden – ironically a parallel fantasy to the militant feminists'. But some of them also have the fantasy wish that a woman will make love to them, will literally get on top, so that they can abandon themselves to erotic pleasure.

But many non-impotent men have these fantasies – that if they let go sexually, and in other ways, they will either become a raging bull, a wild animal, a primitive, not fit for civilized company, or they will be revealed as perverse in their longing for passivity and femininity. This message is a deep one in our culture – the male must be *tamed* if he is to be a civil individual (not too masculine), but he must also be firm and erect (not too feminine). In English fiction we see many echoes of this. In Jane Austen's *Emma*, for example, the key men form a fascinating gallery, a spectrum of gentility and repression.

Emma's father is a pampered hypochondriac, his egocentric tyranny over Emma covered up by genteel manners; her future husband, Knightley, provides a kind of fraternal comfort to Emma, rather than a lover-like excitement ('He is not a gallant man, but he is a very humane one,' Emma says of him[19]); and the man she fantasizes about loving, the glamorous Frank Churchill, turns out to be married to someone else. The women in *Emma* are described with psychological depth and insight, particularly Emma herself, but I find the two key men unbelievable. Knightley is too good to be true; Churchill is a kind of glamorous cad. Male sexuality is either held in check by good manners, or flaunted in a thoroughly disreputable way. The male must be tamed to become acceptable in the drawing room, and presumably the bedroom. To put it in openly sexual terms, the male erection is desired, but has to be concealed, hinted at.

Emma is an astonishing and brilliant comedy of sexual manners, full of deceit, self-deceit, self-discovery, and it provides us with a snapshot of contemporary manners in one contemporary social class, and shows both men and women struggling to simultaneously hide and express their sexuality. For Jane Austen, the ideal man seems to be a blend of father and brother, with a dash of lover allowed. The male is not so much castrated, as *regulated* by gentility.

In her novel *Sense and Sensibility*, the moral is even more explicit: Marianne, the passionate one of a pair of sisters, is attracted to the dashing and romantic Willoughby, who, of course turns out to be a villain. In the end, Marianne is married to the mild and dull Brandon, the perfect gentleman. Thus male sexuality must not be exhibited in too blatant a manner, it must be curtailed, reined in, behind perfect manners and self-discipline. Of course this structure to the novel tells us as much about Austen's own struggle with her own passionate sexuality and creativity and her own masculine side as anything else.

The theme of the attractive blackguard, and the dull friend/husband is a constant theme in English literature. Male sexuality and potency are often seen as intrinsically unreliable or raffish; the decent man is part friend, part brother. It is curious how incestuous sexuality becomes: the husband is often a quasi-brother and therefore safe.

Moving forward to the Romantic era, we find in *Wuthering Heights* a melodramatic image of the virile male, and a passionate love between man and woman that is described by Brontë with full lyrical power:

> My great miseries in this world have been Heathcliff's miseries, and I watched and felt each from the beginning. My great thought in living is himself. If all else perished, and he remained, I should still continue to be. And if all else remained and he were annihilated, the universe would turn to a mighty stranger – I should not seem part of it. My love for Linton is like the foliage in the woods; time will change it, I'm well aware, as winter changes the trees. My love for Heathcliff resembles the eternal rocks beneath – a source of little visible delight, but necessary. Nelly, I am Heathcliff![20]

But in fact the novel does not allow Heathcliff any lasting satisfaction – Catherine turns away from him and marries the vapid Linton, and both Heathcliff and Catherine move towards self-destruction and death. It's as if Brontë, whilst fascinated by such a man, cannot allow him full and free expression and vitality. Again we can suppose that Heathcliff also represents a force within Brontë herself: her sexuality, creativity and aggression, towards which she shows great ambivalence. [21]

In twentieth-century film we find a wide variety of masculine images. On the one hand there is Rambo, brutalized virility; on the other hand, there is the wimp, played to perfection by Woody Allen. But there has also been the attempt to portray the potent male, who is neither effete nor brutal: Henry Fonda and Gary Cooper often played such characters.

Thus conflicting messages bombard men. Be a man, don't be a wimp (Lady Macbeth's message to Macbeth). Be on guard lest you betray your masculinity with a feminine gesture, a remark, a mannerism, an emotional outburst. But on the other hand – don't be brutal, don't be savage, don't be aggressive, be reasonable. These opposing injunctions can act as a vice on men, squeezing them harder and harder until they feel dessicated, lifeless. Front and back there are massive signs that read NO WAY THROUGH. So men try and do a tightrope walk in the middle, but all the time there is an anxious voice inside: 'Have I got it right?' They can easily end up feeling castrated, rendered impotent by the whole barrage of demands and injunctions.

The opposing demands on men can be expressed thus: don't be too potent, for then you might annihilate other people, you'll be a bull in a china shop, you won't be genteel. But don't be impotent, in other words, don't feel helpless, needy, dependent, passive. In my work with male clients, I sometimes say to them that they need to be both potent and impotent with me, and to feel that that's OK. Our human existence contains both feelings – being able to express our personal power through creativity, in whatever form; but also being able to express our ignorance, our fear of the unknown, our utter dependence on others – and there is a whole range of feelings in the middle.

We have seen that aggression and fear and femininity are often repressed in impotent men. But I have found another factor to be crucial – the separation of sexuality and love. Particularly in men over thirty-five, we find a growing need not just to have sex, but to have sexual love. And at this point, impotence can set in, not for any physical reason, but because that man is afraid to give and receive love, and afraid of his need for love.

Younger men often seem to detach sexuality from love. But in the mid-thirties or the forties, there is often this growing need for real intimacy. Whereas the young man is often content with what can only be called fucking (his wife or girl-friend may not be however!), the older man may seek a deeper experience, that can be correctly termed making love.

Some men are emotionally impotent, and may have to do some serious work on their inability to give and receive love.

This brings me to an important point about sexuality. Which is the key sexual organ? We are so used to discussions about the penis, the breast, the clitoris and the vagina, that it's easy to forget that at its most intense, sex is an expression of love. I would argue that the most important sexual organ is the heart. Genitals and heart can be psychologically disconnected, and an adequate sex life goes on. But the sexual experience will not go deep. The orgasm itself will be unsatisfying.

The deepest orgasm is felt in the heart, and this is where many men cannot allow it to penetrate. Do we see here a clue to the prevalence of heart disease in our culture? The heart as an emotional organ is ignored, or given protective armour – and it therefore becomes weaker.

Thus I would argue that sexual impotence (that is, failure of erection) often conceals an impotence of the heart, and this is where we have to direct our therapeutic work if we are to rescue such men from their isolated state. In so many marriages or relationships where sexual problems arise, we have to review the emotional openness between the couple, and not their sexual technique.

CASTRATION

The history of the castration complex in psychotherapy is of great interest. Freud's formulation had the following elements:

(1) the boy supposes everyone has a penis;

(2) but realizes girls and women don't, and sees female genitals as muti-lated organs;

(4) is threatened with castration when he begins masturbating;

(5) has already seen that the breast can be taken away, therefore begins to believe that his penis can be also;

(6) the Oedipus complex is 'smashed to pieces by the shock of threatened castration'.[22]

Thus boys are believed to be terrified by the sight of penis-less women – proving that castration is a fact. And in addition he is threatened with it as a result of wanting his mother, and wanting to supplant his father.

Broadly speaking, we can say that these ideas were taken up by later 'revisionist' analysts, and divested of their anatomical and purely sexual imprint. They were seen fundamentally as ways of talking about how parents and children relate to each other, and less about threats to bodily organs. Thus in an overview by Harry Guntrip of the whole development of psychoanalysis, although he sees the Oedipus complex as one of its foundations, the castration complex itself is not mentioned.[23]

Robert Stoller, one of the foremost analysts working in the area of sexual perversions, has this to say:

> The ultimate danger that I believe lies at the heart of sexual excitement is that one's sense of existence, especially in the form of one's sense of maleness or femaleness, can be threatened (what Freud called 'castration anxiety'). ...
>
> Men do not just fear the body wound to those precious parts. Our genitals represent our identity as males and as masculine.[24]

One might say that Freud had the correct perceptions, but saw them as absolute biological facts ('the biological fact of the duality of the sexes'[25]). Today we might argue that there are no 'biological facts' that are not mediated by human culture. Both penis envy and breast envy reveal the considerable *psychic mutilation* done to men and women: gender itself denies people whole areas of existence and creativity. It is striking how circumcision is practised in many cultures as a symbol of male initiation: surely this deliberate wound done to the penis symbolizes the psychic mutilation demanded by the masculine gender – as clitoridectomy symbolizes the mutilation carried out on women.

We have to be careful not to treat the issue of castration as a purely personal issue – we can't simply argue that 'women castrate men', or 'parents castrate children', or 'men castrate women'. This is too personalistic, and leaves us puzzled as to why the whole mechanism gets going in the first place.

Both sexes are castrated by our culture. Genderization has become a restriction of the whole person, and clearly both men and women are yearning to break down these barriers today. I am reminded here of the title of Germaine Greer's famous book: *The Female Eunuch*. The world is full of male and female eunuchs. Surely one of the great achievements of psychoanalysis has been its recognition of this: 'Psychoanalysis is unique among psychotherapies in asserting the essential castratedness of the human subject'.[26] But again we have to note carefully the apolitical tendency in Freudian thought: whereas psychoanalysis (pessimistically) believes that this is inevitable under any social system, I am (optimistically) asserting that it is patriarchal capitalism that is highly destructive of the human individual and that it is not inevitable.

Thus the family is not only a psychological hotbed of conflict, but also a socio-political microcosm, and contains the same kind of tyranny and hypocrisy as is found in society. Just as the state preaches peace and democracy but practises violence, so many parents would say that they love their children, but actually treat them as personal possessions to be ordered around and interfered with, and forbid the child's natural spontaneity. Obviously children do have to be disciplined, but in our culture this has become punitive – child abuse appears to be very widespread.

And the sexes are busy castrating each other in the internecine war that goes on between them. How is that we have been reduced to this act of mutual sniping and destruction?

I feel an element of gender war is healthy, in the sense that a certain tension and hostility is a natural consequence of the opposition between male and female. But there is no doubt that the culture we live in has exacerbated this opposition to the point of mutual suspicion and hatred and rage and the wish for revenge. Men and women take it out on each other, take out their frustration, their sense of being castrated, being powerless. Everyone feels alienated, dehumanized, and is therefore full of anger and bitterness.

We can see that castration consists of a most complex and paradoxical group of themes. Men's castration is expressed particularly in the fear of their own anger, their own sexuality, and their need for love. I have met many men who live in fear and trembling in case they are provoked to anger and they smash someone to pieces. They have had to hold in their anger all their lives – maybe anger was taboo in their original family, or alternatively they had a father who was destructively angry. There are various causes, but certainly these are men who have an *imploded* anger inside them. This renders them impotent, asexual, infantile, and women know this, and feel terribly disappointed in them. There are quite a number of relationships where the woman goads the man repeatedly, because she is tired of his passivity, but he refuses to get openly angry, and instead is passively aggressive, which is itself infuriating. Then the woman gets angry, and the man can blame her for being irrational. Such relationships usually become very punishing on both sides, as their mutual anger and hatred is concealed, and vented in indirect ways.

In my work as a therapist, I get a number of women clients who try might and main to castrate me – for example, point out what a bad therapist I am, how little I offer them, how much better their acupuncturist is, and so on – but who also desperately want to find out that I can't be castrated by them. It's a kind of power struggle, where the woman wants to know that I can't be crushed by her, but also that I respect her anger, and don't demean it, and won't crush her. The danger for such women is that they can get caught in their own double bind – having relationships with men who do easily fold under. This is a double bind for the woman because she never finds someone who fights back. This leaves her terrified of her own anger – could it castrate somebody? She's left in a state of suspense and fantasy.

In such a relationship the castrated man is an angry man, who has learned to be a victim, that is, manipulatively angry. He exerts power through passivity, through being devious. His actual castratedness is used as a weapon against others – and he often punishes his partner through his moods, his unwillingness to help her, his switched offness, sullenness. It is a terrible position, and completely unsatisfying, since all one's feelings are indirectly expressed. Hence such a man is never directly in contact with other people. This is a double bind for him, for his anger is always bottled up and denied.

We have also seen the macho man as a castrated man – his very caricature of maleness renders him powerless in many circumstances. He is terrified of his own feelings, his own possible 'weakness' as he sees it. He might feel afraid, or panicky, or he might want to collapse – but all these possibilities are ruled out, as he keeps up the fierce disguise of unbending strength. Thus in this case, castration means being deprived of the more 'feminine' feelings. The man who cannot let a woman be on top in bed, who has to retain control sexually, who cannot weep, who must vehemently reject any homosexual fantasies, is in fact castrated quite as much as the man who cannot get angry. External misogyny connects with the denial of the man's inner feminine – in hating women, such men hate themselves.

Castration means being emotionally dead, unresponsive to others, not open to life. The castrated man has no joy in nature, no joy in his own body, or in children. He cannot let himself shake with fear, or weep with exhaustion or grief. Some men permit themselves rage, and this becomes their sole means of emotional expression, along with contempt. The trouble is that such a man despises and hates himself most of all – all those unwanted parts of himself that he sees as unmanly and effeminate.

Castration means that something has been cut off, literally the male genitals. But we also talk about men 'cut off' from their feelings, or simply that someone seems very cut off. So this is a kind of emotional castration: an inability to be present with others, a state of being withdrawn or remote.

This is the true castration of modern men. They function from the neck up. Their bodies are deadened, and therefore their feelings are not available to them. It's hard for them to cry, to be warm, to melt, to love.

At its deepest, castration means being cut off from oneself, divested of a sense of I. This is not specific to men. It is not a fear of not being male, but of not being. It is the feeling of not being a subject, of being an absence, a non-being. It is one of the most terrible experiences in human life: we might say castration approaches death itself. Juliet Mitchell describes this eloquently:

The horror is about the loss of oneself into one's own unconscious – into the gap. ... The castration complex is not about women, nor men, but a danger, a horror to both – a gap that has to be filled in differently by each.[27]

We sense this horror in Hemingway, we see it in Dylan Thomas, Elvis Presley, Jimi Hendrix. Sometimes you can see it in a man's eyes: that terror of not being. As Juliet Mitchell says, it is found in women as well: with men it is combined with, or it is born from, expressed through, the fear of not being a man. There is a kind of slippery slope leading from 'I am not a man', to 'I am not anyone', to 'There is no I'. This is the darkest fear of all – that no one will see me, no one will know I am there, I will not know I am there. Against it men have utilized the massive superstructures of masculine myth and symbolism, as antidote to that sense of absence, non-being, death.

The fragile male comes in various guises. He may be seen ranting and roaring his defiance out, concealing his fear of vulnerability. His hypermasculinity is a paperthin defence against feelings, and against women.

There is the deadened man, who has a kind of strange inert strength. He is not so much fragile as curtailed, reduced. He is able to get through life by shrinking himself to safe proportions. He doesn't feel threatened because he doesn't risk anything, especially intimacy with others. None the less, behind the grim mask there is an inner world that is full of emptiness, loneliness, yearning.

There are a number of men who really look fragile, confused, hesitant. They at least look what they are. There is a kind of authenticity about them.

And some men are like chameleons — they are tough, then feel defenceless and child-like, then deaden themselves. They are often hard to pin down, rather like ageing Peter Pans.

There are no easy solutions. As men, we cannot magically and instantly turn our confusion and vulnerability into strength. We have to go into all the difficult feelings, the not knowing, the helplessness, and then also the rage, fear and need that we have. A truly powerful man is sensitive, emotional, is able to cry, can sometimes admit he can't cope, can allow himself to be passive at times, and can accept feeling powerless, but can also accept feelings of rage, brutality and sadism, indeed the whole spectrum of emotions which human beings are privileged to enjoy.

7 Male Autism

Over the years, I have worked with a number of men who felt trapped by their public face. They had learned to be outwardly unemotional and rational, and in some ways they felt like that internally as well. But they had come to therapy out of a sense of despair and emptiness. Could this be what life was for?

Their condition strikes me as symptomatic of a male malaise – what I loosely call male autism – a state of being cut off from natural feelings and expressiveness and contact with others.

POLITICIANS

In this malaise the public persona takes over the whole personality. For example, it is fascinating to see how political figures are expected to present themselves as mild rational unexcitable people. In America politicians run the gauntlet if they aspire to the Presidency – they are examined minutely for traces of weakness. Men can have their candidacy wrecked because they weep in public (Ed Muskie) or have a psychiatric record (Thomas Eagleton). In 1992, Bill Clinton fought off attempts to smear him as a coward (not fighting in Vietnam) and a philanderer. But after twelve years of Reagan and Bush – a cowboy actor and an ex-fighter pilot – perhaps America was ready for a different male image.

The public is also shocked to see a man in public office who is very like them – with their fears and lusts and needs. They demand a leader who is not like them, who is above human frailties. This is shown dramatically in the courtroom scene in the film *JFK*, when Kevin Costner speaks to the jury about Kennedy with a passionate intensity: 'Remember your dying king!' The scene has undeniable pathos as long as we don't remember the real JFK. The point about the king figure is that he is above us: he is like God, the ultimate autistic male figure in our culture.

A compelling example of American masculinity in the eighties was Colonel Oliver North. He took clean-cutness to an extraordinary degree, and spoke with military precision and virility, and became an instant hero – this was the kind of man America yearned for. He really shoved one up those Iranians and Sandinistas. But watching his plaintive testimony on television, there was also a rather poignant feeling about North – that he was being set up as the fall guy, the man who falls on his sword so that his superiors might live.

In his excellent book on the Nixon years, another fall guy, John Dean, described the way that loyalty to the President, and a kind of masculine code of honour led him on a spiralling vortex: 'Slowly, steadily, I would climb towards the moral abyss of the President's inner circle, until I finally fell into it, thinking I had made it to the top, just as I began to realize I had actually touched bottom.'[1]

Isn't there something rather Hemingwayesque about the blend of masochism and virile posing that is found in Nixon's clique? In Dean's *Blind Ambition*, there is a remarkable description of one of the minor conspirators, Gordon Liddy, who announced to Dean one afternoon on a Washington street corner that he was prepared to take the can for the whole gory mess of Watergate:

> 'I want you to know one thing, John. This is my fault. I'm prepared to accept responsibility for it. And if somebody wants to shoot me. ...' My head shot around. His eyes were fixed and hard, his face full of emotion, his words coming out in bursts, '... on a street corner, I'm prepared to have that done. You just let me know when and where, and I'll be there.'[2]

A truly wonderful scene, straight out of a B-movie. But it really happened, and Dean describes how he is thought of as a bit effete at first, until he agrees to do his share of illegal activity. Politics has really turned into a virility contest – but the most virile is the one who can fight dirtiest and show least compassion. Autism and machismo come together to produce Frankenstein's monsters – men who see life as shoving one up someone else, before they can shove it up you.

Yeats's words come back to haunt us:

> The best lack all conviction, while the worst
> Are full of passionate intensity.[3]

In Britain, the male political image has a very different style. In government circles, it used to be patrician – upper class, austere, courteous, courageous – Anthony Eden, Macmillan and Alec Douglas-Home spring to mind. But in recent years, there has been a shift towards middle-class manners – John Major exemplifies this perfectly. The self-made man, who remembers the hard times in Brixton, but who made it under his own steam. He *knows* that the British people don't want a nanny state. His manliness is more modest than a Ronald Reagan – cardigans rather than cowboy jackets. But this is reassuring to a British public that likes its leaders to be not so much macho as headmasterly. Thus that extraordinary American blend of autism and machismo (exemplified splendidly in Nixon and his cohorts) is less prevalent in British public life: the class system tends to equate overt machismo with vulgarity.

But British politicians still live under the cloud of imperial history – the British Empire enabled its menfolk to colonize other cultures, treat them as inferior, and cultivate a psychological profile that was haughty, unemotional and sadistic. This male image is a very difficult one to let go of, and the collapse of Empire has left British politicians floundering, uncertain as to their identity. The rise of Margaret Thatcher was surely partly a reflection of the crumbling of male political potency: here was a woman who ate men for breakfast, lunch and dinner – and they kept coming back for more!

BAD FAITH

The autistic male reminds me of Sartre's brilliant description of a waiter in a restaurant. The man is not really being a waiter:

> All his behaviour seems to us a game. He applies himself to chaining his movements as if they were mechanisms, the one regulating the other; his gestures and even his voice seem to be mechanisms; he gives himself the quickness and pitiless rapidity of things. He is playing, he is amusing himself. But what is he playing? We need not watch long before we can explain it: he is playing at being a waiter in a café.[4]

This discussion takes place within the context of Sartre's analysis of 'bad faith', which is the condition of being something that one fundamentally is not. As Sartre says, the public does not want a grocer who dreams: 'Society demands that he limit himself to his function as a grocer.'[5]

This gives us a clear insight into the autistic male: he portrays that which society demands. Our politicians are meant to appear stern, rigorous, clean-cut, with perhaps a hint of immorality to add piquancy. No one is actually like that on the inside, so we have the strange spectacle of men playing at something and forgetting they are playing.

But this kind of bad faith isn't the prerogative of men in public office – it is the curse of the Western male. He has learned to be emotionally reticent, to be over-rational, to leave feelings to women, to use logic in arguments instead of his own passions. Often he cannot be tender or loving, he cannot be angry. He has forgotten how to weep. Above all he doesn't know how to be intimate. He is frozen, remote, austere. It's as if he is always in public, never a private man. Furthermore, there is a horrible sense that such men *don't know* they are playing a part, they are so accustomed to it. The persona has devoured them. They only become aware of it when subterranean feelings start to break through – this may well lead to a breakdown. Quite literally, the outer defences have to shatter, before the underlying emotions can get out. Hence the mid-life crisis, or 'male menopause'.

In my work as a psychotherapist, I see men who can think brilliantly, but who actually do not know what they are feeling. They can be having a feeling, and not know what it is. Sometimes I tell them 'You seem to be angry', or 'You seem to be sad', and they are surprised at my comment, and that I can give a name to that strange sensation going on in them. This also means that they often put their feelings into other people, so that while sitting with them, you will find yourself going through a whole gamut of emotions, while the man himself sits there oblivious to it all.

The autistic male is deeply ashamed. He is especially ashamed of his feelings of vulnerability and need, which threaten to betray him. We could say he is ashamed of being alive, and therefore maintains an outer deadness. Spontaneity frightens him, since it threatens his self-control. Enthusiasm disgusts him, since it is too alive.

Everybody suffers as a result of this autism. Their friends and partners suffer terribly, because there is so little open contact with them. And they suffer too, since the core of them remains untouched, unseen. Such men are profoundly lonely, and feel unloved. It is difficult for anyone to love them, since they are difficult to find.

This condition is handed on from generation to generation. The austere father begets austere sons, and so on. Even the influence of a more emotionally alive mother often doesn't counteract the father's influence, since the father is the model for being a male, and his aloofness offers a refuge from mother's influence.

One of my clients was waiting for his mother's funeral, sitting in the house with other relatives and friends. He began to cry about the loss of his mother, and his father came up to him, and in a soft voice, said 'Don't cry. We all feel sad, but we have to hold ourselves together.'

What could he do? It was too awful for him to get angry with his father on the day of his mother's funeral, so he did stop crying, but for years afterwards he conducted furious internal arguments with his father about that day. His father had tried to deprive him of his mourning for his mother. His father castrated him of his grief, and tried to unman him, tried to deaden him, because he was so afraid of his own tears.

I can remember being at a funeral myself, and crying in the car going away, and a little boy looked at me scornfully and told me to stop snivelling. Was he a little carbon copy of his father?

In marriage or other close relationships, such autistic men gradually wear their partner down. They go to work, they are quite friendly, they make love, they carry out their responsibilities well enough. But the person they are with begins to suffer starvation, deprivation of emotional contact, a lack of something deeper, something to do with the heart and the soul. And often such relationships break up, much to the surprise of the man, who feels hard done by. He has never really been with his woman, but he doesn't know that. He has kept himself apart from her, because unconsciously he fears that she will destroy him. He thought that being a real man meant being free of femininity, whereas in fact it means integrating the feminine, and feeling comfortable with women, and accepting that one needs them.

A woman client tells me about her husband:

> He comes home from work, exhausted, looking grey. He wants his dinner and a drink, and then he wants his TV, reads the paper. He takes the dog out later, then we go to bed, sometimes we make love. At weekends he recovers from work, and sometimes we go out for the day. I can honestly say we live like that for months on end, and I feel he has never really seen me, never looked at me openly. If I ask him how he is, he says he's tired. If I say I feel depressed or frustrated I can see the look in his eyes – fear, hostility – that I'll start stirring things up, when he just wants to get through life without thinking about it or feeling anything. Yet I'm sure he's in a kind of blind despair about it all really, he just has to drown it out, and wants me to drown mine out.

It's hard to really convey the sense of deprivation, starvation, about such men. They are good at disguising it, with rationality in particular as an outer mask. They see the world through the intellect, so that they can avoid the terrible void inside themselves. Their neediness is massive, and massively denied. But when – and if – they begin to discover how deprived they feel – emotionally, physically, sexually, spiritually – it can lead to a great crisis for them, since their life appears like a wasteland. They were so good at their job, so efficient, so productive, and now they find inside themselves a blasted landscape, a desert. They find a core of loneliness that is so profound, so unseen, untouched by any other human being, that it can appal and terrify the individual, unless they are given support. At some early age, they had shut a vital part of themselves away from other people, and pretended it didn't exist. They might have been quite extrovert and successful in their life, but still this core was there.

I am sure many men keep it under wraps for the whole of their life, and die with it still intact, and still hidden. We get good at pretending to ourselves that it's not there, that we're not lonely, not needy, not afraid of life.

This is a desolate vision, but it describes accurately the interior life of many men today. We are the hollow men.

I MADE ANOTHER WORLD

I have been using the word *autistic* in a loose metaphoric sense. The more accurate word used in psychotherapy is *schizoid* or narcissistic: 'the problem of those who feel cut off, apart, different, unable to become involved in any real relationships'.[6] The schizoid character approaches an extreme point in the motiveless killer – men such as the Boston Strangler or Ted Bundy in the USA. In Britain the most recent example is Dennis Nilsen.

Nilsen is a strange distant character.[7] From childhood, he was a loner – he never knew his father, and his grandfather, with whom he had had a powerful bond, died when he was six, an event which seems to have been a massive shock to him. He seems emotionally quite cut off from people, so that he was able to strangle young men without a qualm, put their bodies under the floor-boards or in his wardrobe, dismember them and boil their severed heads on his gas stove. He would kill someone, and then sleep all day, or watch TV next to their corpse.

His murders do not appear to be the expression of rage, rather of a wish to achieve a state of oneness with them, a kind of necrophiliac perfection: 'I would sit him in the other armchair next to me as I watched an evening's TV, drinking. I thought that his body and skin were very beautiful, a sight that almost brought me to tears after a couple of drinks.'[8] Eventually Nilsen is forced to burn some of the rotting bodies on a huge bonfire, and his thoughts become almost religious in tone: 'I thought on those who now magnified my empty life seeing their sweetness pervading the London air. I stood like an obedient usher, silenced by them, and their powerful consuming presence ... I remembered them and knew that they were not in the flames but in me, an integral part of me'.[9]

Thus, death has replaced love as the means of achieving contact and union with other people. This theme of oneness and the incorporation of other people into oneself pervades his accounts of the murders, and the way he played with the corpses: 'I lay naked beside him but only looked at the two bodies in the mirror. I just lay there and a great peace came over me. I felt that this was it, the meaning of life, death, everything. ... No sex, just a feeling of oneness.'[10] Nilsen is involved in the most primitive fantasies here: that through death, people become joined together, or physically incorporated into each other. Most of us express this fantasy-wish through sex, where there is some kind of concrete reality to it, and there is a mutuality of feeling and intent. But Nilsen appears frozen at a very archaic psychic level: if he needs somebody to be dead so that his needs are satisfied, then so be it. We can assume that young children have such magical and omnipotent thoughts and wishes, (for example, often wishing their siblings dead), but Nilsen has never left that world, or only superficially.

Nilsen was in the army for eleven years, and in the police force for a year. He was obviously attracted to such traditional male institutions, concerned with order, force, killing. Part of the attraction must have been the degree of structure and formality in such organizations, which would tend to keep his fantasy world in check, and would also express it to a degree.

There is a kind of dissociation about him that is quite chilling – the extremely articulate way in which he can discuss it all is one of the most disturbing features. Yet at his trial, a fierce conflict blew up between the legal and psychiatric professions, and the psychological evidence that Nilsen had a disturbed personality was torn to shreds. Considerable confusion seemed to surround the paradox that a person can rationally know the distinction between right and wrong, can rationally premeditate a murder, yet can still be assessed as disturbed (or mad) because of a lack of emotional connection with people.

Thus in patriarchal society sanity has frequently been confused with rationality. The fact that Nilsen often appears rational, intelligent, is able to talk about what he did eloquently and at length, leads the legal profession to say he is sane. He can distinguish right from wrong. But he isn't aware that the person he is killing is anything but an element in his fantasy world.

We live in a mad culture, where rationality is the hallmark of sanity and sophistication. Is it surprising that we produce people like Nilsen, in whom our dissociation from feeling, empathy, intimacy has reached catastrophic proportions? Nilsen was an exemplary soldier for eleven years – but is that surprising in an institution whose whole *raison d'être* is killing people?

The judge in the Nilsen case brought matters down to a straightforward level: 'There are evil people who do evil things.... Committing murder is one of them.'[11] Well, that lets us all off the hook! It must also have been a relief to a hard-pressed jury, called upon to assess very complex legal and psychiatric arguments. Nilsen says this: 'The decision to kill was never taken until a few moments before it was attempted or transacted. ... I

wished I could stop but I could not. I had no other thrill or happiness.'[12]
The word 'transacted' is characteristic of him – what a bizarre unemotive
word to use of someone's murder. But the final comment rings true – only
in death did he feel joined to others and truly fulfilled.

Nilsen lived in a fantasy world, and he began to kill when this world
spilled over or invaded his external world, which was emotionally poverty-
stricken. He says: 'I made another world, and real men would enter it, and
they would never really get hurt at all in the vivid unreal laws of the dream.
I caused dreams which caused death. This is my crime.'[13] This strikes me
as grandiose: Nilsen didn't 'cause' his own dreams and fantasies. That is
too godlike, and is still part of his fantasy world – that he has the power of
creation and destruction. One would suggest rather that the dream had
Nilsen in its grip: he was its plaything, just as much as the young men who
he so casually killed. He was the toy of the unconscious, since he had never
successfully made the journey to the world of external reality.

It seems impossible to definitively trace back in Nilsen's life the roots of
this separation from reality. Yet it is hard to believe that he was born like
that. One would have to go back to his earliest life, and find out who the
important people were for him, how they related to him, and so on. The fact
he never saw his father is obviously important, but then this must happen to
many people. It does not account for such a chilling dissociation between
fantasy life and real people, and for the replacement of love by death as a
means of bonding with people. One must conclude that Nilsen had never
made firm connections with those around him, and had therefore imploded
into his own fantasies. His fantasies in themselves are not unusual in a
young child, but the pathology lies in their perseveration into adulthood
and Nilsen's inability to separate them from external reality.

One of the striking things about Nilsen's arrest is the degree to which he
began to unburden himself. Not only did he give the police a detailed
account of his killings, he began to write a massive self-examination, fill-
ing fifty notebooks, often writing a letter a day to Brian Masters, the author
of *Killing for Company*. Is it fanciful to imagine that Nilsen was relieved to
be able to explain himself to somebody, and that for the first time in his life,
he had an audience who were curious about him, and interested in his
motives? He began to advance his own, fairly sophisticated – perhaps
suspiciously sophisticated – theories about himself:

> I could only relate to a dead image of the person I could love. The
> image of my dead grandfather would be the model of him at his most
> striking in my mind. It seems to have been necessary for them to have
> been dead in order that I could express those feelings which were the

feelings I held sacred for my grandfather. It was a pseudo-sexual infantile love which had not developed and matured. ... In the post-death awakening these men were as I last remembered Andrew Whyte [his grandfather], the sight of them brought me a bitter sweetness and a temporary peace and fulfilment.[14]

It seems a tragedy – both for Nilsen, and for his victims – that this kind of insight came too late in his life, and that the attention he received after his arrest was in fact what he had always craved, but didn't believe was possible, because he had never had it before.

If he is pronounced to be mad – and how can we believe that someone who can calmly watch TV sitting next to a corpse is sane? – then the awkward question arises: who or what drove him mad? There are several answers to that. Some psychiatrists favour the view that such personalities are genetically warped. This has the inestimable value of allowing us to dissociate ourselves from people like Nilsen: they are simply freaks, abnormalities, nothing to do with us or our culture.

We could argue that his family drove him mad, in the sense of not connecting with him when he was a child, but the whole thrust of this book is that the family is only the encapsulated form of society. Society itself drives men mad, makes them dissociated, emotionally cut off. Society itself is necrophiliac – Nilsen is an extreme version of this, just as Peter Sutcliffe exhibits a psychotic version of male hostility to women. One reason that both Nilsen and Sutcliffe were given massive elaborate trials – when their guilt was incontrovertible and admitted – is *to absolve society*, and label these men bad, not mad. Although they are extremely pathological men, one of the reasons they shock us and fascinate us so much is that they reveal in horrific detail the psychotic tendency in patriarchy and in ourselves.

SEXUALITY AND LOVE

For Nilsen, the only intimacy lay in death, and sexuality was rather tangential, but for many men the fundamental sexual problem is the separation of sex from intimacy. Thus many apparently sexual problems – impotence, fear of women's genitals, fear of orgasm, premature ejaculation – resolve themselves into problems to do with relating. Of course, there are specifically sexual areas of difficulty – shame and fear about being a sexual being, having a penis, wanting to penetrate women, and about having feelings of desire, aggression, sadism, masochism, homosexual desire, and so on – but even these are closely connected with relating to someone else. A man who is disgusted by his own penis has obtained that attitude from somebody else – he wasn't born with it! And the only way he will shift it is by working on it with someone else. For example, fear of orgasm often stems from a very early frightening experience to do with excitement and pleasure, when the child's feelings were not contained by the parent.

In our culture, there is a tremendous amount of sexual fetishism – sexuality is turned into a thing in itself, and becomes technologized and commercialized. All manner of devices are on sale to increase sexual potency, penis size, duration of erection, and so on. All kinds of substitutes can be bought, from vibrators and artificial vaginas to rubber women. But isn't there something extraordinarily lonely about all this, something desperate, even? The orgasm is pursued at all costs as if it offered a transcendent vision in its own right, no matter how achieved, and no matter with who. It is a kind of behaviourist paradise – buy this contraption, and experience sexual nirvana. Sexuality is technologized and dehumanized.

But male sexual autism is much older than this new technology. It is traditional for men to view sex narcissistically – as women have said to me, men masturbate inside them, ('I feel like a sperm-bucket'). This has involved a denial of female sexual pleasure, and a refusal to meet the woman in and through intercourse.

Sexuality has been connected with lust not love – to let feelings get involved was embarrassing or shameful or frightening.

In my work with people in therapy, I don't see them as desperate to attain sexual bliss, but above all to be accepted, received, met. That matters more than sex. Sex can be a wonderful expression of intimacy, but in our culture is so often used to take its place. Clients have frequently told me that they went to bed with a woman because they didn't know what else to do, or they felt embarrassed just sitting with her and talking. At least in bed they could get on top of her, stare at the pillow, have a good fuck and ignore her!

Indeed in psychotherapy, sexuality and sexual feelings can often be seen as a cover, behind which deeper needs lie buried. In our culture sexuality has been emphasized partly as a result of the increasing isolation and emotional autism of people. Sexual pleasure is fetishized, since contact with people seems too difficult and too painful. It's easier to get in bed with someone than be intimate with them.

We meet this most often with the womanizing male. Such men usually feel intense dissatisfaction in their life. The constant sex momentarily relieves the dissatisfaction, but does not really touch its core. But if such a man stops his womanizing – a different picture emerges. All kinds of difficult feelings emerge – intense need (which he fears), hatred of women, baby-like feelings of dependence. His promiscuity both expressed and concealed these feelings. He had to go on the run, going from bed to bed, woman to woman, terrified that if he stayed with one woman too long he would begin to show his feelings towards her. We see this clearly with Hemingway – the hatred, the need, the infantile feelings – Hemingway hated himself for having such feelings.

Let me briefly describe one of the men who I have worked with for a lengthy period in therapy. Ian has been married four times, and has had many other relationships with women. He complains that they become 'boring' after a period, and he is forced to leave them. He has had affairs with women at work, or women he met in the pub which he frequents, even with a cousin. All women are eroticized.

But in the therapy we also find that Ian begins to be 'bored'. I press him to stay with this feeling, and not evade it, as he usually does, by finding some new stimulus. He is tempted to stop seeing me ostensibly because of the boredom, but he is sufficiently desperate about his life and his tormented life with women in particular, to listen to me say that this feeling of boredom could be a key that will open up other feelings. His womanizing is still going on, at times in a desperate way – for example, sleeping with three different women in the same week.

What strikes me as he goes into the boredom more and more, is that there are other feelings around. I start to pick up a kind of despair, and anger, and grief – there are times when I myself feel overwhelmed by a kind of dark inarticulate pain when I am with him.

Eventually a tirade of feeling bursts out on me – I haven't been a proper therapist to him, I've neglected him, I'm only doing it for the money, I'm not very good anyway, I have no suggestions as to what he can about women, probably my own sex life isn't up to much. I can hear a desperate child in all this, screaming and yelling that it feels uncared for, but also terrified that somebody might get too close to him. Ian has been caught in a classic double bind – emotionally starved, yet dreading real intimacy, because then he will be exposed as this needy little boy. Thus although I am not a woman, the same process has gone on with me – the boredom came up as a defence against his deeper feelings, and then he was tempted to leave me and by implication dismiss me as yet another failed partner. We then began to explore his relationships with his parents, both of whom had been very austere people.

Eventually Ian was able to realize that he had eroticized his need, his anger and despair for over four decades. And this eroticization could be traced back a long way – he remembered as a ten-year-old having desperate erotic fantasies about his mother, who was emotionally quite cut off. He had developed a strong voyeuristic feeling about her, tried to catch sight of her undress, in the bath, and so on. He had gone through a period of putting her clothes on.

Every time Ian left a woman, he was expressing both his sense of despair and disbelief that anyone would ever meet him or accept him, and he was punishing women for being so unhelpful. And he also was protecting them from his own hatred and need, which he felt was absolutely unacceptable, as it had been to his mother. But any woman who got near him got the cold shoulder as well. He went through a lot of grief over some of the failed marriages – he had been the remote one, rather than the woman. At bottom, he couldn't bear to be loved – it made him too raw, and brought back so much grief and loneliness, and revealed his childhood to be a wasteland.

Sex now began to dwindle in importance in Ian's imagination and life. When he felt the ancient yearning and need and anger, he was prepared to experience the feelings in themselves, and not eroticize them. This was a crucial turning point – sexuality was no longer a hiding place from other feelings.

To balance the womanizer, I should refer to another man, Jim, who was fifty years old, but had never been to bed with a woman, but felt himself to be heterosexual. He had held women at arms' length, and had never had a woman friend. But again I found that he held me at arms' length and treated me rather courteously and dispassionately as a 'professional helper'. It took years before we could get round to looking at the way he related to me – he was so frightened of contact and intimacy, and I had to respect that fear and not press him too much.

But eventually we were able to look at the way he was with me. And again a great deal of anger and need began to come up – feelings which he felt were unbearable to others, as they had been to his parents. In some ways his remoteness towards me functioned to protect me from his horrible feelings – also one reason he had cut off from women. He was furious with me, and furious with women, and wanted to punish them – and also wanted them to punish him. But all these tempestuous feelings appalled him, and made him retreat from people.

He began to confess to a variety of sexual fantasies – and felt great guilt about them. They were sadistic and masochistic, often involving anal and oral sex. There were feelings of disgust about female genitals, and about his own genitals. He expressed a keen interest in my own sex life, partly in the hope, as I see it, that male–female sexuality could be all right, and also as a covert way of having sex with me.

And then he found a girl-friend – totally platonic, as he kept telling me, but allowing him to explore his feelings towards her, which were very passionate in a strange way. As I write Jim is still at this point – whether he will be able to go beyond this kind of relationship and have a sexual one remains to be seen.

FREUDIAN SEX

One of the great shifts that has taken place in psychoanalysis and therapy has been from the biological standpoint of Freud to a more truly relational approach to human affairs. Thus for many (although not all) therapists, sexuality itself assumes much less importance now, or to be more exact, sexuality is seen as a means of relating to others. Infantile sexuality itself can be seen as one way in which babies and young children passionately seek to express their need and love of their mother. Harry Guntrip describes succinctly the move away from the psychobiological theory of 'instincts': 'The psychosomatic whole of the human being does not begin as a bestial layer of animal instincts blindly seeking detensioning.'[15]

Within this approach, sexual problems themselves, such as male impotence, are seen primarily as problems to do with relating to people, not problems about the physiological sexual act, or problems with 'instincts' or 'pleasure'. Thus the Reichian emphasis on the orgasm as the ultimate goal seems rather childlike: it is being able to have an orgasm *with someone* that is important. In other words, the core of the psychotherapeutic work is to do with intimacy, and our ability and inability to sustain it.

From this standpoint, the modern obsession with sex can itself be seen as an alienation from relationship.

But psychoanalysis itself is often used – in areas such as film criticism, literary criticism, gender studies – to isolate and reify notions such as desire, pleasure, language. For example, Jeffrey Weeks, in his discussion of psychoanalysis in *Sexuality and its Discontents*, states: 'we become fully human through the entry into the order of language and meaning.'[16] One problem with this is that it ignores much post-Freudian psychoanalysis, which is concerned above all with the profound effects of early relationships on the unconscious and thence on the way we live our lives and relate to others as adults.

Weeks is referring to a particular form of psychoanalysis which strikes me as somewhat autistic in itself. Language is reified in this theory as an absolute thing. But speech and language do not emerge in a vacuum, but in that first intense relationship with mother. Language is one of the ways we find out that there is an 'I' and a 'Thou'. But some of the French psycho-analysts have divorced language from human contact.

In an article on pornography and psychoanalysis, Elizabeth Cowie puts forward a similar kind of analysis: 'sexuality is characterised as a desire for pleasure, rather than simply the satisfaction of biological sex'.[17] This also strikes me as an arid use of psychoanalysis, very much derived from the French school. What is noticeable in Britain is that it is often used by people who are not analysts or therapists. Psychoanalysis has been turned into a particularly intellectual way of analysing culture – for example, it is used extensively in the analysis of film – and in the process has become extremely convoluted and divorced from people. Such writers never quote clinical material – but then many a Lacanian seminar doesn't either. It is a kind of philosophy of psychoanalysis – but one cannot do philosophical therapy with someone! They will object, quite rightly, that they are being seduced back into their own intellectual defences or into the therapist's. Indeed this use of psychoanalysis is characteristic of the academic main-stream, which has exalted thinking and ideas, and split them off from the rest of life. For example, academic philosophy itself has, from the psycho-logical point of view, adopted a disastrously schizoid emphasis on logic and language.

The isolation and reification of 'sex' and 'sexuality' and 'pleasure' is itself, ironically, patriarchal and hypermasculine, a kind of splitting of bodily pleasure from relationship. It is interesting that masturbation – often, of course puritanically condemned as harmful in previous centuries – can now be celebrated as a self-loving act.[18] It may well be at times – but the way my clients talk about masturbation, it is also often an expression of loneliness and need that can reach the point of despair: I have to have sex with myself because there is no one who loves me.

One might contrast Cowie's view that 'sexuality is a desire for pleasure' with the view of Guntrip: 'A baby's hunger can be satisfied, but it still needs to stay at the breast, not for food *but for relationship*' (my empha-sis).[19] But writers such as Weeks and Cowie are distorting not simply post-Freudian thought, but also Freud himself, who throughout his life tried to balance two different notions: that of the instinctual drive, 'the impulses that were manifestations of man's biological nature, demands generated by the body',[20] and the notion of object relations, particularly relationships with other people. If we crudely extract from Freudian thought two im-portant strands: drive theory, and the Oedipus complex (a set of family relations), then it is the second group of ideas that has stimulated the object-relations school, and analysts such as Klein, Winnicott and Guntrip.

If sexuality is a desire for pleasure, why do people desire intercourse? Why not simply masturbate for pleasure? But then some feminists have targeted intercourse itself as a main plank in male domination, and have argued that women's sexual pleasure is increased outside intercourse, free from that abominable penetration. Lynne Segal points out that Shere Hite in her *Hite Report* seems rather disappointed when women express their appreciation of intercourse with men, even if they do not thereby achieve multiple orgasm![21] The separation of pleasure from relationship has achieved startling dimensions here. But is it not a fact that most women do want to be with men, not simply because this brings sexual pleasure, but because it brings intimacy, sharing, and family life?

Men such as Ian the womanizer devote their lives to pleasure, but this comes to seem increasingly hollow, for what it avoids is relationship – or more simply, it avoids women! Thus the definition of sexuality as the search for pleasure, or the search for 'the signifier of pleasure' – is itself a fetishism, since it overlooks the possibility that in sex, people not only project their unconscious fantasies onto each other, not only find pleasure, or find (or construct) important symbolic structures, but do actually meet each other: 'People need contact with other people not for pleasure and tension-reduction but simply *as contact*. Often the contact is sought not through pleasure but in pain'(original emphasis).[22]

I have had a number of clients in therapy over the years – of both sexes – who have experienced great sexual happiness in their life, but who still find their way to therapy because of a deep sense of incompleteness or deprivation inside them. They are not suffering from a lack of pleasure in their lives, but are still suffering from a very early lack of holding, containment, nourishment which impairs their capacity for intimacy and fulfilment as adults. One might argue that this must also damage their capacity for pleasure, but the cure for that damage is not pleasure! Indeed, we are compelled to go into the deepest feelings of despair, emptiness, fear, and loneliness that have probably always existed underground.

On the other hand, there are also quite a number of people for whom sexual pleasure is terrifying. Here again one can point to a failure in early relatedness and containment – pleasure seems uncontainable or will provoke envy or punishment.

Perhaps the greatest stumbling block to the theory of sexuality as pleasure is masochism. Large numbers of people conduct their sexual and other relationships in self-destructive ways. How can this be? Arguments that the pain itself is pleasurable are merely tautologous. But a theory of sexuality as contact has a profound grasp of masochism: it represents the perseveration of old ways of relating. The child who is offered negative or painful contact from its parents has no choice but to accept it – it cannot walk away. As an adult, that individual will tend to repeat the same kinds of contact, not out of some perverse pleasure, but out of loyalty to the parents' way of living, a disbelief that others ways of relating are possible, out of an unconscious wish to repair the faulty relationship, and as a covert communication: 'I am deeply hurt.' Thus masochism is a memory, a history, that yearns for a new beginning and the end of pain.

CAUSE AND CURE

There are two key questions about autistic men, both 'normal' and pathological. What causes their remoteness, and can anything cure it?

As I have said, it would be simplistic and persecutory to lay the blame for male autism at the door of male children's parents. It is also absurdly circular: those parents were themselves damaged by their parents, and so on.

Surely we have to point the finger at Western civilization. These are the men that industrial capitalism demands. These are the ideal units for industrial production. They are functional and efficient. Who cares if they have no soul? There is no doubt in my mind that the autistic male has evolved over the centuries since the Renaissance, and since the Industrial Revolutions. These two massive movements separated thinking from feeling, and created modern society and its requirement for efficient economic producers and consumers. They also began to atomize society, to break up its bonds of community and extended family, and to reduce us to pure individuals. The logical end-point of this is the *laissez faire* fallacy – that there is no society, that we are a bunch of single units, who band together occasionally out of self-interest.

The people who live like that become deeply unhappy, become mad, enraged, dissociated, but often hide their unhappiness under an iron control, a mask of impassivity. A question of great interest here concerns the division of labour between men and women. Why is it that men took on this burden of being dehumanized producers, and women were able to retain some emotional reality?

Partly because women were allotted the role of child rearer. Anyone who brings up children must be connected with primitive needs and fears, must be able to comfort children, must be able to love. Women have been closer to the earth, closer to feelings, closer to life and death. Men have moved amongst abstractions, have invented things such as steam-engines, computers, have split the atom.

Thus the gender system in our culture imposes such powerful emotional identities on men and women, quite unconsciously, that it becomes very difficult to break from them. In the first place, most people are not aware that they are conforming to a gender system – it just seems natural that women are allowed to cry, and men aren't. Secondly, if one does acquire a degree of awareness of gender, one fears ridicule, rejection, if one attempts to step outside its normal expectations.

There is also an argument that this division is innate – that men are innately logical and abstract, women innately emotional and concrete. I find this implausible, since there are quite a number of men and women not like this, and I meet men and women who go through profound changes. Autism is an attribute of masculine gender not biological maleness.

One gets some sense of the historical relativity of these issues from a poignant article by Karen Hansen about a nineteenth-century American man.[23] Brigham Nims, who lived in New Hampshire before the Civil War, did sewing, quilting and household chores regularly, wrote loving letters to his male friends, shared a bed with a sick male friend, but was not, Hansen concludes, considered in any way odd. Hansen suggests that the greater fluidity and overlap between men's and women's lives that is revealed in Nims's diaries are partly due to his rural location – capitalism had not organized and regimented people in the farming community at that time. Furthermore, the division between home and work does not exist for Nims.[24]

The thesis of innate male autism is a bleak one, particularly as it means that there can be no cure. But this is contradicted by the evidence that such men do have breakdowns, do build a new kind of life for themselves, we might even say do build a new personality on the ruins of the old one. There is a kind of conversion experience that autistic men can go through, when they discover, not Jesus, but their own emotionality and vitality.

There is no doubt that therapy can help the autistic male to discover his emotional aliveness. But therapy is not a magic cure – the man must want and need to change, must feel so desperate with his present condition that he has to change. In other words, change must come from within. It is usually no good hammering at the defences of such a man, as many a wife or girl-friend has found. He digs in deeper, and pulls up the drawbridge and the portcullis. But with some men, the tension of maintaining that iron poise takes its toll, and chinks emerge in the armour, or they have a breakdown. Perhaps they are the lucky ones? The unlucky ones carry it to their grave, and even die with a stiff upper lip, forbidding themselves and the people close to them the chance to grieve or feel angry about death.

But it is a most moving experience to see a hitherto autistic man begin to discover his emotions and let them out. Often there is enormous grief at all the wasted years of emotional deadness. And also great rage that this deadness was imposed on him, or demanded of him. The key to the therapeutic relationship is safety – does such a man feel safe enough with the therapist to begin to explore his feelings? Then the walls of autism can begin tumbling down.

In fact, I would go so far as to say that only psychotherapy or analysis can deal with severely withdrawn men, whose inner loneliness is untouched. No friendship, or love relationship or marriage can deal with it. It is too inaccessible, too primitive. Even if a loving partner can nourish that side of a man, eventually he will feel betrayed or abandoned by her, since she cannot love him in that way continuously. Then it is very tempting for such a man to blame his partner for failing him, and to leave her.

Only therapy offers such a continuous and safe environment where such vulnerable areas can be explored, where the deepest need for recognition and love can be allowed to surface in its own time, and where all the accompanying rage and hatred can also be expressed. I meet women who have a Messianic need to heal such men, but their task is doomed.

8 Rippers, Muggers, Soldiers

Men are not simply fragile and autistic – they are also frequently violent, and male violence has become one of the most important topics in feminism. It has caused anger, sadness and perhaps above all bewilderment: why do men go to war, rape women, beat each other up?

Men such as the Yorkshire Ripper – who terrorized and killed women in the North of England during the 1970s – bring up very sharply differing views on male violence. If men are innately violent towards women, then Peter Sutcliffe merely took this to a logical end-point. Some feminists would therefore see the Yorkshire Ripper not as a psychotic murderer, but as the male incarnate. He simply does what other men dream of. At the time of his trial, I remember the graffiti on the walls in London: YORKSHIRE RIPPER: NOT MAD, JUST MALE. Joan Smith verges on saying this in her essay on Peter Sutcliffe when she concludes: 'when the trees are so dense, who can with certainty pick out the really rotten timber?'[1]

The French feminist Nicole Jouve has done an analysis of Sutcliffe which is more circumspect than this, employing, as she does, sophisticated methods of semiotic analysis. She sees Sutcliffe as symptomatic not so much of maleness as patriarchal society: 'It is as if, in hearing the voice of God, Sutcliffe had heard the secret voice of Society. ... For Society supported him: it did not stop him.'[2] Elsewhere she states that Sutcliffe was, of course, responsible for what he did, but so was his father for being 'a very bad husband, and a dreadful father', and also: 'the whole aura of aggressive macho values is also responsible'.[3]

Jouve therefore presents a much more thoughtful feminist analysis, which does not simply say 'Men are violent rapists and killers', but explores the social values that lead to violence against women.

When we look more closely at Sutcliffe, he is far from being a man exulting in male triumph over women. He hates women because he is unsure about his masculinity. He is described as being close to his mother, quiet and introverted, or in Jouve's words, 'weak, weedy and oversensitive'.[4] He is described as a mummy's boy, clutching her skirts. He is bullied at a tough Secondary Modern. He is shy of girls – his wife Sonia is his first girl-friend.

But there is also compensatory activity to all this lack of masculinity. He gets interested in motorbikes, he buys a bullworker and develops his muscles. Most significantly, on the window of his lorry (he is a long-distance lorry driver), there is this bizarre notice:

In this truck is a man whose latent genius if unleashed would rock the nation, whose dynamic energy would overpower those around him. Better let him sleep?

Here is the dark Superman theme: beneath the shy rather feminine man lurks a potential genius. But it is the very cult of manhood that torments Sutcliffe, since again and again he fails to pass its tests. Thus he isn't the champion of masculinity, but its failure, its victim. His violence is a desperate psychotic assertion against his own unmanliness.

Jouve sees the relationship between mother and son thus: 'Peter must have given her much of the emotional and material satisfaction she failed to get from her rowdy and unreliable husband.' He is actually called her 'favourite daughter'. Jouve describes him as a 'man possessed by the desire to be a "Real Man"'.[5] He is a great disappointment to his father, a man who projects an image of working class masculinity – drinking, occasional fighting, womanizing, burglarizing houses. When his wife has an affair he humiliates her publicly and in front of the children. Thus there is a violent vindictive streak towards women in Sutcliffe's father.

Sutcliffe appears to be very identified with his mother, and linked with her in an incestuous husband-like bond, but he also conceals a deep hatred of her, because he feels she has not allowed him to become a man, or become separate from her. When he kills his victims he attacks their bellies and abdomens, he bites their breasts, he shoves things into their vaginas – a direct attack on the woman's body, that body that dominates him. He is proving his manhood by punishing the woman, destroying her, who he feared had destroyed him. He is also destroying the feminine part of himself – Joan Smith comments: 'The common denominator in the attacks is Sutcliffe's obsessional destruction of those parts of the female body which signal gender.'[6]

There is a relevant comment by the psychoanalyst Marie Bonaparte, concerning the little boy's fantasized attack on the mother:

What the small boy apparently yearns to accomplish is an anal, cloacal, intestinal penetration of the mother; a bloody disembowelling even. The child of two, three, or four, despite, or rather because of its infancy, is truly then a potential Jack the Ripper.[7]

Thus, murders by men such as Jack the Ripper and the Yorkshire Ripper are a literal enactment of the attitudes that babies have towards their mother. Jack the Ripper used to eat organs from his victims' bodies – here we get a grisly echo of the cannibalistic feelings in children: 'the oral-biting fixation ... is very much concerned with cannibalistic tendencies'. Klein also makes the point that such tendencies are repressed not destroyed: 'One of the bases of psycho-analysis is Freud's discoveries that we find in the adult all the stages of his early childish development ... the deepest repressions are directed against the most unsocial tendencies.'[8]

Further evidence can be gleaned from anthropological studies, which show that such tendencies are expressed in many societies in various ritualized ways. The Jungian analyst Te Paske, describes in his book on rape how the Aztecs used to sacrifice prisoners and eat them:

> The treatment of victims in this ritual context displays in full archaic flower a ritualized form of behaviour ... characteristic of the sadistic rapist, including the cropping of hair, keeping of mementoes, washing or cleaning of the body ... forced behaviour, cutting and execution, flaying and dismemberment, the religious fantasy and the tendency to appropriate parts of belongings of the victim.[9]

Thus, we can posit a picture of human society over thousands of years gradually developing an ability to symbolize and *deliteralize* such universal primitive fantasies, and therefore not needing to act them out. Te Paske describes this as a kind of sacrifice in itself: 'Of crucial importance for consciousness and for the individuation process is the gradual deliteralization and internalization of potential acts through the sacrificial process of reflection.'[10]

Human beings develop a use of symbols and a detachment from the symbols that precludes a total acting out of primitive feelings – for example, instead of carrying out human sacrifice, our culture became content with a symbolic sacrifice of the Son-God: 'Take, eat; this is my body' (Matthew 26:26). None the less, very primitive acts can still be carried out in certain conditions, for example wartime or psychosis. The possibility of regression to such archaic levels is never absent.

As we saw in Chapter 5, the role of the father in redeeming the son from a primitive masculinity is crucial. In isolation, the son can feel overwhelmed by his mother and his need for her. He has a sadistic reaction, and attempts (in fantasy) to dominate his mother. Left at that, the boy's future relations with women look doomed. But hopefully the father is present to demonstrate another way of relating with mother: not sadistically and defensively, but accepting his own need and love of her. In other words, father shows concretely the possibility of not being destroyed by, nor destroying, the woman. This redeems the son from his archaic fantasies where mother and son confront each other in a desperate struggle for sur-

vival. But Peter Sutcliffe lacked this influence and was swamped by those
fantasies, and was encouraged in them by his father, who acted out his own
violent hatred towards women.

I have referred earlier to one of the key problems with the psychological
analysis of sadism and violence – it is often militantly asocial. It focuses
almost exclusively on the intrapsychic sources of hatred, and totally
neglects society's demand for aggression. Thus psychoanalysis has a rather
undistinguished record in the analysis of war: if war is simply the accumulated mass of many individuals' sadism projected onto a huge screen, how
do we explain the social roots of war?[11] If the enemy in wartime is seen
simply as the recapitulation of the hated father or mother, it seems to
suggest that the occasion and cause of war are almost random. The notion
that social conflicts cause war is therefore conspicuous by its absence.
Unfortunately, psychology has often taken this stance, and reminds us
again of Margaret Thatcher's celebrated dictum: 'There is no such thing as
society.'

Another good example of psychotherapy's weak historical understanding is its treatment of Fascism. This has often been analysed as an outburst
of semi-psychotic irrationality. Thus, Jung was fond of citing the cult of
Wotan prevalent in Nazism as indicative of their mystical orientation: 'Hitler's power is not political; it is *magic*' (original emphasis).[12] No doubt the
Nazis did use German myth to give historical credence to the Third Reich,
but something that Jung has failed to consider is that from the point of view
of capitalism/imperialism fascism is perfectly rational. It smashes and
atomizes the working class, turns women into breeding machines, insti-
gates witch-hunts against scapegoats (Jews, homosexuals, Communists)
and pursues foreign conquests. Of course it has its own kind of mystifica-
tions, but big business tends to back it because it's good for profits!

Thus the asocial psychological view takes violence out of context.
Violence becomes an absolute, a kind of thing-in-itself. What is ignored are
the social roots of violence. This is also true of some feminists' analysis of
violence – it is seen not as something demanded of men by patriarchal
society but innate in men.

Returning to the theme of infantile cannibalism, is the baby's sadism
simply an innate reaction, or is it also often a reaction to poor parenting? In
the former view, Sutcliffe's psychosis becomes simply an exaggeration of
inherent masculine attitudes. The second view sees it first within the family
context, and secondly within the context of the social pressures on men to
be tough and unfeminine. This pressure tormented Sutcliffe since he felt he
was too feminine (too identified with mother) – and therefore tried to
destroy the feminine externally. As his father had persecuted his mother for

being an adulteress, Sutcliffe began to clean up the streets of prostitutes. He was the product of a marriage in which there was little communication, and in which he was used as a pawn. His mother used him as a prop to compensate for her violent husband; his father filled him with ideas that women should be punished for their misdeeds, thereby reinforcing his infantile fantasies.

In her book *'The Street Cleaner'*, Nicole Jouve shows a reluctance to see a damaging influence in the mother–son relationship, even when it is self-evident. She herself presents masses of evidence to show that Sutcliffe had a deep hatred of women and of the way he had been feminized by the close relationship with his mother:

> Sutcliffe must have wanted to deny the femaleness he found in him-self, and must deny the mother he loved. Because the femaleness made him the butt of persecution, a foreigner among men. It was because he was like his mother, on the side of his ill-treated mother, that he was ill-treated.[13]

Jouve is similarly perceptive about the nature of Sutcliffe's violence: 'It would make sense to argue, in the face of Sutcliffe's violent assaults (armed with a knife, a screwdriver) on women's abdomen's and bellies ... that a deep hatred of the mother's body was venting itself'.[14] And on the same page she quite happily quotes Melanie Klein on the importance of very early infancy on the development of psychosis.

But there is a quite contradictory strand in Jouve, which can be defined as 'It's the father's fault' – 'To the original image of the Father as persecu-tor ... for which other figures could be substituted, in the place of whom other people could be "felled" ... he now substitutes another female figure, the prostitute'.[15] This strikes me as bizarre: Jouve never shows convinc-ingly why Sutcliffe should hate women because he had been persecuted – by his father. Surely the prostitute 'stands in for' the loved and hated mother?

Jouve never really decides whether Sutcliffe's psychosis is a result of (classical) Oedipal or pre-Oedipal conflicts. Many feminists have focused on the classical Oedipal complex, since the father looms large in it as would-be castrator of the young boy – it's men who corrupt boys and turn them into violent men. On this subject Erich Fromm describes Freud's 'blind spot' towards mothers:

> Freud's idea – that the child especially fears the father – reflects another of Freud's 'blind spots', based on his extreme patriarchal atti-

tude. Freud could not conceive that the woman could be the main cause of fear. But clinical observation amply proves that the most intense and pathogenic fears are indeed related to the mother; by comparison, the dread of father is relatively insignificant.[16]

This bias of Freud's has had the bizarre result, as we saw in Chapter 5, that feminism has felt more favourable to his conservative and patriarchal psychological model of the family than the more radical and less patriarchal model of analysts such as Fromm and Horney. Freud was simply unable or unwilling to grant women that much power – for him they are second-class-men – and feminism has been able to argue that Freud in his prejudices held up an accurate mirror to patriarchal society. But later analysts were to find through empirical observations of mother–infant interaction (unknown to Freud) how powerful a figure mother is to the one- and two-year-old child, and how the seeds of psychosis are often sown here. One might also suggest that Freud was involved in an unconscious denial of the power of his own mother over him.

Jouve does have the honesty to see that Klein's analysis of psychosis as evidence of a very early disturbance in the mother–son relationship fits Sutcliffe very accurately. In fact, at one point, Jouve presents a most cogent analysis of Sutcliffe's schizoid vision of women: 'He's learned to fear and hate all behaviour in his women that will show him up to be weak. Yet he loves his mother and wife, and he wants to be good to them, so his fear and hate will be vented upon substitute images of them.'[17]

That is well put. Sutcliffe exhibits a psychotic split: there are good women ('His mother is good. His mother is an Angel'[18]) and bad women, who must be 'cleaned up'. But the latter are surely symbols of *the seductive mother*, who made Sutcliffe very feminine, tied him to her in a symbiosis which threatened his masculine identity. But the hatred of the seductive mother is split off so as to protect the good loving mother – Klein's notion of the paranoid–schizoid split involves the perception of quite separate good and bad mothers.[19] This split perception is characteristic of the first year of life and in the psychotic is never relinquished.

But Jouve then contradicts herself in her zeal to nail the father: 'the father is, I think, more than anyone else, after Sutcliffe, also responsible'.[20]

I am not out to nail the mother. Indeed it is surely incorrect to lay blame in this way at the door of either parent. We have to say that it was the whole relationship between Sutcliffe's parents that somehow failed him, and in particular, failed to give him a solid masculine identity. Yes, he was too close to his mother – but his father did not intervene, and when he did, he presented an image of violent brutality. Did his mother have to turn to her son as a substitute for a husband who wasn't there for her? There is also a hint that a deep hatred existed between the parents – shown explicitly in the father, but hidden in the mother.

But there is also an element of mystery about Sutcliffe's psychosis – many boys have violent fathers and a close relationship with their mother, but don't kill women. We will probably never know now the true story of Sutcliffe's very early life which might shed light on his subsequent madness. But certainly, in the effort to put the blame on Sutcliffe's father – so that a genealogy of male violence can be constructed – both facts and psychological theory have to be considerably distorted. Indeed it can be argued that it is precisely the father's role in rescuing the son from his primitive fantasies towards mother that was missing for Sutcliffe. To put it simplistically, he didn't feel masculine enough to be able to live with women comfortably.

FEMALE VIOLENCE

I was talking about these issues with a woman psychotherapist, and she said to me, 'yes, but what you are leaving out is that little girls want to cut their mother's breasts off and gouge out her vagina as well'. I was taken aback, partly by the obviousness of what she said. Anyone who has studied children reports that both boys and girls are sadistic, cannibalistic, envious. Let me cite a brief comment by Klein: 'The earliest feelings of guilt in both sexes derive from the oral-sadistic desires to devour the mother, and primarily her breasts.'[21]

But in men this destructiveness is exacerbated by the threat that mother poses to the development of a masculine personality, especially if father is unable to help him achieve this.

Men also fulfil their time-honoured role of proxy for the rest of society. Men are socialized to be aggressive and violent – indeed Sutcliffe's fear was that he wasn't a real man, and therefore he could prove he was by being violent. He conformed to a social stereotype, albeit in a psychotic way.

But the really militant feminists also corroborate the view that both sexes have feelings of hatred and violent anger. They feel murderous towards men, they detail the horrible crimes and bestial feelings of men, and become enraged.

Valerie Solanas, in the famous *SCUM Manifesto*, shocked people because she didn't intellectualize or deny her rage, but merely presented it:

Simultaneously with the fucking-up, looting, couple-busting, destroying and killing, SCUM will recruit. SCUM, then, will consist of recruiters:
the elite corps – the hard core activists (the fuck-ups, looters and
destroyers) and the elite of the elite – the killers.[22]

Solanas took herself literally, and nearly killed Andy Warhol, thereby
showing the immense dangers in acting out one's feelings. There is a
middle ground between this and denying them. In this middle ground we
feel our feelings – we don't project them onto others, and we don't turn
them into blind action.

It is worth pointing out that evidence is beginning to accumulate to show
that women are not the pacifist doves they are claimed to be by some feminists. For example, lesbian relationships are not immune from domestic
violence – battering takes place in a rather similar manner to heterosexual
relationships.[23] Crimes of violence amongst women have been rising
sharply; female intake into the US Army is rising fast, and there were
women soldiers active in the Gulf War. In my experience as a therapist,
child abuse – physical, emotional, sexual – is frequently carried out by
mothers. In the many terrorist groups in the world, women are a minority,
but they are not insignificant – the IRA have used women to plant bombs.
In the Mafia, women are beginning to assume powerful positions: 'a new
generation of tough, ambitious women have begun to share power with
men and play a leading role in the Camorra [the Naples Mafia]'.[24] Women
political leaders – such as Margaret Thatcher, Golda Meir, Indira Gandhi –
have not been noticeably tender-hearted or pacifist.

One can also point to the divisive history of feminism itself, constantly
riven by internecine struggle: Lynne Segal describes in *Is the Future
Female?* how 'the disputes between feminists of different racial, ethnic,
class or national groupings proved extraordinarily divisive and painful'.[25]
This would be surprising only to someone who had the fantasy that women
were exempt from normal human conflict and hostility.

Thus although women have been socialized not to be physically violent,
this gender distinction itself may be breaking down. Would this not demonstrate conclusively that violence is not linked to hormones, but social
role and gender? This is being shown in many films now, where women
are permitted to take violent roles, for example, the avenger (*Sudden
Impact*, *Fatal Attraction*).[26] Of particular note is the character played by
Sigourney Weaver in *Alien* and *Aliens*, who alone has the knowledge and
the courage to fight off the alien creatures, while all around her American
soldiers are whimpering in terror. A post-feminist heroine indeed! But the
alien creature itself is also portrayed as female – the trailer for *Alien³*

announces triumphantly 'The bitch is back!' The quasi-vaginal quasi-penile monster opens her fanged jaws, and men quake – but Sigourney does not quake! In *Alien³*, Weaver eventually sacrifices herself to save humanity from the alien she carries inside herself: the female is both Christ-like and demonic.[27]

One of the significant psychological developments in feminism is that women begin to own their own feelings of anger, hatred, violence towards men. Surely this shows us that a profound and unconscious development is going on, affecting not only social functions such as the work/home split, but also the differing emotional ascriptions to men and women (men are big and strong, women are little, demure and frail). We now begin to see that men can be demure and frail, and women can be tough, violent and brutal.

VIOLENCE AGAINST MEN

In recent years, domestic and sexual violence against women has been exposed as very widespread, and not confined to Western countries – it is found in India, Africa, Latin America.[28] But in the process of highlighting this, attention tends to shift away from the violence directed by men against other men – as if this was somehow to be expected, or men can 'take it'.

The *British Crime Survey* regularly reports that many kinds of crimes, including thefts, assaults, threats, and robbery from the person, are more common against men than women. The same kind of statistics are reported in America.[29] But there is plenty of evidence that such surveys underestimate violence against women – for example, *The Islington Crime Survey* (*ICS*) shows women suffering more from assault and theft than men[30] – but particular forms of violence such as mugging seem to be directed primarily by young males against other young males. The *ICS* also reveals the extent of police harassment of men: a third of young white males and a half of young black males had been stopped and searched by the police in the previous twelve months.[31]

The *ICS* also surveyed people's beliefs and perceptions about crime – for example, many people expected that the main victims of street robbery would be elderly women, whereas in fact amongst white people they are the least likely. Significantly, men are not expected to be victims of street robbery. Here the authors of the survey make an interesting comment:

Perhaps people, on a common sense level, expect that kind of experience [street robbery] to happen to young men and understand that its
impact, and the ability of young men to recover from that kind of
experience, is qualitatively different from that of women ... it is unsur-
prising that people are more likely to 'hear of' street robberies involving
victims who are more vulnerable than male adolescents.[32]

This is a fascinating statement. Three claims are made: first, that men
have to endure crime as part of their normal life experience; secondly, it
doesn't have so much impact on men as women; and thirdly, that men
recover better. It is not quite clear if these views are those of the survey
respondents, or are the survey authors' – certainly the presupposition that
male adolescents are less vulnerable than women appears to be uncritically accepted. What a condensed mythology about men this represents!
Men just have to put up with robbery and violence – and in any case we
all know (common sense really) that male adolescents are pretty invulnerable! Hidden somewhere in these comments is surely the subtext: 'men
are violent, therefore they have to expect to be treated violently – serves
them right'.

The same kind of unwritten morality often seems to exist as regards war:
men perpetrate war, therefore have to expect to be killed. Women and children are 'innocent victims' – by implication men are 'guilty victims',
because they started it. In her book *The Demon Lover* Robin Morgan sees
men as 'thanatotic', loving death – yet she ignores the evidence that men
are reluctant soldiers and even more reluctant combatants (see Chapter 4,
section on 'War').[33]

War is a holocaust for men – ordered to go and kill other men, and to risk
being killed. During major wars, men become the property of the state, and
any who refuse to fight are severely punished – often killed. An example of
this occurred in the early 1990s in the wars in Croatia and Bosnia, where
young men were press-ganged into military service, and draft-dodgers
were frequently sent to the front without weapons to dig trenches.[34]

MALE VIOLENCE

Thus to the question 'Why are men violent to women?' I want to counter-
pose the question 'Why are men violent to men?' In other words, why are
men violent at all? What must be tackled is the amount of violence that
men commit – football hooliganism, war, terrorism, mugging, murder.

My answer is straightforward: men are conditioned and trained to carry out the violence of the whole culture. In this sense, women who are obsessed/fascinated by male violence are actually projecting their own violence onto such men. And we all project our violence onto 'violent men'. As Jung said, in a discussion about the Second World War: 'We love the criminal and take a burning interest in him because the devil makes us forget the beam in our own eye when observing the mote in our brother's, and in that way outwits us.'[35]

Jung's words are wise: we love the criminal – he blinds us to our own criminality, and at the same time expresses it. Just watch the British Conservative Party Conference every year baying for blood in the law and order debate: hang them, flog them, punish, punish, punish. There is tremendous zest and energy in this debate every year – naturally it is justified by references to escalating violence on the streets of Britain, and the need to control this. But this is humbug – the hangers and floggers exist *sui generis*. They don't need crime statistics to get their blood up – it's already up. To a degree we all share this feeling – there is a macabre pleasure in seeing the guilty caught and punished. Why else do we all sit down every night and watch an endless diet of crime thrillers, police series, and so on, on our televisions? It's a way of having our own violent feelings in safety, and feeling reassured because the guilty are (usually) punished. There is also the thrill of seeing the guilty go free (*The Silence of the Lambs*). The murderer as hero is an ancient theme in art (as in *Macbeth*), but today we do seem unusually obsessed with the interlocking themes of sadism, guilt and punishment.

Thus to my mind, those feminists who are most zealous in proving men to be born killers and rapists are revealing their own fascination with violence. The anti-pornographer would rather not read the stuff, you know, but is compelled to, it's all so beastly. Indeed, she feels compelled to quote great chunks of it at you, so that you really get a feel for it.

But we all do this – we are fascinated by what we deny in ourselves. We want to claim that the troubles in Ireland are caused by 'psychopaths' or that the Germans are an unreliable lot, and caused two world wars, or that young people today have no discipline. In other words, there is a universal tendency to blame and project. The problem is 'out there' somewhere. There are these violent people, who for some reason keep on rioting, killing, mugging, starting wars, and so on, while we feel afraid but also morally superior (and watch the salacious *Crimewatch* programmes on British TV).

To follow Jung's image, it is our *denied criminality* that feeds the criminal, since he acts out our own anti-social delinquency. At some deep unconscious level, society approves of the criminal, and needs him, as it approves of Sutcliffe cleaning up the streets of prostitutes. Why are so many people fascinated by him, both men and women? Or indeed why is murder such a fascinating topic – witness the number of violent films being made today, such as *The Silence of the Lambs*. There can be little doubt we find relief and enjoyment in them from our own long-buried fantasies of killing and dismembering people. The character of Hannibal the Cannibal in that film actually eats people, devours their faces with his wolf-like teeth, and penetrates them with his remorseless intellect. Significantly, at the end of the film, he has escaped from prison, and is at liberty in a sunny exotic place – he is the hero of the film.

Therefore I insist: it is not men who are intrinsically violent, but certain human societies which are violent and warlike and genocidal. Our culture prepares and selects its males to carry out its warlike aims, to be its warriors, its rebels, its rioters, its psychotic killers. Our unconscious anger, hatred and destructiveness is acted out by such males, as society's misogyny is acted out by men like Sutcliffe. And misogyny is not peculiar to men – many women have a deep hatred of other women.

This isn't 'psycho-babble'. It's common sense. It's prevalent in families and relationships. One person acts out a certain group of feelings for the whole family, or for both partners in a relationship.

For example, it is quite a common occurrence to find that when someone recovers from a severe depression, or from some addiction, for example, alcoholism, their partner often then becomes depressed or disturbed. We can say that the partnership hinged on one partner being 'sick', so that the other partner could act being 'well'. But the sickness was in both of them, so that when the overtly depressed person recovers, the underlying disturbance in the other one appears. People marry alcoholics, drug addicts and potential suicides precisely so that the 'sick one' becomes the carrier for the unconscious misery and self-destructiveness of the apparently healthy partner.

In large families, it is common to find that different members are given different emotional duties. Jimmy is the clown, Jane is the quiet one, Fred the crazy one, Bob closest to his mother, and so on. There is a psychic distribution of talents and abilities.

Projection is thus a vital element in the engine room of the human psyche, but, of course, it is often denied. The militant feminist can view her own denied and projected violence and hatred in the shape of men, and can castigate it, lacerate it, while feeling pure herself, just as the medieval churchman could blame his lust on lascivious women, and then banished them in the vain hope of destroying his own lust.

RAPE

For some feminists, rape has become not just a shocking assault on women, but a central defining characteristic of men: 'Rape ... is an exaggerated expression of a fully accepted sexual relation between men and women. ... Force is intrinsic to fucking.'[36]

The more left-wing view considers rape to 'stem from social conflicts', and that 'rape is a historically specific phenomenon linked to women's relative degradation as capitalism arose'.[37] Thus, in the first view rape is simply a universal attribute of the male human; in the second view, rape is a relative indicator of the social oppression of women.

But from the psychological point of view, there is a further important point to be made about rape: is it, as the radical feminists assert, an expression of rampant masculinity? Is the rapist the male red in tooth and claw?

In his book on rape, the Jungian analyst Te Paske makes a contrary assertion:

> The rapist is a weak, impotent, angry and depressed individual compensating for just these deficiencies with fantasies and demonstrations of virility, power and possession. His battle is with forces of the unconscious with which he is unable to deal internally.[38]

The last point about the unconsciousness of such men is crucial. They are people who have such a weak ego that they are unable to separate unconscious images and feelings from deeds: one gets translated into the other directly, whereas most people are able to distinguish them. Having homicidal feelings in most people does not lead to homicide: there is a boundary between the unconscious and the conscious sides of the psyche.

This does not, let me emphasize, absolve rapists of their responsibility in committing their violent assaults. We are not saying 'they can't help it'. But we are saying that there are specific psychological reasons for perversion, including rape, and most crucially, that this kind of analysis offers hope of treating such people. They can be helped to explore their sense of inadequacy, so that they do not have go around punishing women for it, helped to build up their inner ego strength, and helped to change the relation between fantasy and reality in their inner world. One also has to uncover their own sense of having been abused, which compels them to abuse others. What is much more difficult is to change our culture so that damaged people do not exist in such large numbers.

Of course many people – both men and women – have rape fantasies, and both men and women have fantasies of being raped and doing the raping. People often feel guilty about such fantasies, and get worried that maybe they will put such an image into action. But the fantasies happen anyway, and in most people are harmless and enjoyable, again because we are able to distinguish fantasy from reality.

The rape fantasy itself often contains a blend of feelings of domination, fusion and identification. If I imagine raping somebody, or being raped by somebody, there is both the sense of power over someone, or being over-powered, and along with that, the need to merge with someone, to become one with them. Te Paske describes this as 'breaking the bounds of subject and object in a frenzied assault'.[39] This image no doubt revives an aspect of our desires as infants, when our primitive love for mother partly involved an attack on her body.

Actual rape has the same emotional roots. As the lover through his tran-scendent emotions experiences the dissolution of his own boundaries, so the rapist, in his hatred, attempts to forcibly burst through those bound-aries. He erupts into the woman in a crazy and hopeless wish to overcome his feelings of impotence, a wish to merge with her, to annihilate his and her separateness. Rape is a kind of perverted symbiosis. The rapist con-cretizes those feelings, whereas most of us are able to express them in a sexual manner which is not coercive.

Hence, I would argue that the rape fantasy *does not cause rape* (nor the homicidal fantasy homicide), since the rape fantasy is widespread, possibly universal, in Western culture amongst both sexes.

What causes rape, and a whole range of other perverse acts by men, is first, the man's own gender confusion (at some level he is uncertain about his masculine identity); secondly, feelings of impotence and inadequacy, combined with sadistic revenge fantasies; thirdly, the inability to be inti-mate with women (or indeed with anyone), and fourthly and crucially, the non-discrimination between image and deed, between unconscious and conscious modes of existence. There has been a faulty development of psy-chic structures, a lack of separation between omnipotent fantasy and realis-tic deed. And there is often an underlying rage at having been abused that explodes into compulsive action. Rapists are therefore often psychologi-cally primitive men, who are dominated by their own unconscious and unable to separate from it. The unconscious itself has become a kind of mother, with whom they are locked in a deadly symbiosis. As with Sutcliffe, one can often point to an emotionally primitive relationship between mother and son unrelieved by good fathering. David Lisak, in his study of American rapists, found that 'the worse the subject's relationship with his father, the more did he express hostility towards women'.[40]

Furthermore, when society as a whole is lurching towards greater instability and conflict, as ours seems to be doing, such individuals tend to erupt into violent behaviour more readily – for there is a tacit social license to do so. For example, one can argue that in the Gulf War, Iraq as a country and a culture was raped – the Cruise missile is a particularly horrifying phallic destroyer. Political and military rape is repeated at ground level by individuals. And in many wars soldiers begin to rape women. The culture of soldiering implicitly condones such perversities – if you are allowed to kill people, indeed encouraged to kill, then other violent acts become less taboo as well. Indeed war is implicitly not only misoygnous (anti-women) but anti-feminine – to become a soldier, a man has to erase his own non-masculine feelings and attitudes. The inner woman is raped and annihilated in military training.

Here we come to a by-now-familiar dividing line between political and psychological analysis. Rape is undoubtedly part of patriarchy's humiliation and oppression of women. But for the individual, male rape is often an expression of pseudomasculinity, that stems from feelings of inadequacy, of *not being a man.*

Rape is an expression of impotence not potency – and I don't just mean sexual and emotional impotence, but feelings of powerlessness in society. Thus one could predict that in cultures and subcultures where men feel devalued, the incidence of rape will increase. Surely this is one factor in the high incidence of rape by black American men?[41]

We see that the masculinity demanded by patriarchal society is a masculinity gone wrong. In fact it represents men's identity denied, castrated, annihilated. A man who is in contact both with his own personal power and his own vulnerability has no need to carry out acts of violence or oppression, has no need to act out attitudes of contempt or denigration. *But the state needs to crush men* to create its brutal warriors, who will crush others. This can be found in all armed forces: military training, to a large extent, consists of humiliation and depersonalization, so that the individual male ceases to question the motives for what he is doing. He does what he's told, and he's brain-washed to believe that being a man means being brutal. Joan Smith describes the brutalized songs and poems of US air pilots in her essay 'Crawling from the Wreckage', but concludes that these women-hating pieces are not simply expressions of male domination, but also attempts to deny their own feminine side: 'For them [the pilots], emotion is truly overwhelming, a threat to their carefully constructed masculine existence; is it surprising that the dreams of such men are dreams of dead women?'[42]

The association of brutality and manhood is also brought out by the Beirut hostage Brian Keenan when he describes being savagely beaten by his Lebanese captors, which he describes as a kind of rape:

> Abed now became our tormentor every other night. Occasionally in the afternoon he would come in and play out a game, his role as torturer. He would take great pleasure, having beaten us, in jumping up and down on our outstretched legs. We never spoke or cried out. It was becoming apparent to us that this perverse individual had more need of us than he understood himself. He was attempting to make himself a man. He thought by beating and brutalising us, that his manhood was assured.[43]

THE VIOLENT STATE

The condemnations that most governments make about violence are hypocritical: they condemn what they practise. Which modern sophisticated state does not have a fearsome fighting force? Which does not practise state terrorism, overtly or covertly? Which does not periodically require its young men to kill? But the same state will then turn round and say: 'Ah, but that is violence condoned by the state, and necessary for its defence. What we cannot have is private violence.' This may be a cogent argument in government circles or philosophy seminars, but it tends to break down in the back streets of Belfast or Beirut, or for that matter, Los Angeles. How can a state which carries out mass killing in Iraq then preach to its citizens that violence is 'outside the law?' Rambo is Rambo is Rambo, whether in Baghdad or Los Angeles. In Britain we have had the unedifying spectacle of a British prime minister exulting over victory in the Falklands War, and then turning round to condemn 'football hooligans', 'juvenile criminals', and so on. Then violence is blamed on computer games or TV violence!

The state legitimizes and sanctifies violence, whilst claiming to abhor it. Every modern state possesses a standing army, a police force, a secret service, a prison service, paramilitary militias, and so on. We can argue that the state has arisen precisely to control the social tensions that are part and parcel of class society, and therefore must always have force at its disposal. This is part of its *raison d'être*. Lenin, in his usually trenchant fashion, went so far as to define the state as 'special bodies of armed men, which have prison etc. at their disposal'.[44] In every modern state therefore, a certain number of men are required to become expert in killing, forcible arrest, and other uses of violence. In times of social tension, their numbers increase dramatically.

But what is the origin of the violent state? We are faced with a philosophical parting of the ways. Some feminists can argue in their idealist manner, that this armed state has arisen out of the inherent violence of the male psyche. One cardinal problem with this is that there have been, and still are, many societies where there is no such state, not even a chief. In his anthropological survey of different kinds of political regimes, I. M. Lewis describes the Nuer people of Sudan: 'We cannot locate chiefs and other obvious positions of political leadership, for there are none.'[45] Indeed the British Empire had considerable problems with such societies, since there were no obvious rulers with whom the British could deal. Are we to surmise that such peoples have less aggressive males, who presumably have less testosterone in their bodies? In fact, chiefdom and statehood are relatively late developments in hominid development – at least three million years elapsed before the local autonomy of bands, tribes and villages became subsumed into larger units.[46]

There are also societies which have not been warlike, and other societies which have been very warlike[47] – it seems unlikely to say the least that these differences were due to biological differences between the men involved. Rather one must point to environmental and social differences. Otherwise we get locked into a bizarre kind of racial theory of violence, for example, that Germans are intrinsically warlike, or that the 'white man' is warlike.

The alternative view to idealism or biologism is to say that the state arises as the arm of a ruling social group, and then trains 'its' men to be its warriors both against other states and against its own citizens.

The modern state is inevitably involved in hypocrisy: it must condone its own violence, while condemning the violence of others. Thus the IRA are 'murderous cowards', the French Resistance were heroes, the carpet-bombing of German cities in the Second World War is celebrated by a statue to 'Bomber' Harris in Central London, the warriors of Desert Storm were 'defending democracy' (not oil) with their Cruise missiles. This is the inherent contradiction in the state today. It must frequently use forcible suppression, but must pretend otherwise, or glosses over it with rhetoric.

Surely the bloodthirsty history of the British Empire and more recently of American expansionism should not be ascribed to the biological or psychological make-up of the British or American male, but to the specific social and political oppression of other states.

Historical examples abound testifying to the social/political basis for violence – consider, for example, European colonialism in this century.

One reason Mussolini attacked Abyssinia in 1935 was that Italy was felt to lag behind other European states such as Britain and France in colonial possessions. But again we cannot ascribe this to the greater rapacity of British or French men, but to the different historical development of British, French and Italian capitalism and imperialism. One might, of course, argue that the colonial urge was itself a male one – but then many cultures have not practised colonialism.

Marx posed the issue starkly: does social being determine consciousness, or does consciousness determine social being?[48] Male violence must either be seen as a question of original sin (ordained by biology or psychology), or as a social construction required by patriarchal society. Ironically if the first thesis is true, then we cannot blame men for obeying their biological destiny. But there is a lot of evidence to suggest that it isn't true, and that violence is a product of social conflict and exploitation.

9 Male Images and Stereotypes

Women have complained long and hard about the qualities they have traditionally been expected to display, such as demureness, compassion, care, receptivity, and so on. But not so much attention has been paid to the stereotypes that are attached to men, or there has been an unspoken assumption that these are preferable. Of course, as I have said before, one cannot blame the women's movement for not looking at men's position with sympathy – that is something they want to get away from. It is up to men to articulate their anger and frustration at being stuck again and again with the same attributes. Here is a cogent feminist argument:

> As a result of their socialization, most women have over-developed certain attributes such as warmth, compassion, tenderness, intuitiveness, nurturance and flexibility at the expense of certain others equally important for effective human functioning, for example, assertiveness, endurance, initiative, industry, risk-taking, and self-reliance.[1]

The argument is well put. My point is that it can be reversed equally well – men have overdeveloped the qualities of being assertive, tough, hardworking, self-reliant and so on. I think a lot of men are tired of having to go out to work all of their lives, having to support a wife and children, make insurance provisions, pay mortgages and other bills. Of course, today there is a lot more sharing of these responsibilities as women have become economically more powerful. But this sharing is not only of benefit to women – it releases men from the exclusive burden of looking after families.

Some men are fed up and angry at being constrained in these ways, expected to be the provider, the strong rock, the sexual performer, expected to always cope, not to collapse, expected to be chivalrous, to mend fuses and flat tyres, to make the moves in courtship, expected not to be passive or weepy or frightened, expected to go to war and be killed, or be prepared to kill others.

This is the obverse side of all the justified complaints that women have had in the last two decades. Sometimes men's position has been assumed by default to be all right, that all the things men are supposed to enjoy makes their life a bed of roses. It doesn't! Men die earlier than women, die of heart attacks because they are conditioned not to feel from their heart, they get ulcers because they are conditioned to keep their anxieties to themselves. They suffer great anxiety and depression because they are not 'manly' in the stereotyped manner, or because they have feelings that seem forbidden to men. They are very lonely because they do not know how to communicate to someone openly about feelings, and hence always remain cut off. They feel deeply abused, although often they don't know how, or why, or from whom this happened.

According to some feminists, men enjoy power, influence, domination, lord it over women and other men, and generally feel like the king of the castle. But most men that I see in psychotherapy feel desperately inadequate, lonely, out of touch with people, out of touch with their own feelings and bodies, sexually unsure of themselves, bored with the job prospects that are available to them. You might argue that that is a biased sample of dissatisfied men, and that most men are living it up, but I doubt it. Everywhere we see signs of frustration, loneliness, despair, lack of fulfilment in men.

Men have been brainwashed to think they are never unhappy, and if they are, they keep it quiet. Thus they bottle up their feelings and develop physical symptoms instead, or they become violent, or criminal or anti-social in some other way.

Why is it young males who vandalize public property, who steal cars, go in for joy-riding, get in fights, carry knives, and so on? Don't tell me it's because of testosterone – that's like saying women are 'naturally' submissive. I think these male youth are expressing their utter frustration and their feeling that they aren't wanted except as factory-fodder, if they are lucky enough to get a job. Their expression is utterly inarticulate and unconscious, but then they have hardly been educated to express themselves.

Men are not supposed to get depressed, just as women are not supposed to get angry or aggressive. The psychiatric hospitals are mostly full of women, and the feminist thesis that women are being punished through psychiatry has some truth in it. But it is also true that men are forbidden to show feelings other than aggression. Men go on and on until they have breakdowns, or they project their depression into their partner, or they drink, or find some other way of anaesthetizing themselves. Thus such indices as suicide, drug addiction, alcoholism are all much higher among men than women.[2]

Men are not supposed to want to be cared for, and this is another reason they haven't gone into mental hospital as much as women. For a man to take to his bed and go through a regressive period, where he doesn't do much, goes through heavy feelings, weeps, feels sorry for himself – this is extremely taboo, and I believe, is more available to women. Men have self-reliance bred into them, and they turn into fortresses, repelling anyone who might sympathize with them, terrified of emerging from the fortresses, yet desperately lonely within it. They are hollow men, and the prizes that seem to be offered to them in our culture are often experienced as hollow. A middle-aged business men said to me – 'Sure, I can go in the wine bar and flaunt my money, and my expensive suits, and my portable phone, but no one in that bar knows that I wake up at three in the morning with a terrible dread inside me, and sometimes I cry without knowing why.'

SUPERMAN, FREDDY AND SCHWARZENEGGER

If we want to look more closely at the stereotyped images of men in our culture, it is very illuminating to examine those found in the media and in the arts. Here we find images which provide an insight into the expectations of the culture, and also into the unconscious depths of masculinity. That is, we find both images that consolidate or reinforce the stereotypes of masculinity, and those images that subvert it. We find both the macho man and something quite different.[3]

One image that has been resurrected in the cinema is Superman. This is a typical ambivalent model: behind Superman is Clark Kent, bespectacled, diffident, hopeless with women, rather clumsy. So here we have a polarity between the male who is nice but useless, and the male who is omnipotent. Of course, Superman is basically a modern rendition of an archetypal figure, who solves insoluble problems, puts disasters right, and can actually control nature. This is man the scientist, the space explorer, the accumulator of knowledge and technology – but in Superman he is totally positive. Superman doesn't cause pollution or war, but prevents them.

Superman is a kind of jokey image: we smile when we think of him in his tights and underpants, and his cape, and Clark Kent's quick change in the telephone booth, and the films tended to encourage the rather camp humour. But there are also some serious ideas about men here: that beneath the outer surface of competence, knowledge and sureness there is someone less assured, more nervous about himself. But then the polarity in this fantasy can be reversed: Superman is the fantasized compensatory image for the man who feels inadequate.

An opposing male image is provided by Freddy Krueger, star of the *Nightmare on Elm St* series of films. The first of the series was based on a brilliant image: Freddy first appears in a girl's dream, and gradually emerges into her daylight reality, persecuting her and her friends. One of the most disturbing things about the film is that it is often difficult to tell if a particular incident is really happening, or is part of the girl's dream. For example, at the end, when Freddy appears to have been vanquished by the heroine, he suddenly reappears, spreading mayhem again. But is this really happening, or is she dreaming again? That blurring between fantasy and reality which many people experience is captured vividly in these images.

What kind of man is Freddy? He is macabre, violent, with a fiendish sense of humour, and a deep desire to mutilate people – his body is adapted to this, with its massive claw of razors.

One of the fascinating things about Freddy is that he became a cult. You could buy all kinds of Freddy Krueger paraphernalia – masks, hands. My own son fervently desired a Freddy hand, and walked round the house for days brandishing his claw. He totally enjoyed the fantasy of being a mutilator, and having this power to terrorize people. This is one way children can find a cathartic relief for their guilt about being full of nasty feelings towards Mum and Dad. It's interesting that some parents don't let their children have such fiendish toys – believing like some feminists that fantasy leads to reality (or fantasy is reality), whereas on the contrary it's through the working through of aggressive fantasy that children learn to distinguish it from actual violence. Surely this is one reason that fairy-tales, cartoons and comics are tremendously violent.

In *Nightmare on Elm Street II* (subtitle: *Freddy's Revenge*), the theme is given a new twist, in that now a young adolescent male continually dreams of Freddy, and has the fear that he is Freddy. He finds the claw in his room, finds himself in his girl-friend's bedroom with the claw attached to him. Here is the male nightmare – that his sexuality is a ravening monster, that will savage and terrorize women. This is a particular fear at adolescence, but many adult men retain it. Along with the fear is a deep unconscious wish to be a Freddy, to be a scourge and destroyer and rapist towards women. But in fact, in *Freddy's Revenge* most of the victims are men – possibly suggesting that deep-seated homophobic fears are being expressed.

A rich body of images about men has been provided in recent years by the Schwarzenegger films. Aided by excellent special effects, his later films – including *Terminator*, *Total Recall*, *Terminator II*, *Kindergarten Cop* – provide a highly complex set of fantasies about being male.

In *Terminator*, Schwarzenegger is a machine in a man's image, and the plot of the film revolves around his hunting down a woman who is to give birth to a new leader in the future. In the end the man-machine is himself destroyed, and broken into pieces. Here is the theme of man as machine, robot, conformist, obeying authority, attacking women, becoming dehumanized in the process, and eventually destroyed.

In *Total Recall*, the process has gone further: the protagonist's mind has been stolen, and he sets out to recover it. Here is a kind of male lament: his mind has been raped by the culture, and the struggle is on to reclaim his individuality, and to assert that he is something distinct from the implanted and alien mind structures. 'Your life is a dream' his pseudowife (herself an implanted memory) tells him – but can he work out which is dream and which is reality?

In *Terminator II*, the robot hunter takes a new twist: there are now two of them, one good, one evil. This is a fascinating extension of the Terminator theme: now the male is part destroyer, part restorer and creator. This undoubtedly reflects many men's unconscious unease about their ambiguous nature, loving but hating, kind but aggressive. How can we be both?

Special effects in this film are the star, as the evil Terminator, a man made of liquid metal, dissolves and reformulates himself as different objects or people. Thus destructive masculinity is seen as protean: able to assume any shape. Reassuringly, Schwarzenegger is the good Terminator, who is rapidly humanized by a young boy – he asks the boy 'Why do you cry?' A vital question for the autistic male.

In this film, Schwarzenegger also carries out the time-honoured male ritual of self-destruction – he spectacularly descends into a vat of molten steel, in order to destroy the chip in his brain that might condemn humanity to nuclear holocaust. This film contains an amazing synthesis of male roles: the invulnerable machine, the masochistic Christ figure, the destroyer, the young boy. When the liquid Terminator is himself terminated (also in molten steel), he goes through a macabre series of transformations, before totally regressing to a pre-human, pre-life stage of formlessness.[4]

The image of the male as robot is widespread in modern cinema: replicants in *Blade Runner*, androids in the *Alien* trilogy, See Threepio and R2D2 in *Star Wars*. A related image is that of the disembodied male intellect: Spock in *Star Trek*, speaking computers in many films such as *Solaris* and *2001*. But this theme has long antecedents: Sherlock Holmes, the desiccated misogynist solver of crime puzzles; the cerebral Houyhnhnms in *Gulliver's Travels*. But in *Gulliver's Travels* Jonathan Swift also describes the Yahoos – depraved filthy beasts – and the image of the male as animal is often counterposed to the desiccated intellect. In *Star Wars*, we have Chewbacca, the inarticulate companion for Harrison Ford; and in Shakespeare's *The Tempest* we find Caliban, the noble savage, contrasted with Ariel, the spirit of the air. Thus reason and flesh are often portrayed as split: the male is both rational and bestial.

American films as a whole have given us a remarkable and profound analysis of maleness – there are numerous studies of love between men (*Butch*

Cassidy and the Sundance Kid), or of male solitude and autism (*A Fistful of Dollars*) or male brutality (*The Dirty Dozen*; *Dirty Harry*). The male psyche has found one of its major vehicle of expression in Hollywood.

There are such a rich variety of images that spring to mind: one thinks of Jack Lemmon in *Some Like it Hot*, playing a woman who gets engaged to a man who doesn't mind that 'she' is a man ('nobody's perfect' his fiancé says). Or Kevin Costner in *Dances with Wolves*, rediscovering male cama-raderie with Native Americans and his connection with the wolves and the earth; Antony Hopkins in *The Silence of the Lambs*, ruthless, intellectual, cannibalistic; Dustin Hoffman in *Tootsie*, allowing free rein to the wide-spread male fantasy of being a woman; from an earlier period, Gary Cooper at the end of *For Whom the Bell Tolls*, wounded, waiting for the Fascist troops to arrive, ready to sacrifice himself to save the others – mar-tyred, Christ-like; Gregory Peck in *The Gunfighter* (1950), austere, sombre, utterly doomed; Henry Fonda in *Once Upon a Time in the West*, sadistic, extremely un-Henry Fonda-like; Paul Newman at the end of *Hud*, arrogant, abandoned, cut off from humanity. Marlon Brando, Montgomery Clift, Robert de Niro, Al Pacino, Hoffman, Micky Rourke – these artists have given us fascinating and sometimes profound analyses of masculinity.

THE BUFFOON

Superman, Freddy Krueger, Terminator, Hannibal the Cannibal – these are larger than life images of man as god, demon, destroyer. But there are other, less inflated images as well. For example, there is the buffoon/clown figure.

In British culture, one of the finest examples of the buffoon has been John Cleese's portrayal of Basil Fawlty in *Fawlty Towers*. This was a masterly performance by Cleese: Fawlty is emotionally castrated by his bitchy wife, but nurses perennial grudges and thoughts of revenge against her, constantly makes a mess of things, but retains grandiose fantasies that he will get it right next time. This summary cannot do justice to Cleese's comic genius – one thinks of the episode where Germans arrive at his hotel, and Cleese ends up marching up and down swearing that he will not sing old Nazi songs, but compulsively begins to, and does a gro-tesque and utterly tactless imitation of Hitler goose-stepping in the middle of the restaurant.

It is a superb portrait because we all recognize the truth of it. He is a man at war with himself, desperately wanting to perform well and surprise his wife, but again and again sabotaging himself. It is also supremely uncomfortable to watch: Cleese has that ability to tread on the razor's edge between farce and anguish.

The buffoon has a rich tradition in British humour. One thinks of Tony Hancock, *Steptoe and Son*, the *Mr Bean* series by Rowan Atkinson, Tommy Cooper, Michael Crawford in *Some Mothers Do 'Ave 'Em*, the TV series *Only Fools and Horses* – the inadequate man has been a deep vein in British comic art. But the comedy is a catharsis and relief against the fear that we are like that – we are clumsy, we are terribly dependent on our wives and mothers, we are child-like, petty, peevish, but also grandiose, inflated. Men fear that they are little boys at heart, and the comedy enables us both to mock ourselves in the form of Fawlty, or Del, and to laugh in relief: perhaps it's not so awful being a man.

In America, there has been a more surreal vein of comedy: one thinks of the Keystone comedies, Laurel and Hardy, the Marx Brothers, Chaplin, Jerry Lewis. There is still the image of the useless male, but it is portrayed more physically and more wildly than in British comedy (and in Chaplin, much more romantically). The inept male is transformed into an extravagant image of anarchy, that ultimately seems to subvert bourgeois order itself – he becomes heroically and splendidly chaotic.

Woody Allen has presented a more intellectual study of inadequacy and pretension – he has raised impotent self-consciousness to a new and agonizing pitch of comic art: 'I'm the only man I know with penis envy.' The remark is typical of Allen: self-deprecating, wonderfully exaggerated, narcissistic. He is not strictly a buffoon or a clown, but a man ludicrously obsessed with himself and his own insecurity: 'don't knock masturbation – it's sex with someone I love'.

But all of these comic geniuses provide a catharsis against our own inadequacy and pretentiousness. They raise our deepest fears from the unconscious and turn them into burlesque – what a relief that we can laugh at them!

MALE LOVE

Male love is one of the dominant themes in American film. In many films, women are peripheral: the central dramatic tension concerns the possibility of men discovering their love for each other. The 1988 film *Rainman* is a classic example – Tom Cruise discovers that he has an autistic brother (Dustin Hoffman). At first, he simply wants to use him to get his share of an inheritance, but comes to love him. But there are innumerable studies of this theme, often based on two men who have become distant from each other, and must refind their mutual need. Examples are *Midnight Cowboy*, *Thunderbolt and Lightfoot*, *Pat Garrett and Billy the Kid* (describing an ambivalent love/hate relationship between Garrett and Billy), *Dances with Wolves* (the white man and the red man discover each other and their need for each other).

The whole western genre, or the police thriller genre, or works such as the massive *Godfather* trilogy, take as their central focus men living together, struggling to work through their mutual love and hate. In the *Godfather* stories, women are there as lovers, mothers and wives, but the real passion exists between men. There is a scene in *The Godfather* when they have 'gone to the mattresses': they are in siege against other warring families – the men sit in the kitchen, one of them cooks a spaghetti sauce. Sonny (James Caan) is fired up with war-like emotion, there is a feeling of warmth, comradeship. Michael (Al Pacino) returns to the bosom of the family, and becomes his father's avenger.

Yet there is also something dismaying in this homoeroticism – not because it is homoerotic, but because it only allows the full intensity of male love to develop in the proximity of death and suffering. Again and again we find this equation of love and death in writers and filmmakers. We find it in Hemingway, who courted death all his death, and finally succumbed to it, and whose novelistic heroes court death – think of Robert Jordan in *For Whom the Bell Tolls*. We find it in Lawrence, whose strange sadistic/masochistic fantasies about sexuality and death can be found graphically in his story 'The Woman Who Rode Away'. We find it in many novels and films about war – men finally discover their need for each other, are able to care for each other, as they lie bleeding in the trench, mutilated by the grenade, or indeed at the point of death.

We might say that death is both a symbol of orgasm – which presumably many men unconsciously desire with other men, but are also terrified of – and also symbolizes a kind of ultimate point in life, when there is no point any more in concealing one's deepest feelings. A client of mine described how he saw in his dying father's face the deep love for himself – a love that had never been spoken of between them, and was still not spoken of at the moment of death. But many men have the fantasy that finally, as they lay dying, they will be able to express their love for others, and receive it – a love too painful to bear in life.

Death can also be equated with the womb – going back into the safe darkness, where there is no struggle, no identity. Death is a great and final non-separation – it strikes me that in the western film, for example, male love is simultaneously so intense yet so taboo that the only gift that men

can give to each other is death. This is almost explicit in a film such as
Gunfight at the OK Corral (1957), which is really concerned with the
intense mutual need and dependence of Wyatt Earp and Doc Holliday (Burt
Lancaster and Kirk Douglas). The film ends with Earp saying in anguish
over the dying Holliday: 'I need you Doc'. This is the great unmentionable
need of man for man – but in *OK Corral*, it becomes acceptable since Doc
is a doomed man.

The death–love connection reveals the deep-going masochism that exists
in male psychology. It is OK for one man to love another if they are mor-
tally wounded – suffering permits the stripping away of the normal mask of
impassivity. Indeed, the masochism is the expression of love: 'Greater love
has no man than this, that a man lay down his life for his friends' (John
15:13).This is a profound perversion: love equals suffering. But male love
has been perverted, such is the fear surrounding it.

Yet how attractive such films as the western and the thriller can be: they
are Zen-like, positing a world that is anti-Christian, anti-domestic, anti-
feminine.[5] Precisely through their concentration on death, and their rejection of the normal liberal definitions of the meaning of life, they appeal to
that part of the human spirit (particularly in men) that yearns for a more
primitive kind of life. Isn't this why men climb mountains, go pot-holing,
hang-gliding? I don't think such activities are simply masochistic or defensive: they reveal that something has been lost in male existence, a kind of
concreteness, a living in the present, and a lack of concern for the future or
for a life after death.

WESTERNS

The most significant film genre describing male love is undoubtedly the
western, which became increasingly sadistic and quasi-psychotic in the
post-sixties period. The directors Sergio Leone and Sam Peckinpah
developed a luxuriant eroticism of violence, photographed with stylistic
bravura.

For example, at the beginning of *Once Upon a Time in the West* (Leone,
1969), three men wait for Charles Bronson to arrive on a train. No words
are spoken; the heat and barrenness of the day is conveyed brilliantly: one
man traps a fly in his gun; another collects water dripping onto his hat.
Bronson arrives and shoots the three men: the gunman explodes in orgasmic violence. Later in the film three gunmen – Bronson, Henry Fonda,
Jason Robards – compete for the attentions of Claudia Cardinale. As in

hard-core porn, the competing men, whilst ostensibly pursuing the central heroine (whore with a heart of gold), also use her as a mirror in which to refract their mutual fascination. One might suggest that the voluptuous savagery of Leone and Peckinpah reflects an increasingly tenuous suppression of homosexual desire.

Just before the climactic shoot-out in *Once Upon a Time in the West*, Bronson and Fonda have one of those enigmatic dialogues which mark the western, and which the Italian western exaggerated to operatic/farcical proportions:

BRONSON: You're not a business man.
FONDA: Just a man.
BRONSON: An ancient race.
FONDA: Nothing matters now, not the land, not the money, not the woman. I came here to see you. I know you'll tell me what you're after.
BRONSON: Only at the point of dying.
FONDA: I know.

Then the Morricone music goes into overdrive, the two men stalk each other in the heat and dust. The camera dwells on the two men's faces – Bronson has a flashback to the sadistic killing of his brother by Fonda – and kills Fonda. Robards dies of gunshot wounds, and Bronson takes his body off for burial. The woman is left in the new railroad town as the custodian of civilization.

What does this archetypal sequence reveal? These two men are merely husks, emptied out of compassion, personality, meaning. Bronson is consumed by revenge; Fonda is heartless, seductive, dazzling in his inhumanity. The western – which in the B-movie gave us such artless charm – has become not merely tragic, but has gone beyond tragedy into nihilism and despair. Whereas in the classical western – say *Shane* – there always seemed to be some point to the violence (Shane kills the cattle baron's gunman so that the homesteaders can farm and build their homes), now in the decaying brilliance of Leone, for men everything has collapsed. They can only look at each other, and kill.

The looking is crucial – in many westerns, men continually stare at each other, held in each other's gaze with a passionate intensity quite different from their regard for women.[6] At the beginning of *Shane*, Alan Ladd says to the young boy who worships him: 'I like a man who watches things going round. Shows he'll make his mark some day'. Men watch and wait upon each other, ready for the climactic moment, when they find love – or death. And there seems to be little difference between the two – since male love cannot be found in life, it must be found in death. American Marines have sometimes used the term 'eye-fucking' to denote the intense experiences they found in war – the western is the opera of eye-fucking.[7]

In one sense such films as Leone's are impassioned expressionist poems; in another sense they are both ludicrous and sinister. They shrink male existence down to a tiny arena, where exotic and ritualistic dramas take place – nothing like real life, one might say. At the same time they do illuminate dark and unconscious areas of masculinity, as do the Japanese samurai films. I find them both repellent and fascinating. Are they not a shriek of pain and rage against the strait-jacket placed upon men by modern society? Yet they have no real solution except an atavistic nostalgia for an era when 'men were men'.

If we go back only ten years before Leone's masterpiece, the homoeroticism in the western is less strained, less apocalyptic. In the splendid *3:10 to Yuma* (Delmer Daves, 1957) the gunfighter Glenn Ford is waiting with his captor Van Heflin for the train that will take him for trial in Yuma. In a brilliant scene the two men are closeted in the bridal suite of the town's hotel, while Ford cajoles, bullies, seduces Van Heflin to let him go. At the end of the film, however, Ford turns against his own gang, who have come to release him, and jumps with Van Heflin into the train, out of respect for his goodness, tenacity and manliness. The seducer is seduced – and after six months' drought the heavens open and the rain pours down. The coming together of the male couple is celebrated by nature.

The director handles this relationship with affection and humour – while they are eating, Van Heflin cuts up the meat for the handcuffed Ford, who implores him plaintively: 'cut off the fat, I don't like it'. The bridal suite is of course a witty yet significant symbol: the two men are trapped in it, and have to break out to find their real identity.

The western rejects bourgeois society as a castrating feminizing instrument that takes men away from this particular moment, this concrete instant, and from each other. The western never explicitly theorizes or speculates: it presents action set in landscape; it is utterly sensuous. Above all it celebrates beauty – I doubt if there is a more beautiful film genre, constantly dwelling on the shape of the land, the mountain, the river, the desert, within which stylized choreographed male violence is depicted.

The remarkable thing about the western is how universal its appeal has been. How odd that a few insignificant characters from the American West (Billy the Kid, Buffalo Bill, Wyatt Earp) became worldwide cultural icons, and that the actors who have played in the western – John Wayne, Gary Cooper, James Stewart, Clint Eastwood – are instantly recognizable.

This suggests that the rise of the western was not simply due to certain American historical developments (the frontier, the clash between the white man and the Native American), but reflects more universal feelings and needs. The western reveals the repressed: the male couple, the male family, enrapt in their visions of love, death, empty deserts, horses, huge skies, the far country.

ANDROGYNY

Homoeroticism has generally led a hidden life in the western and other films depicting a male world, but in the post-war period a new generation of American film actors began to openly subvert the masculine image portrayed by John Wayne and Rock Hudson. Montgomery Clift, Marlon Brando and James Dean depicted a different kind of man: full of anguish, yearning.[8] A new kind of acting emerged: neurotic, dangerous, searching for authenticity, not afraid to look weak or clumsy. And these three actors also projected a narcissism, a femininity, that produced something highly charged and intense on screen. They seem locked in some private self-dialogue, fascinated in their own bodies, their eyes full of veiled meanings, uncertain about what kind of man they are. In Graham McCann's book *Rebel Males*, there is an extraordinary picture of Clift: he stands against a desk, his head turned towards a woman sitting there.[9] The body stance, the tilt of the head, the hand resting on the desk, the lowered eyelids is very like a woman, yet Clift is dressed in the white T-shirt that became the uniform for macho film actors. This ambiguity in fact gives these three actors a considerable erotic fascination – it's like watching a man and a woman in the same body It's surely no accident that Clift, Brando and Dean were all obsessed with their mothers, and Clift and Dean in particular had strenuously bisexual lifestyles. They portray men haunted by uncertainty, perplexed by gender, full of anger and anguish.

Early rock 'n' roll was characterized by either the macho type, such as Elvis, or the clean-cut boy-next-door type, for example, Ricky Nelson, Fabian. In the late sixties and early seventies, singers with a more unconventional image began to emerge: David Bowie, Marc Bolan, Alice Cooper, Freddy Mercury. Here were men who cultivated a 'camp', feminine, or bisexual image. Thus in 1971, Bowie visited America for the first time, wasn't allowed to perform because of visa problems, but 'gets plenty of publicity when he wears dresses in Texas and Los Angeles'.[10] In 1972, Bowie openly declared his bisexuality.

In the eighties, British bisexual singers such as Boy George and Freddy Mercury were quite open about their sexuality, and there was also a plethora of gay singers: Pet Shop Boys, Erasure, Jimmy Sommerville, Frankie Goes to Hollywood.

It's not so much that such groups and singers blazon their bisexuality and homosexuality, but rather that it is accepted within the music world. You don't have to be a butch male to be successful as you did in the fifties, and to a degree in the sixties.

Some of these singers became extremely popular because they propagated an image entirely at odds with the old macho image. David Bowie, Boy George, Freddy Mercury – these were men with an ability to project theatrical fantasies that teeter between masculinity and femininity. Young people have obviously enjoyed and, to a degree, imitated such play.

One might of course argue that such presentations are entirely ephemeral and unimportant, but I disagree. Popular art, precisely because it is more naive and less solemn than 'serious art', reflects directly and rapidly shifts in the collective unconscious. And in pop, the statement we have been getting is that men are not as constrained by the old 'masculine' role. I am not suggesting that men will suddenly start walking around in dresses or being camp – that isn't the point. Rather that in pop we see fantasies and images that stretch our conceptions of being a man, and allow some elasticity within traditionally hidebound stereotypes.

The opposite of androgynous pop has been heavy metal. This is 'hard-on' music, it is so virile and aggressive, the singers are so insistently masculine – leather, shaggy hair, gold chains, crucifixes – that it gets wearisome, and easily crosses over into misogyny. But at its most authentic it gets close to the blues, it has a kind of elemental rawness (Gary Moore, Extreme).

GAY MAN

Male homosexuality is surrounded by ambivalence in our culture. To be sure, there are any amount of negative images of it – the spread of AIDS allowed all kinds of myths to surface – the 'gay plague', the man who had sex with two thousand men. The association of the HIV virus with blood lent a grisly and sinister overtone to the notion of 'bad blood' in homosexuals.[11] There was also the suggestion of 'God striking back' at gay men for being so unnatural. At times, the British tabloid press have had a field-day with their 'poofters' and 'queers' and 'dykes'. In Jeffrey Week's book

Sexuality and its Discontents, the section on AIDS is called 'Sex as Fear and Loathing.'

Yet since the 1970s the gay and lesbian communities have also seen a powerful growth in self-assertion and confidence – 'gay pride' has become a focus for festivals, demonstrations, books, and so on. This suggests that the self-hatred of gay men has been considerably reduced.

One of the interesting things about the death of Freddy Mercury (1991) was the considerable feelings of sadness, warmth and love towards him that was expressed beyond the gay community. I sensed among some heterosexual men strong protective feelings towards gay men – not that they want to become gay, but that they are glad that some men are. Perhaps male love is finding its feet in the world – for the heterosexual man, the gay man represents something important, something he has had to deny, that he has lost and mourns. This can be referred back to every man's love for his father – but also to the possibility of love between friends, going beyond the normal emotionally strangled 'Hail fellow well met' kind of contact that we see in pubs and elsewhere.

Of course there have also been severe backlashes – certain newspaper editorials accused Freddy Mercury of being a murderer! But the massive pop concert at Wembley in his memory was shown on TV, and there was no attempt to hide the fact that he died of AIDS, and that money from the concert would go to AIDS charities. The same thing happened as Rock Hudson lay dying of AIDS in 1985 – he was amazed at the thousands of letters that poured in, some from very unlikely people.[12]

The vitality of the gay community is a sign of the psychic health and unity of the whole community, since attacks on gays fundamentally represent self-attacks on the homosexual component that exists in everyone. We see on the other hand that societies where gays are persecuted are always repressive, dictatorial and self-hating societies. Think of Nazi Germany, Stalin's Soviet Union – sexuality becomes a front-line weapon in any authoritarian state. The right wing in any society will always attack homosexuality, since totalitarian thought wishes to discipline and constrict human beings into rigid categories, and at a deeper level is compelled to attack those parts of itself that don't fit the prescribed image. This reached ludicrous and savage proportions in Nazi Germany – men were virile blond warriors, women were breeders, and gay men were killed in the death camps. Splitting, projection and scapegoating were institutionalized into the fabric of the state.

At the unconscious level I would argue that patriarchy actually finds male homosexuality very exciting – and threatening. Lesbians have not been the subject of persecution in the same way because it is the gay man who irritates, stimulates and excites the conservative heterosexual males who form the backbone of patriarchal rule. Like pornography, the fantasy of homosexuality promises an orgiastic release from the straitjacket of marital heterosexuality – hence male homosexuality is often associated with the fantasy of promiscuity. This strange mixture of fascination and horror can be seen in nineteenth-century works such as Krafft-Ebbing's *Psychopathia Sexualis* (1886) which almost lovingly records details of sexual 'perversion'.[13]

But sexuality is a political weapon in patriarchal society – revealed explicitly in the dictatorships, but also found in our culture. The notorious Clause 28 in Britain shows this – the family must be protected from single mothers, homosexuals, and other riff-raff. Yet as Jeffrey Weeks says, 'far from diminishing the public presence of lesbians and gay men, it greatly contributed to an enhanced sense of identity and community'.[14] It strikes me that we are at a very delicate stage in the acceptance of homosexuality – or perhaps we are at a crossroads. Will the macho heterosexual jackboot reassert itself, or will the masculine gender become more and more relaxed? Thus the future of homosexuality is closely tied up with the whole future of men and masculinity.

THE MALE BODY

The female body is a modern icon, used to sell all kinds of commodities, and used as a sexual fetish. Women have rightly complained about this fetishism, that is completely unreal, and demeans real women. But what about men's bodies? They are not exempt from this process. Although they are not blazoned across our TV screens or in magazines and newspapers as much as women's bodies, none the less there is a significant amount of use of the male body. Particular areas that are used in advertising are the face and the upper body, but attention has also moved to buttocks, thighs, belly, particularly in TV advertising The famous Levi advertisements, which show a young man taking his jeans off and washing them in a launderette, has a fascinating strip-tease theme – will we get to see his penis?

The two critical areas of the body for many men are the head and the penis. The head is the instrument of thought, and therefore the source of intellectual and organizational power; and the penis, while potentially the most potent, is also the most vulnerable area. In between these two organs is the heart – which for many men is no man's land, alien territory. Yet ironically, heart disease and failure is a common cause of death in men, as if male indifference to matters of the heart reaps a savage reward.

In certain men that I work with in psychotherapy, one might say that their existence is both cerebral and 'penile', but not heartful. There is thinking and there is sex – but what is in between? An emptiness, a hollow, an embarrassment, a shame about feeling.

If one made a drawing of some men's bodies that was psychologically rather than physiologically accurate, there would be a huge head balanced above an erect penis, perhaps with exaggerated biceps and pectorals. But the legs would be dwarfish, the feet minute, the face immobile. This is a ghastly caricature, but then aren't some men just that? It is striking how little many men know about their body, compared with women. For example, prostatic disease – which is commoner than breast or cervical cancer – often goes on for years before men do anything about it as they are either too embarrassed to seek help, or just assume that it's an inevitable part of growing old. By contrast, women's health has become an important issue in our society, and 'Well Women Clinics' are part of the British health service – as far as I know, there is no screening for prostatic disease.

HEAD

Many men get stiff necks, from carrying around that enormous head, full of its information, its built-in Filofax of data, appointments, birthdays, shoulds and shouldn'ts, and so on. What an enormous weight!

I have often heard women joke that their male partners think with their penis. One can reverse this, and say that they probably also make love with their heads. Or indeed, that all experience is perceived as happening in the brain. This is also true of many women, but amongst men it is epidemic. Men will actually argue passionately that since the brain is the focal point of the nervous system, that experience really is in the head.

Behaviourism, which is surely the pinnacle of patriarchal reductionism, triumphantly announced in the forties and fifties that the mind was only a series of stimulus response connections – and therefore (like God) was dead. Not the triumph of mind over body, but brain over mind. Emotion was only a series of synaptic surges in the cortex.

What about men's bodies? The body is for sport and sex and eating. When it's tired, it sleeps. Thus it is quite an efficient functional instrument for many men.

The idea that the body is an amazingly sensitive emotional register is totally alien to them. They just look blank if you talk about it. That the body feels as well as senses, emotes as well as digests – this is unknown.

Sometimes if a man in therapy says he is angry, I might say 'Where do you feel the anger?', and I get the blank look. They feel it in their head – where else?

When I was a kid, I used to read a comic which had stories about Mekons. These were creatures on another planet with enormous swollen heads and huge eyes, and dwarfish bodies. When I talk to men who are academics or computer programmers, accountants or business men, I sometimes have the fantasy they are Mekons. They experience the world through their eyes, ears and intellects, but the whole front of the body is numb.

It is interesting to consider what kind of subjective body-image such men have – I am sure some of them actually experience themselves as 'talking heads'. Thought reigns, logic holds sway, rationality is king. Such men are disdainful of women and their emotionality and irrationality, and feel bewildered when women attack them for their aloofness.

At some point in their development, their awareness, which as a child is naturally spread all over the body, got shrunk, compressed into the head. Excitement, joy, despair, rage – which are all orgasmic feelings that suffuse the whole body, became miniaturized into the cortex, where life seems like a video game, fast and furious, but bodiless, heartless.

What kind of orgasm do these men have? They have orgasms in the head. Can they cry? Can they explode in rage? All the time the force of rationality exerts its cold baleful pressure on such bodily experiences, which become strangled and alien.

But on the other hand it is amazing to watch a man begin to experience feelings in the heart region – there is an opening up, a new sensitivity to other people and the environment, feelings of warmth and love, and often deep pain, a sense of heart-break. From the body having been an efficient machine, or a piece of meat that is taken for granted, it can become the seat of emotion, a remarkably sensitive indicator of one's openness to the world. This can be a revelation to many men, who have tended to ignore the body except as an exercise area, or the arena of sexual athleticism.

It is interesting to note in parenthesis that working as a therapist with people, I continually use the front of my body as a kind of radar, to tell me what is going on with them. My face, heart region, stomach, belly, genitals – all the time these are registering the other person, being emotionally responsive to them and their feelings. It is a kind of transmission system between my unconscious feelings and their unconscious feelings. With certain people, a particular area of my body becomes numb, since theirs is, but with others feels totally alive. With some men, I find that my head feels excited, but the rest of my body is blank.

PECS, BICEPS, TRICEPS, DELTOIDS

At the beginning of the film *Total Recall*, Schwarzenegger is in bed with his 'wife' (like everything else his marriage is a memory implant). She starts to unfasten her nightdress to expose her breasts, and the interesting question arises (for this viewer anyway): 'Who has the larger breasts?'

Later in the film Schwarzenegger goes to Mars, to find out if his memories of it are also implants or real and he arrives disguised as a woman. In the best scene in the film 'she' stands in the arrival hall, her head begins to peel open, and there stands the grinning Arnie, ready for some more orgasmic violence. This is a classic 'transformation scene', of which there are many in Hollywood cinema, and illustrates nicely the ambiguity about the male musculature, at one level, emblem of 100 per cent virility, yet at another, envious of, competing with, imitating the female torso. And later in the film there is a male pregnancy – the leader of the Martian guerrilla army is a baby encysted in the belly of a man. (The film *Alien* has a bloody male childbirth scene.)

Schwarzenegger's physique reflects the considerable amount of narcissism about the male musculature in our culture, comparable with the attention paid to women's breasts, thighs, buttocks, and so on. But with men it tends to be justified as to do with sport, keeping fit, being active, consolidating the image of the male as invulnerable warrior/athlete. Remember the old adverts for Charles Atlas – 'Don't be a seven stone weakling.' In the ad, a man with muscles bulging like car tyres poses, infatuated with his own image. Such a man is in love with himself. He is self-existent; he neither loves nor needs love.

Such a body can be seen both as a massive penis, but can also be construed as quasi-female. In body-building the pectorals become massive, jutting breasts which are flaunted. I notice with pop singers such as Prince and Michael Jackson that there is a vogue for lifting the T-shirt up suddenly to expose their chest, in a grotesque parody of centrefold girl exposing her breasts. Michael Jackson also frequently clutches his crutch while dancing, as if to reassure himself and us that his penis is intact. Thus we end up with a man with breasts and penis. He is truly self-sufficient!

Body-builders usually have narrow hips, admired in men partly, I would think, to distinguish them from women's child-bearing hips; while the hefty shoulders denote 'upper body strength', that phrase so beloved of sports commentators. This contrast between upper and lower body is shown most grotesquely in American football players – above the waist, gigantic Goliaths, minotaurs, inflated by all the body armour, but below the waist like tiny dancing dolls with petite buttocks. There is both an ultramachismo and a girlishness combined in this body-image.

Considerable attention has been paid in modern psychology to the penis-like qualities of such a body, connected with the 'phallic character'.[15] It is erect, always ready for action. It is deeply veined, ribbed, with a massive head. It tenses itself, ready to explode. But crucially it is rigid, since the man himself is emotionally rigid.

This means, amongst other things, that ironically such men often feel sexually permanently dissatisfied, since their rigidity does not permit a full emotional and physical surrender during intercourse. Alexander Lowen comments: 'The phallic male finds no deep satisfaction on any level of activity and he is forced into continued pursuit and conquest.'[16]

They are often narcissistic, obsessive men, who are unable to relax, or be spontaneous. The fetishism of the body is in fact a defence against other people, who are actually experienced as frightening, and a defence against the body's spontaneous rhythms. The phallic male wants to control life, and must therefore be permanently on guard.

BEERGUTS

French and Saunders – the British female comedy duo – have a biting sketch where they play two gross men, complete with enormous beer-guts, sitting in front of the TV, making lewd comments about the women they see: 'Cor, I could give her something', complete with obscene gesture.

These men are pathetic, because their defences are so paper-thin – that is the point of the sketch. They are only fooling themselves. No woman would possibly be interested in them, they are so corpulent, so gross, and so narcissistic.

Of course this is cruel parody. But what about the real beerguts, sitting in the pubs, or sitting at home with the six-pack? What makes them tick? Does anybody care?

The beergut is a formidable defence. You walk through a crowd, and people have to get out of the way because your gut precedes you. You can hide behind it, you can almost hit people with it. It is also a badge of manliness – I can drink sixteen pints a night, and I wear this to prove it. Never mind that it could easily kill me, the sheer effort of carrying it around – I'm proud of it. It shows I'm a real man.

It also hides my penis, which is good, because then I won't frighten people with it, and I won't frighten myself with it. In fact if I look down I can't see it! That's a relief because then I don't have to think about being a man, and having a penis. I can just heave all this weight around, sit in the pub and fill myself with liquid, and hide my needs.

I take it to the pub with me, and prop it against the bar, and I sit behind it, and it's my best friend. And it keeps me warm at night, I can cuddle up to it as if it was a woman.

Such men look like pregnant women – they develop pendulous breasts and huge bellies. I wonder if they are unconsciously envious of women's ability to bear children and be creative with life itself? Is the beergut a fantasy pregnancy?

PENIS

The penis is the source of a man's greatest vulnerability, and his greatest feeling of power. It is a place from where he expresses love, hate, fear, tenderness, contempt, friendship, disgust, and also a place where he can become completely expressionless, without feeling. It is used as a battering ram against women; as a weapon of revenge; as an expression of love and adoration; it is also a little boy's willy, a dick, a shlong, the python, prick, rhythm stick, ding-a-ling.

It can be anything. We might say: the penis is the man. One cannot talk about penises separate from their owners, just as we cannot talk about 'sexuality' in abstract, or talk about 'sexual problems' separate from the problems that people have in relationships.

So men feel about their penis as they feel about themselves: proud, shy, afraid, disgusted, ignorant, loving, hating, angry – the whole gamut of human feeling is potentially found between a man and his penis.

Sexually a penis enables a man to penetrate deeply into a woman (or a man) and caress her (him) there. Thus the penis in this respect is bound up with relating to others: it is a means of contact. But as a baby or a boy, the male finds the penis as a source of comfort for himself, maybe a substitute for the breast, something he can manipulate at will. He discovers masturbation, which again can mean so many things to different men – comfort, company, desolation, lust, fear, love.

Thus the penis is, as it were, poised between narcissism and altruism. It can be used to relate to oneself, or to others. Quite often these two directions get confused, and one hears a woman angrily accuse a man of masturbating inside her during sex. So one can go through the motions of relating sexually but in fact remain completely in a world of one's own. In that world, the penis may loom large as a kind of fantasy friend, or lover, or mother or father.

The penis is also connected with performance. It gets erect, remains erect during sexual intercourse and then subsides. But what anxiety is aroused in men about this! The erection becomes a fetish, that measures one's manhood, virility, athleticism, or whatever. How afraid many men are not to have an erection, when in fact that often signifies something emotionally important: I don't want to make love, I don't want to relate to you, I feel afraid, I feel childlike, and so on.

'Keep your pecker up' men say to each other – reflecting the desperate need to keep the damn thing erect. Never mind if you feel depressed or sad or lonely, or bored or angry or uninterested – keep the flag flying, make the python do its tricks, hoist the top-sail, expand the gland – what a mythology surrounds penis performance! Mae West celebrated and mocked it in her famous gibe: 'Is that a six-gun in your pocket, or are you just pleased to see me?'

It is interesting that images of the erect penis are still considered beyond the pale. Thus in pornography one may legally peruse women's genitals and breast and anus, but the male penis must be photographed in a crestfallen state. Why is this? Is the erect penis so dangerous that it cannot be photographed? Or is the ban for men's benefit, so that they do not run the risk of being defaced or mutilated or even desired? It is also possible that in patriarchal culture the erect penis is considered too exciting for other men to view.

At my secondary school we were all compelled to swim naked in the school swimming-pool. This caused anguish for new boys, but as we got older, it provided great interest, in that we could compare the many penises that one saw. The difference between the circumcised and non-circumcised exercised great debate: which was superior? Some boys reckoned that the uncircumcised penis provided much greater sensitivity – the circumcised scoffed at this, for they had a penis on display all the time, not a flabby piece of skin. The argument was never satisfactorily solved, since direct experiential comparison was impossible!

The first pubic hairs provided an initiation rite on their own. The first boys to get them were in fact derided not admired – was this an expression of our fear about sexuality?

But there is also a fatigue factor that sets in pretty rapidly – watching thirty or forty penises becomes tedious. They all look roughly the same. This is a complete contradiction to how they felt for each individual, who tended to scan their own for every minute blemish, and regarded it with a

mixture of adoration, fear and disgust. Philip Roth describes the adolescent
boy's fascination with the penis wonderfully in *Portnoy's Complaint*:

> It was at the end of my freshman year of high school – and freshman
> year of masturbation – that I discovered on the underside of my penis,
> just where the shaft meets the head, a little discolored dot that has since
> been diagnosed as a freckle. *Cancer*. I had been giving myself cancer.
> All that pulling and tugging at my own flesh, all that friction, had given
> me an incurable disease. And not yet fourteen! In bed at night, the tears
> rolled from my eyes. 'No!' I sobbed. 'I don't want to die! Please – no!'
> But then because I would very shortly be a corpse anyway, I went ahead
> as usual, and jerked off into my sock.[17]

That hits the tone exactly, if in a rather mordant way: the fear, the com-
pulsiveness, the horror, the ferocious guilt, the excitement that one had this
thing that could be manipulated again and again. Of course in this amazing
novel, socks are not only the thing that get jerked off into – Roth has a
fierce eye for detail and surreal realism – sister's bra, the bathroom mirror,
his own mouth, urinals, empty chocolate wrappers, cored apples, empty
milk bottles, and the family dinner, all become receptacles. Roth captures
with great comic invention that male adolescent madness, craziness about
masturbation.

If the breast is our first experience of nourishment that is ultimately controlled by somebody else, then for a boy the penis is a trail-blazing experience of something he can control. And masturbation can become for some
men their only source of sensual comfort and love. If you are cut off from
people it is ideal: perfectly narcissistic, perfectly controllable, and replete
with fantasy. It is also a notoriously lonely, not to say desolate experience.

Roth has another lyrical passage describing the penis of his hero's father:

> I stand at attention between his legs as he coats me from head to toe
> with a thick lather of soap – and eye with admiration the baggy substan-
> tiality of what overhangs the marble bench on which he is seated. His
> scrotum is like the long wrinkled face of some old man with an egg
> tucked into each of his sagging jowls – while mine might hang from the
> wrist of some little girl's dolly like a teeny pink purse. And as for his
> *shlong*, to me, with that fingertip of a prick that my mother likes to refer
> to in public (once, okay, but that once will last a lifetime) as my 'little
> thing', his *shlong* brings to mind the fire hoses coiled along the corridors
> at school. *Shlong*: the word somehow catches exactly the brutishness,
> the *meatishness*, that I admire so, the sheer mindless, weighty and

unself-conscious dangle of that living piece of hose through which he passes streams of water as thick and strong as rope. ... If only I could have nourished myself upon the depths of his vulgarity, instead of that too becoming a source of shame.[18]

This is magnificent prose, rich, dense, following the rush of thought and feeling, and rising periodically to ironic and almost tragic heights: the teeny pink purse, the fire hoses, the 'living piece of hose' – and expressing the profound lament of the male boy for the lost maleness of his father, the 'depths of his vulgarity'. The whole novel is based on the shame of the boy about his maleness, a shame taught him by both mother and father. Roth expresses a crucial aspect of modern life for men: their unfathering.

Is there something intrinsically comic about the penis? As I write this I can feel in myself a compulsion to start making jokes about penises – this shows the embarrassment I have about it, and the fear, and the vulnerability also. If I make lots of penis jokes, then I am safe, or rather my penis is safe! For then you won't joke about it – I've pre-empted your mockery with my own.

Thus the penis leads us to castration. Classically, the boy fears castration from the father for desiring Mum. But having worked with men with castration fears for over fifteen years, there is no doubt that for many boys Mum also wields the scalpel of ridicule, or the axe of disgust, or whatever her chosen instrument is. Men also recall their mother being fascinated by their penis, desiring it, coveting it. This can make a man terrified to have genital contact with a woman – she might mock his penis, then again she might devour it or take it off him.

There is also something majestic about the erect penis, there is a grandeur in it, which some men find difficult to claim for themselves, out of fear that they are being sexist in some way. This is ludicrous. Sex between a man and a woman, or between two men, or two women, is at its best when both feel that grandeur in their bodies, including the genitals. It is a nobility, an animal beauty, a power that our civilization shuns.

Here is one of the sources of shame about the penis. It is inescapably animal, primitive. You can think with your head all day, and maybe all night, but you must go to the toilet, and pull out your penis. You wake up early in the morning and it's hard. Think your way out of that one! Of course it's all too easy to do that – to retreat into the head and treat the penis as an unfortunate by-product of evolution.

Isn't this another reason for the legal barring of the erect penis in pornography? It is too aggressive and too obvious in its intent. When it's erect, it has no intention of urinating – after all, little boys are allowed to do that by the road-side – it wants to penetrate somebody. Both the would-be penetrator and the would-be penetrated feel some qualms about this being made too explicit perhaps? This was one of Freud's great discoveries – how much we all dread and yearn for the sheer animal side of being alive.

Thus men today need to reclaim this sense of beauty and power about the penis. Part of our celebration of it, and its primitive grandeur, lies in a healthy ribaldry about it, which accepts the animal quality of it with affection. Mae West again: 'a hard man is good to find!'

10 Growing Up

We all write our own stories. Even the most abstract philosophical treatise comes out of the heart and belly of the man or woman who wrote it.

So rather than be ingenuous about my own investment in the issues that I am discussing in this book, I would prefer to describe briefly my own story as a boy growing up.

I grew up in a working-class Lancashire culture, where there were certain fixed ideas about how men and women behaved, and what their respective roles were. To deviate from those roles was to risk being condemned or ridiculed. For a woman to roll home drunk from the pub, for a man to cry openly, for a woman to fight in the street, for a man to feel depressed – these were 'counter-cultural'. They just didn't happen, or if they did, there was swift judgement passed.

At the same time, there could be a considerable amount of tolerance for eccentrics and people who didn't fit the stereotypes. For example, when I worked in factories, I saw gay men treated sympathetically and with friendliness. There might be some joking and horseplay, (partly revealing other men's fascination with homosexuality), but I was often surprised at how much tolerance there was. The same was true of people who seemed 'retarded' in some way – people were very kind to them.

There was a considerable segregation between the sexes. I remember when I started going in pubs at about the age of 15, there were men-only bars, where women were explicitly not allowed in. Landlords said to women who were about to cross the threshold of such a bar: 'Sorry, love, ladies aren't allowed in there.' Of course, today that is considered sexist, but I wonder if we haven't gone too far the other way. Why shouldn't each sex have their own preserves? Indeed we've reached the bizarre position where for women to have women-only clubs, meetings, health clubs, swimming-sessions, etc., is 'right on', but not for men! Of course many pre-industrial societies have very powerful segregation between the sexes.

The men-only bars made it explicit, but there were whole areas of life where only men congregated – football matches, certain pubs, heavy industry – and there were areas where women dominated, such as shopping, offices, the kitchen.

Of course children belonged mainly to women, and babies almost entirely. Men would admire babies, pick them up, but they would put them down again soon. They wouldn't really hold them for long periods, or sing them to sleep, as women did. And they didn't change their nappies, feed them, read them stories, or take them to school.

So as a young boy I lived in a woman's world, my mother's. Before I started school I remember long summer afternoons, that seemed to go on for ever and ever. My mother would be making something for tea – scones or a cake – and I would be playing on the floor. I can remember very clearly the feeling that this was perfection, this was life. I'd finally understood what life was all about: this was my life, and it would stay like this for ever. It was a state of mutual adoration. Things such as school and work were inconceivable.

Then gradually I became aware of worlds that were different. Obviously my father went to a different world, but I don't think I was interested in it until I was of school age. It didn't really sink in that he had another existence, entirely with men. And school seemed like an extension of home, since it was only round the corner.

When I was a young boy my father's factory had an open day, so that everyone's families could go along and look round. I was amazed when we went. It was the first time I'd seen where he worked. It was a whole universe of men, who not only worked together, but obviously liked each other, had fun with each other, made fun of each other, went in for horseplay and practical jokes, and so on. There were lots of apprentices, young boys, who were treated with a mixture of kindness and mockery. My father was obviously popular and respected through the whole factory – managers would come and ask him questions about some problem in the factory, because he had been there all his life and knew it all inside out.

It was a rich world, with its values and culture quite distinct from the values of home, wife and family. I think I was shocked that there was this other world, which my father went to. It was as if he lived in two different worlds, a kind of schizophrenic existence.

Yet later in my life, when I worked as a lecturer, I found that it was a relief to have two different worlds. I enjoyed going off to work and getting away from home. I enjoyed having a sphere of my life that my partner didn't engage in. And I also enjoyed coming back home and leaving work behind. So although schizophrenic in one sense, this split life is also quite pleasing in another.

As I got older I also became aware that my father was a bit of a loner as well. He could joke and laugh with the men on the shop-floor, but he had a sensitive side that he hid from them. He liked classical music, he read the

Guardian, he mulled over ideas a lot. I'm sure if he'd been born thirty years later he would have gone to university. When I was older he told me that he often felt like an innocent amongst his mates at work. So for him masculinity wasn't a cut and dried thing, he couldn't just relax into being a working-class man. He felt a bit of an outsider, because he saw the world in a different way from them.

Being an outsider for me was made more explicit once I went off to Manchester Grammar School at the age of eleven. I began to develop two different views of being a man. My dad worked in a factory, worked with his hands, came home physically tired, got a wage-packet every Friday with his money in. But I was setting off on an entirely different journey, where men worked with their brains, didn't get their hands dirty, used long words and less four-letter words, and got paid invisible salaries. I developed two identities: working-class male and middle-class male.

In some ways, I can see now it as an enriching experience, but that's not how it seemed then. It was bewildering, and I felt afraid I wouldn't ever belong anywhere. In some ways that fear was justified. It represented a kind of uprooting that is permanent. I never feel quite at home now in any social class. And I am not sure what kind of man I am socially. Do I belong down at the football match, in the public bar, wearing a flat cap? Or do I belong in the art cinema, the concert hall, reading the *Guardian*, frequenting book shops?

At university, my split nature was at times almost comical. One night I would be in the bar with my engineering, rugby-playing friends. We would down pint after pint, talk about women with a mixture of awe and condescension, shout, vomit, crack jokes, make fun of each other, get excited and aggressive. The next day I would go for 'tea' with a group of my intellectual friends, mostly women. (At home in Oldham 'tea' was the cooked meal you had at six o'clock.) They were people who read novels and poetry, talked about them, watched the latest *nouvelle vague* French cinema, talked about Godard, visited London art galleries. This was a new world to me, and I listened, kept quiet and learned. And eventually I went with them to the French films, and I talked with them about novels and poetry. So what kind of man was I altogether? I had no idea. I felt a mishmash of different elements, and how they all hung together – that has taken me all my life to figure out.

The struggle for me has always been how to live harmoniously, with these disparate elements inside me. At school and university, I protected each side of me from the other. My boozing pals didn't know my intellectual friends, and vice versa. Occasionally the two groups would meet somewhere, say at a party, and there would be mutual incomprehension and distaste. But I had these two elements inside me, presumably competing for attention, attacking each other, trying to be top-dog to the other. Only in the last few years has this civil war within me calmed down and developed into a more civilized state of co-existence.

WOMEN

There was a kind of woman in my childhood who we were all afraid of, who was exemplified by our next-door neighbour, Mrs Edrich. She ran a fierce regime in her house. She cleaned fanatically, dusted, hoovered, scrubbed the flagstones outside the house, and glared at my mother if she forgot to do the same, and if you went in her house, commanded you not to sit on certain chairs so as not to spoil them. She had a front parlour that was like a mausoleum, never used, full of stuffed furniture, dated pictures, ornate wallpaper. You felt like tiptoeing through it, as if corpses were the only permitted residents. And in those days probably that was their major use – the corpses of the man and woman of the house would lie for one night before burial in a room never used in life.

Towards me, she turned a gimlet eye, watching for grubby finger marks, muddy feet, boyish antics, that might mar in any way her pristine palace.

You could say with hindsight that she was squeezing all her frustration, her lack of creativity, her insularity, into this fanaticism about the home. She was repressed, bitter, hawk-like, a domestic tyrant. Mr Edrich was an entirely shadowy figure – I have hardly any memory of him. He went to work and came home again, and was careful not to get marks on the furniture. So to the local kids, and to adults as well, Mrs Edrich was formidable, vulturine. Her tyranny has two faces: it expresses her utter powerlessness; and yet to me, and I think to my parents, she instilled genuine fear. We walked in dread of her, lest she spy out that our household wasn't up to scratch. Devotees of the British TV soap *Coronation St* will recognize an echo of Ena Sharples here.

Here is a woman who is both powerful and powerless. For the feminist, she illustrates the repressive nature of woman's role as housewife, and that is an accurate analysis. But to a boy, to all boys in that neighbourhood, she was something terrible. And it seemed that to Mr Edrich she was something terrible, although he obviously had made a kind of *modus vivendi* with her.

Mrs Edrich showed the split between home and work, between women and men, to a pronounced degree. The home was her territory, and she ruled over it. Of course to boys, the home was the only world there was, except for school. So in our world, it seemed that women were dominant. They did all the things that mattered to boys: they cooked your food, cleaned your clothes, washed you, listened to your stories, your complaints, told you off for misdemeanours, cuddled you, put you to bed, attended to your ailments. What did it matter to a young boy that there was another world out there where men dominated? That was a far-off world, whereas this world was immediate. It was the only real world. Your feelings, your food, your clothes, your illnesses, your play – these make up the world of a child, and in these areas women were experts.

In some ways, women were like servants in working-class households: they waited on everyone, cooked their food, cleaned the house, cleaned everyone's clothes, paid bills probably. Again, there is an ambiguity about this: it can be seen as an utterly servile role, and also as utterly powerful. Husbands were like little boys, pampered, yet ordered about.

There was often a kind of sexual mythology about women in the factories where I worked in the holidays. In one factory, where I worked in the stores department, the men would swear that some of the canteen women would freely give their sexual favours, and in fact had a bed in a back room of the canteen, where great antics took place. I never found out if there was any reality to this fantasy, but the men in the stores delighted in embroidering on it. There was a mixture of admiration, fear, awe and contempt for such sexual harridans, if they existed.

Such women were portrayed as lustful Amazons, with enormous power over men, rather like Roman emperors. One wink of an eye, and you were in the sacred hut, treated to a sexual orgy; but arbitrarily you could be rejected.

It is an astonishing fantasy – the woman as sexual monster, at the mercy of her own lust, but treating men imperiously. She has what they want, and they know it, and she knows it. Hence the men's admiration and hatred for her. This was the woman you would never marry – soiled goods. But also who would want a wife like that – how could you endure her sexual demands, how could you trust her not to favour other men?

Female sexuality is seen here as something terrifying and devouring, never-ending, gobbling up penises, and demanding more. It is both titillating and eerie. I wonder how many men unconsciously view women in this way?

There were also sexual mythologies about men. I worked in the same factory with a black guy who delighted in walking round the stores with his penis in his hand sticking out of his overalls. All the other men enjoyed this, I suppose partly because it brought together gender and race fantasies. Henry had a big black dick, and was he going to give those canteen women some stick with it! This is like the beergut fantasies I described: men fanta-size about making these Amazons beg for mercy. So to balance the myth of the sexually rapacious woman, there had to be the myth of the battering-ram man. The black man who seemed to fulfil this fantasy was both admired and feared. He could give the canteen women some stick, but you wouldn't let him near your wife – she might also fancy his big black dick! (There were also, of course, hidden homosexual fantasies going on – he wasn't actually showing his penis to women, but to men!)

It is the whore/madonna split all over again. Men want to marry a madonna, because she won't weary them with her sexual demands, nor will she go off with other men, nor will she make him face his own sexuality openly and honestly. But secretly they fancy the 'whores', who promise orgiastic abandon, a rejection of all social values and norms, a chthonic merging in flesh. But of course this is the split in their own sexuality, pro-jected conveniently onto women, who have historically often take the burden of lust and evil on the one hand, and an impossible purity on the other: the witch and the Virgin Mary.

When I was in my teens, there was a similar view of girls at parties, coffee bars and so on. If you could get a girl to let you walk her home, you expected to be allowed to 'feel her up', i.e., touch her breasts at least. Going to the cinema often involved a tortuous struggle to touch a girl's breast, or undo her bra strap, or kiss her. What were we really after? Affection, our mother's breast, sexual conquest? I guess a blend of the whole lot.

I can remember being in bed with a girl at a party, and some other man staggered through the room – we were all drunk - and put his hand under the blankets and squeezed her breasts! Did such things really happen? They did. Women were like meat, and you prodded them, and squeezed them. But the girls treated the men like meat as well; they were neither more or less brutal and mechanical. That's why I've always found the feminist attack on men treating women as sex objects one-sided. I can remember girls who grabbed at you in the same way, would grab your penis as if it was a razor-strop or a tap to be turned on. I never saw sexual brutality as a male preserve.

I think I was bewildered by all of this, scared, but putting on an air of bravado. I would go with my friends to dances at the local Co-op dance-hall, but first we would go to the pub and drink ourselves silly. Then, and only then, we would go to the dance, walk round and round, making highly critical remarks about the girls who were all dancing in the middle. But of course we were completely terrified of them. We could only ask one to dance if we were absolutely plastered with drink. The worst thing was that you could never admit you were frightened. You would stagger out when it finished, and say something derogatory about the girls – 'They weren't up to much', 'What a load of slags', but secretly disappointed, lonely, bitter at not having met anyone. But who could you talk to about your fears and need of women?

Eventually I managed to break through this level of fear, and actually meet some girls as people, although still fascinated and obsessed with their bodies.

I had an experience with my first girl-friend that seemed to confirm the fantasies of the men in the factory. I was terrified of having actual intercourse, whereas she was very keen. We would repeatedly approach the critical point, and I felt too frightened to go on, but also unable to tell her I was frightened. I went on holiday in the summer for several weeks, without her, and when I got back, the first thing she told me was that she'd found someone else, and he was a great fuck, and they'd done it standing up against a wall round the back of Barclay's Bank. I felt humiliated, totally rejected. It was like a reversal of all the myths of the reluctant virgin and the importunate lover: in our case, I was the former and she was the latter. She was the brutal one; I was the wounded one. You can see why I raise my eyebrows at some of the things the feminists say. I didn't feel like a marauding male at all, I felt marauded!

My reluctance recurred with a later girl-friend, but in desperation I went to see the family doctor, who gave me friendly words of encouragement, whereupon I jumped in bed with the girl and away we went. It's interesting that I wanted a man's approval before I could have intercourse. It was as if he guaranteed to me that I wouldn't come to any harm inside her, and also that I wouldn't damage her with this penis of mine. I wasn't sure if a penis was an instrument of love or a weapon of war, or whether a vagina provided a welcoming embrace or a deadly bite.

I felt I was a sexual nincompoop, and the girls I met seemed to be knowledgeable and self-assured. I was the virgin, I was the one saying no, I was the one who felt guilty because I wouldn't – or daren't – open my legs!

You could argue I was exceptionally retarded, or sexually pathological, or whatever, but I've talked to a lot of men subsequently who had similar experiences. That early relationship with mother is confusing for the male, since he knows that mother is sexually taboo, even though he may have intense love and sexual desire for her. Thus he becomes familiar with an emotionally intense but sexually suppressed relationship; and often will later have the converse type of relationship, sexually intense but not intimate. There is also the Oedipal memory of being sexually rejected, being a little boy who isn't 'man' enough for Mum – this often connects with men's fears about their penis being too small.

It makes me wonder if a lot of male fantasies about being Casanovas or inexhaustible lovers stems from this fear that they are also nincompoops, or that they are weaklings, confronted with women's voracious sexuality? Pornographic fantasies about the man with an eleven-inch penis, or a penis like a steel bar, unbending, incorruptible, eternal, inexhaustible – surely these are compensations for the dread of being not enough, not big enough, not man enough. Lawrence expresses this fear and hostility in the character Michaelis in *Lady Chatterley's Lover*, who makes love to Connie Chatterley, but is bitter towards her afterwards:

> 'You couldn't go off at the same time as a man, could you? You'd have to bring yourself off! You'd have to run the show!'
> 'What do you mean?' she said.
> 'You know what I mean. You keep on for hours after I've gone off ... and I have to hang on with my teeth till you bring yourself off with your own exertions.'
> She was stunned by this unexpected piece of brutality, at the moment when she was glowing with a sort of pleasure beyond words, and a sort of love for him. Because, after all, like so many modern men, he was finished almost before he had begun. And that forced the woman to be active.[1]

Here is Lawrence's fear and anger at women 'running the show', and his distaste for women wanting to have an orgasm as well as men. He also points the finger at men, who have no endurance, and 'force their women to be active'. Thus Lawrence sees the modern woman's desire for emancipation and for recognition of their own sexuality as stemming from male inadequacy. If only the men were really men, the women wouldn't want all this freedom and power!

Later in the same novel, Mellors, who initiates Connie into Lawrence's version of phallic nirvana ('the phallic hunt of the man'[2]), complains in the same way about his former wife:

> When I had her, she'd never come off when I did. Never! She'd just wait. If I kept back for half an hour, she'd keep back longer. And when I'd come and really finished, then she'd start on her own account, and I had to stop inside her till she brought herself off, wriggling and shouting, she'd clutch clutch with herself down there, an' then she'd come off, fair in ecstasy. And then she'd say: That was lovely! Gradually I got sick of it ... and she got worse ... she'd sort of tear at me down there, as if it was a beak tearing at me. By God, you think a woman's soft down

there, like a fig. But I tell you the old rampers have beaks between their legs, and they tear at you with it till you're sick.[3]

One of the interesting things about Lawrence is how his prejudices are flaunted in the mouths of his characters – here in Michaelis and Mellors we find his massive fear and hatred towards the vagina, described as a 'beak'. And in the phrases 'wriggling and shouting', and 'she'd clutch clutch' there is such intense dread and loathing of the woman's own sexual power and needs. Lawrence's ideal is the woman who is passive, who worships the penis, and submits to its penetration. But the vagina must not have its own life, its own motion, its own vitality. Mellors even trots out that old saw: 'Seems to me they're nearly all Lesbians.'[4]

However, Connie is not a Lesbian, and dutifully she sets to, to worship Mellors's penis – in Lawrence's terms she's a real woman. She worships at the shrine: 'A man! The strange potency of manhood upon her!'[5] She gazes reverentially at Mellors's penis: '"So proud!" she murmured, uneasy. "And so lordly! Now I know why men are so overbearing." '[6]

This would be comical, as Lawrence often is unintentionally comical, except that behind it is Lawrence's real torment over his masculinity, which as an adolescent I identified with. He seemed to suffer agony over two issues: his emergence from the working class into an intellectual, creative, middle-class milieu. And he suffered all his life from that dichotomy between the woman's world and the man's world. *Sons and Lovers* shows us how Lawrence (Paul Morel) was very immersed in his mother's world. But none the less, he was a man, not a woman, and struggled all his life to find out what that meant, and why his masculinity felt so threatened by women.

Lawrence never solved these problems – indeed one could almost say they killed him. He looked for more and more bizarre solutions, including primitive cultures and religions, and his own half-baked and semi-fascist ideas about sexuality and the relations between men and women.

But his essential problem was that he never fully recognized his hatred, fear and need of women, (and how much he had lost his father), and so he just blamed them, as Mellors does, for being rapacious, domineering, using men as instruments for their own pleasure. This is an odd mirror image of militant feminism: there is the same hate, the same blame, the same fear, the same imputing of terrible power, to the woman in this case. There is the same desperate and denied need and disappointment. These are real feelings, based on real experiences. They are not just fantasies – they come out of that whole culture that Lawrence came out of. He felt utterly castrated as a man, but couldn't admit that, couldn't take responsibility for it and do something about it, apart from blame women, or produce compensatory characters such as Mellors. Mellors's phallicism in fact reveals Lawrence's dread that his own penis – and his manhood as a whole – was a damp squib. It's magic via fiction – I mean that Lawrence magically turns himself into the man that he knew he wasn't – the virile gamekeeper. Comical? Yes, but also very sad, and desperate.

In my early manhood I would have agreed with Lawrence, that women wanted to tear at you, and you had to fend them off. It has taken me a long time to let myself actually experience my feelings about women, and not simply blame women, or even worse, act out my feelings.

The way I acted them out was to go from relationship to relationship. There would always be something I could cite as wrong with the last woman – but the present one, ah, she was different – until disillusionment set in. The sheer repetition of this eventually took its toll on me, and I stopped, as much in exhaustion as anything else.

When I stopped, the feelings began to surface, very painfully and slowly. What came up were my fear of women, my great need of them, my rage at them – and I could see that one reason I had broken up relationships was to avoid these feelings. I couldn't actually bear needing and hating a woman – like Hemingway, I wanted to put a million miles between me and the woman I needed. A lot of this was guilt – I wanted to protect her from myself. So I would get into a 'good woman/bad woman' pattern. The last woman was bad, and the present was good – until inevitably she became bad, and I could get away again.

I also wanted to hide from them the fact that I didn't feel I was a man. Deep down, I had no idea what masculinity was. I was totally confused, but pretty convinced I didn't measure up, whatever the criteria were. I couldn't stand the demands that women made on me because I felt I was inadequate, and I would never be able to meet their demands, so it was their fault for making them. And I hated the woman I was with because I needed her so much. I felt that need marked me out as unmanly – surely men didn't need other people so much? That's what I'd learned from my culture. Men were resourceful, self-sufficient, took life's knocks with a shrug of the shoulder and a stiff upper lip. They didn't want to cry on somebody else's shoulder, they didn't want to collapse sometimes. They were copers.

When you're young it's so much easier to run away from all this, or simply blame other people, and make them bad. Isn't this what the militant feminists are doing? I was a mirror image of them.

But eventually I realized that one of the big projects in my life was to find out what being a man meant, what manhood and masculinity were, and who I was. To call this project 'big' is an understatement. It's a lifetime's project, and I often feel that I've only just begun. I feel relieved that at least

I was able to give up all the answers that I thought I'd found, and admit that I was only just discovering what the question was.

Something has been taken away from men in our culture, something very important – not Lawrence's phallic narcissism, something deeper, closer to the heart. Indeed Lawrence's penis fetishism is no solution. In a curious way it merely mimics the feminists who say that men are just thinking penises. It isn't the penis that's missing – it's the heart. This is the organ that lies between the head and the genitals, and connects them psychically. The tragedy for many men is that it's been anaesthetized, so that they think and they have sex, but they don't feel. Part of the desperate need that men have for women is that they want them to do their feeling for them, so that they feel complete. But that leads in the end to frustration and hatred – because it's emotional experience by proxy. You can't really get someone else's heart to function as your own.

MEN

Both my grandfathers fought in the Great War. My father's father was captured by the Germans, and worked for the next two years in a salt mine. To the end of his life he could still recite odd bits of German – he could count in German, and he had funny phrases such as 'Machine nix arbeit'. He also used to say that the German guards were very friendly to them. But he had several brothers killed in that war.

My mother's father was in the trenches for the whole war, and he wrote home regularly. I still have his letters. They are quite bitter. 'The officers treat us like dogs.' 'We never know what we are doing, and I don't think anyone else does really.' Remarks such as those abound. He describes a sergeant in his company being shot for cowardice. One can sense his disbelief that these things were going on, and the shrinking belief that it was worthwhile.

They both survived. My father's father came home and worked in cotton mills for the rest of his life, and contracted severe byssinosis, and eventually got a byssinosis pension. He also had injuries from being caught up in the huge moving belt that you found in cotton mills then, that drove the machinery. He was lucky to survive that, as it killed most people who had similar accidents.

He was a sentimental kind of man, prone to tears after a few halves of bitter in the pub, and especially if he started to sing 'Danny Boy'. I have a sentimental streak like him.

He told many stories about growing up in Victorian Lancashire, the games they used to play, and the practical jokes. I always wish I'd tape-recorded them, but now they're lost, except the ones we can remember. There was the time their dog jumped up onto to a butcher's open-fronted window and grabbed a leg of lamb, and ran home with it. My grandmother used to supply the punch-line to that story, when you asked, 'What did you do with it?' – she'd say 'We washed it and cooked it and ate it.' As a young boy, grandfather and his pals used to get hold of a dog and put his legs down the storm drain in the street so that it couldn't move. Then they knocked on the door of the owner and said 'Hey, missus, your dog's had an accident and had its legs cut off.' Some of the humour was quite cruel and aggressive in this way. I wish I could remember more of his stories, they're like fading photos in an album.

My other grandfather had green fingers – he had a magic way with plants, and used to grow a lot of vegetables and flowers. He also used to keep a pig in the back garden, and periodically someone would come round and kill it for him.

He was a strange man: stern in many ways, but also very affectionate to me. I used to sit with him for hours and play cribbage. I can still hear his Yorkshire voice saying 'Fifteen two, and the rest won't do. Fifteen four and the rest won't score.'

He hated royalty and vicars. If any royalty came on the TV, he would start abusing them as parasites. And if any kind of churchman knocked on the door, he would really argue with them. As a kid, I didn't really understand the vehemence of his views, but I can see now that he was quite bitter about the Establishment, and the way they treated the working man. This wasn't a theoretical position – he felt bitter about the way he'd been treated, and with good reason. The First World War, especially, permanently altered his view of life – he saw in the army the same class-divisions perpetuated. The duty of the working-class man was to die, or if they survived, come home and work hard and not complain, so that the rich could enjoy life.

About that generation, who were born in the Victorian Age, there was a feeling of great deprivation. They were barely educated, left school at eleven or that sort of age, to get jobs in factories or on farms. Life was harsh for them. They grew up expecting to be deprived – it was in their blood. If they were sick, they paid to see a doctor, or if they had no money, they went without. They had one day off at Christmas, and then went straight through to Easter without a break. They worked six days a week – and often compulsory overtime as well. When they retired they were exhausted, worn out.

When I hear people speaking of the warmth and the culture of working-class people, and becoming very romantic about it all, I always take it with a pinch of salt, because so often they leave out this sense of starvation – emotional, cultural, spiritual. It's like the old plantation-owners talking of their happy blacks singing as they pick the cotton – and living on pittance wages, in miserable shacks, with no education or health provisions.

There is a kind of sentimentality that creeps in when people describe working-class culture, and a kind of snobbishness about present day conditions – too bad that the workers now want videos and microwaves, when in the old days they sat round the piano and sang! This is all nonsense, a complete romanticizing of the past. It's like the argument that life down the coal-mines was comradely and full of male warmth. Yes it was, but it was also bloody dangerous! There was plenty of comradeship in the trenches as well, while you were dodging the bullets.

When we come to the next generation, we find men out of work in the Great Depression, and then – more war. My father's brother, at the age of fourteen, was put on a bus to London with several pounds in his pocket, and told to find a job and get on with his life, as there was no hope of work in Lancashire. So he did just that, and eventually worked at Rolls Royce. But think of that fourteen-year-old boy's fears, sitting on the bus to London, leaving behind him everything he knew.

My own father started work at fourteen and worked in the same factory for forty years, which was closed down by a take-over company, which then started to build factories in Korea for the cheap labour. But since he stopped work, he has been fitter, happier, healthier than he ever was.

But about this generation there is still the feeling of deprivation. They knew decades of unemployment, great poverty, war. For them, life was tough, and you buckled down and got on with it. There were times when my parents literally didn't have enough money for the next meal, or had a shilling left to their name. It's something that can never be eradicated from their minds and bodies.

Then there is my generation – what to make of them? They are more puzzling, since they began to escape from the old straitjackets to an extent. One of my cousins ended up as a film producer, another worked as a physicist at British Nuclear Fuels.

But were we different? We grew up in the sixties, we seemed to escape all that deprivation, the unemployment, the grinding poverty. We got into pop music, we enjoyed ourselves, we had money to burn apparently. 'You never had it so good,' Macmillan said in 1959. But I don't think the deprivation altered really. At the emotional level, it was still the same.

I come from a line of working men, who made things with their hands. My father made textile looms; my uncle, Rolls Royce engines; my grandfathers, cotton and chemical products. My parents wanted me to get out of that world, and for better and worse, I did. But I want to honour these men, and to celebrate them, and their terrible struggles. They were sent to be butchered in wars, they were killed, taken prisoner, then they came home and worked in factories and cotton-mills, and then they retired and died.

When I think of the notion of patriarchal society, which I believe is a powerful and correct concept, I get angry at the way some have portrayed it simply as a system designed by men to exploit women. It does exploit women, but it also exploits men. It grinds them into the dust; it kills them; it dehumanizes them. It reduces their life to work, and exhaustion, and the factory hooter.

I don't believe patriarchy was invented by men like my grandfathers or my father or my uncle, in order to subjugate women.

I also get angry when feminists argue that men like the Yorkshire Ripper are simply being men – as Joan Smith says, 'Peter Sutcliffe was always different, but not by a wide margin.'[7] I think there is a wide margin between Peter Sutcliffe and the men in my family, and my male friends – a very wide margin.

I have so many stories about men. If I began to recall male friends that I've had, this book would swell to ten books. Such a variety – Frank, who couldn't face university, hit the bottle, and went back to the North and lived over a fish and chip shop. Dave, who became a journalist and was shot dead at a crossroads in San Salvador, trying to get that final story for his paper. He got good obituaries. Jim, who came down from Glasgow, and became a psychiatric social worker, and counsels the suicidal. Shekhar, whose first sexual experience was being seduced by a temple prostitute in India. George, who I last heard had been imprisoned in Ghana for taking part in a coup-attempt. Alan, who I betrayed, and who never forgave me.

Norman, who came home from the Second World War, embittered like my grandfather, and swore he would never be anybody's lackey again. And he never was. Jon, my old mate the carpenter, who now sells computer equipment – he's moved with the times! My great friend Schmuel, who went back to Israel. I used to see his name in scholarly journals, but I'm sure I'll never see him again – what a strange feeling it is to say that.

Adam, my own son, who loves guns and mock-fights with his friends, but who is one of the sweetest tempered and kindest boys I've ever met.

It's almost overwhelming to bring up this gallery of men I have known. How much I love them! How much I mourn the ones who have died, who I will never see again. And feel sad about the ones who are alive, but who I will probably never see again. How much I enjoy the ones who are still my friends.

How rich it is to be a man, how difficult, how confusing. It would be impossible to generalize about all these men, to draw sociological or psychological conclusions. Even if it were possible, it would be somehow sacrilegious. It would dishonour them.

11 Conclusions

The issues in this book can be divided into two groups – certain concrete ideas about gender, and some wider themes to do with how gender can be studied.

There are three concrete issues that have been central to the book: first, that patriarchal masculinity damages men. This is not an original idea at all, but I think it is often sidelined in books on gender, which have been generally, and understandably enough, concerned with the deleterious effects of gender inequality on women. I am not therefore saying 'men suffer as much as women' – it is pretty clear that women have suffered the double oppression that Marxism has talked about.

But the effects of patriarchal gender on men are not inconsiderable. The split between rationality and emotion that exists in Western culture tends to propel men into the role of thinker and doer, rather than experiencer of feelings. This tends to make them bad at relating to people, and leaves them rather isolated and cerebral.

Men are also trained as the shock-troops of patriarchy, that is, trained to practise violence against women, other men, and any 'enemies within', in Margaret Thatcher's memorable phrase. This involves the considerable brutalization and dehumanization of men. A further consequence is that men themselves receive an enormous amount of violence, in the form of killings, suicides, muggings, and so on. War in particular shows the masochistic quality to masculinity: was ever a more chilling phrase spoken than this – *dulce et decorum est pro patria mori*?

I have commented on the great fragility of the masculine gender: it does not seem to be a comfortable identity for many men. To say it is 'unnatural' begs the question as to what is natural: let me say that there is a forced quality about some types of masculinity that suggests a considerable inner conflict – the masculine gender is partly a defence against feminine identity.

This book shows that in becoming accomplices and agents of the patriarchal oppression of women, men are themselves mutilated psychologically. Thus the militant forms of masculinity represent a considerable self-abuse and self-destruction by men. As I have said before – but I repeat it because I think it is a crucial idea that connects the social and psychological analysis of masculinities – in hating women the male hates himself.

The second idea that I have explored is the notion that female power is palpable and potent in certain areas of life and that men are in awe of it. This tends to go unexplored in gender studies except as an aside; however, in psychotherapy and anthropology, there has been plenty of empirical research to back it up. Psychologically we can connect the idea of women's power with several things: first, the importance of mothering in early childhood in our culture; secondly, the greater emotional awareness that women seem to show; thirdly, female sexuality and reproductive ability are perceived by many men as enviable and frightening. Fourthly, and probably most importantly, women remind men of their own internal feminine identity, which many men feel compelled to crush and punish.

In the history of psychoanalysis and psychotherapy it is now clear that the 'maternal revolution' has been a massive one – many great thinkers and analysts such as Winnicott and Melanie Klein turned their attention to the intense mother–infant bond and its effects on adult life. It marked a most significant shift away from the paternal bias of Freud's castration theory. Why did this shift happen? Has it been an attempt to blacken women as the instigators of mental illness in their children? I don't think so – ironically, we could argue that it showed a shift towards a more female psychology, away from the obsession with the penis. Phallic psychology has been replaced by the psychology of the breast.

The third core idea I have worked with is that masculinities are not innate. I have rejected an essentialist view of gender. Thus, in my view, the notion that men are basically rational if violent creatures, whereas women are gentle and caring, is false. There is now a massive amount of evidence to contradict it, and certainly post-Freudian psychotherapy does not work with such presuppositions. It seems truer to say that social systems construct, indeed embody, gender systems, and produce the 'men' and 'women' required for the perpetuation and maintenance of such societies. Gender is therefore as inviolable as society; and there are signs today that patriarchal gender is not inviolable, since patriarchal capitalism is in a serious crisis.

This brings us to the psychological and social structure of the family. Freud's great discovery was that the patriarchal family produces enormous conflict and repression in infants, and that these conflicts are unconsciously reproduced in adult life. In Western culture at the moment part of this conflict stems from the 'too much mother, not enough father' pattern that seems very common. Boys are immersed in a proto-feminine identity for the first years of their life, but then must move away from this towards a masculine identity of some kind. Thus masculinity itself – particularly the militant varieties such as machismo – is shown to be partly a defence against the feminine.

But don't boys need to become not-feminine precisely because they live in a patriarchal culture and have to be inducted into the systems of male power? This is obviously true, but I have also devoted some attention to those studies which seem to show that a less militant masculine identity is possible in a less abrasive culture. The psychological analysis of gender offers this penetrating insight: that to carry out the oppression of women demanded by patriarchy, men are compelled to castrate themselves and split themselves into fragments.

WIDER THEMES

The wider themes that have pervaded this book are to do with studying gender. It seems pretty clear that psychotherapy and feminist sociology approach gender very differently. Therapy in the main does not look at gender politically. Thus, whereas a feminist sociology analyses gender in terms of the male *political* domination of women, psychotherapy looks more dialectically at all the contradictory currents of power and domination going on between people.

Each side in this debate can be criticized for having shortcomings. Psychotherapy has traditionally been asocial, and, for example, has simply taken the family as a 'given'. This is as much a question of pragmatics as anything else, but it does reflect a conservative quality to therapy that can slide into an adaptive stance – being happy means adapting to patriarchy. Thus therapy can learn a lot from 'social construction' theory in feminism and sociology: the notion of gender as a cultural artifice liberates us from notions of unchanging male and female attributes. This accords well with those psychological studies which reveal, for example, women's latent aggression/sadism, and men's latent vulnerability.

But feminist sociology and political studies strike me as psychologically naive at times. Or perhaps 'naive' is the wrong word – 'homogeneous' is a better one. For example, descriptions of pornography as 'violence against women' are one-dimensional – it's rather like saying that a dream in which you kill your father is actually about killing your father. In fact only the dreamer knows what that dream is about. Phenomena such as rape, sexual harassment, domestic violence exemplify the oppression of women under patriarchy; but we cannot infer that the men involved feel powerful. Public power shrinks personal power. The patriarchal shock-troops become zombies, or what in German is called the *Unmensch*, the monster, the non-man.

But I have also argued that the social and psychological analyses of masculinities, which often seem opposed in methodology and subject-matter, need each other's insights as a kind of cross-fertilization.

If one were fantasizing about setting up a massive research project on gender and sexuality, it should surely be a multidisciplinary one. Certainly in the writing of this book, time and time again I have been surprised by the ways in which non-psychological studies of gender – in feminism, sociology, anthropology, Marxism, evolutionary biology – enrich the psychological perspective. The same themes seem to crop up again and again, even if they are dealt from different points of view. For example, the topic of menstruation has been analysed in very interesting ways in anthropology and biology – and their insights are highly relevant to the psychological study of menstrual taboos and envy in men. Two other topics that positively demand interdisciplinary study are incest and machismo itself.

Any critique presupposes the notion of change. I have not spent much time on this, but many of my criticisms of the masculine gender have implied that things should be changed. But how? How are men to change?

It is a truism in therapy that people don't change unless they're desperate. It strikes me that more and more people are desperate today, and our culture often has a desperate air about it. Surely it's not too optimistic to say that the feminist challenge to patriarchy will not go ignored by men, for it is in their interests too to deconstruct patriarchy – not theoretically but concretely. And the challenge to gender inequality cannot be divorced, it seems to me, from an overall challenge to all social inequalities.

The Roman gladiators used to chant to the emperor: 'We who are about to die salute thee!' Incomparable masculine gesture! – a blend of stoicism, masochism and bravado that Hemingway would have been proud of. But today perhaps we can coin new songs and sayings – we refuse to die, and we refuse to salute our executioner!

Appendix:
Films Cited

Alien (Ridley Scott, 1979)
Aliens (James Cameron, 1986)
Alien³ (David Fincher, 1992)
Angel Heart (Alan Parker, 1987)
Blade Runner (Ridley Scott, 1982)
Butch Cassidy and the Sundance Kid (George Roy Hill, 1969)
Dances with Wolves (Kevin Costner, 1990)
The Dirty Dozen (Robert Aldrich, 1967)
Dirty Harry (Don Siegel, 1971)
Fatal Attraction (Adrian Lyne, 1987)
A Fistful of Dollars (Sergio Leone, 1964)
For Whom the Bell Tolls (Sam Wood, 1943)
The Godfather (Francis Ford Coppola, 1972)
Gunfight at the OK Corral (John Sturges, 1957)
The Gunfighter (Henry King, 1950)
Hud (Martin Ritt, 1963)
JFK (Oliver Stone, 1991)
Kindergarten Cop (Ivan Reitman, 1990)
The Last of the Mohicans (Michael Mann, 1992)
Midnight Cowboy (John Schlesinger, 1969)
The Missouri Breaks (Arthur Penn, 1976)
Monte Walsh (William A. Fraker, 1970)
Nightmare on Elm Street (Wes Craven, 1984)
Nightmare on Elm Street II (Freddy's Revenge) (Jack Sholder, 1985)
Once Upon a Time in the West (Sergio Leone, 1969)
Pat Garrett and Billy the Kid (Sam Peckinpah, 1973)
Rainman (Barry Levinson, 1988)
Shane (George Stevens, 1953)
The Silence of the Lambs (Jonathan Demme, 1990)
Solaris (Andrei Tarkovsky, 1972)
Some Like it Hot (Billy Wilder, 1959)
Star Wars (George Lucas, 1977)
Sudden Impact (Clint Eastwood, 1983)
Taxi-Driver (Martin Scorsese, 1976)

The Terminator (James Cameron, 1984)
Terminator II (James Cameron, 1991)
3:10 to Yuma (Delmer Daves, 1957)
Thunderbolt and Lightfoot (Michael Cimino, 1974)
Tootsie (Sydney Pollack, 1982)
Total Recall (Paul Verhoeven, 1990)
2001: A Space Odyssey (Stanley Kubrick, 1968)
Unforgiven (Clint Eastword, 1992)

Notes

Notes to the Introduction

1. For example, Alice Jardine and Paul Smith, *Men in Feminism* (London and New York: Methuen, 1987); Joseph A. Boone and Michael Cadden, *Engendering Men: The Question of Male Feminist Criticism* (New York and London: Routledge, 1990).
2. Jeffrey Weeks, *Sexuality and its Discontents* (London and New York: Routledge, 1989), and *Against Nature* (London: Rivers Oram Press, 1991).
3. David Thomas, *Not Guilty – Men: The Case for the Defence* (London: Weidenfeld & Nicolson, 1993).
4. David D. Gilmore, *Manhood in the Making* (London and New York: Yale University Press, 1990).
5. See David Morgan, *Discovering Men* (London and New York: Routledge, 1992) pp. 44–7.
6. M. Roper and J. Tosh (eds), *Manful Assertions: Masculinities in Britain since 1800* (London and New York: Routledge, 1991).
7. R. J. Stoller, *Presentations of Gender* (New Haven and London: Yale University Press, 1985); R. J. Stoller, *Sexual Excitement* (London: Karnac, 1986).

Notes to Chapter 2: Exploring Gender

1. Simone de Beauvoir, *The Second Sex* (Harmondsworth: Penguin, 1979) p. 15.
2. D. Morgan, *Discovering Men*, p. 46.
3. Ibid., p. 2.
4. Jane Tompkins, *West of Everything: The Inner Life of Westerns* (New York: Oxford University Press, 1992) p. 42.
5. D. H. Lawrence, 'The Real Thing', in *Phoenix: The Posthumous Papers of D. H. Lawrence*, ed. E. D. McDonald (London: Heinemann, 1961) p. 200.
6. 'The Good Man', *Phoenix*, p. 752.
7. Ibid., p. 751.
8. T. S. Eliot, 'The Metaphysical Poets', in *Selected Prose*, ed. John Hayward (Penguin, London: 1953) p. 117.
9. See Susan Bordo, 'The Cartesian Masculinization of Thought', *Signs* **11**:3 (1986).
10. Jeff Hearn, *The Gender of Oppression* (Brighton: Wheatsheaf, 1987) p. 6.
11. J. Lorber and S. A. Farrell, 'Principles of Gender Construction', in Lorber and Farrell (eds), *The Social Construction of Gender* (Newbury Park: Sage, 1991) p. 9.
12. Lynne Segal, *Slow Motion: Changing Masculinities, Changing Men* (London: Virago, 1990) p. ix.
13. Lynne Segal, *Is the Future Female? Troubled Thoughts on Contemporary Feminism* (London: Virago, 1987) pp. 37 and 246.

14. Mary Midgley and Judith Hughes, *Women's Choices* (London: Weidenfeld & Nicolson, 1983) p. 219.
15. Mary Daly, *Pure Lust: Elemental Feminist Philosophy* (London: Women's Press, 1984) p. 164.
16. L. Segal, *Is the Future Female?*, p. 44.
17. Robin Morgan, *The Demon Lover: On the Sexuality of Terrorism* (London: Mandarin, 1990) p. 100.
18. Caroline Ramazanoglu, *Feminism and the Contradictions of Oppression* (London: Routledge, 1989) p. 14.
19. See Donna Haraway, *Primate Visions: Gender, Race and Nature in the World of Modern Science* (New York and London: Routledge, 1989); Chris Knight, *Blood Relations: Menstruation and the Origin of Culture* (New Haven and London: Yale University Press, 1991) pp. 129–36.
20. D. Haraway, *Primate Visions*, p. 309.
21. Jane Flax, 'Postmodernism and Gender Relations in Feminist Theory', *Signs*, **12**:4 (1987) p. 627.
22. D. Morgan, *Discovering Men*, pp. 28–9, 43, and Chapter 3.
23. Joan Smith, 'Women in Togas', *Misogynies: Reflections on Myths and Malice*, revised edition (London: Faber & Faber, 1993).
24. See R. Morgan, *The Demon Lover*.
25. See the collections by J. Lorber and S. A. Farrell, *The Social Construction of Gender*; T. Threadgold and A. Cranny-Francis (eds), *Feminine/Masculine and Representation* (Sydney: Allen Unwin, 1990).
26. R. W. Connell, *Gender and Power* (Cambridge: Polity Press, 1987) p. 61.
27. Ibid., p. 215.
28. Ibid., p. 215.
29. See J. Weeks, *Sexuality and its Discontents*, and *Against Nature*.
30. Harriet Whitehead, 'The Bow and the Burden Strap: A New Look at Institutionalized Homosexuality in Native America', in S. B. Ortner and H. Whitehead (eds), *Sexual Meanings: The Cultural Construction of Gender and Sexuality* (Cambridge University Press, 1981).
31. R. W. Connell, *Gender and Power*, pp. 278–9.
32. Sam Keen, *Fire in the Belly* (London: Piatkus, 1992); David Cohen, *Being a Man* (London: Routledge, 1990); David Jackson, *Unmasking Masculinity* (London: Unwin Hyman, 1990).
33. See Ean Begg, 'Animus: the Unmentionable Archetype', in John Matthews (ed.), *Choirs of the Gods: Revisioning Masculinity* (London: Mandala, 1991) p. 152.
34. See R. J. Stewart, *Celebrating the Male Mysteries* (Bath: Arcania, 1991); Robert Bly, 'The Horse, the Hawk and the Rider', in John Matthews (ed.), *Choirs of the Gods*; Robert Bly, *Iron John: A Book about Men* (Shaftesbury: Element, 1990).
35. C. G. Jung, *Memories, Dreams and Reflections* (London: Flamingo, 1983), Chapter 9 'Travels'.
36. John Matthews, 'Introduction: Revisioning Masculinity', in *Choirs of the Gods*, p. 12.
37. R. Bly, 'The Horse, the Hawk and the Rider', in J. Matthews (ed.), *Choirs of the Gods*, p. 28.
38. R. Bly, *Iron John*, p. ix.

39. See the essays in S. Cohan and Ina R. Hark (eds), *Screening the Male: Exploring Masculinities in the Hollywood Cinema* (London and New York: Routledge: 1993).
40. R. J. Stoller, *Sexual Excitement*, p. 167
41. See the special issue of *Anthropology*, **9**:1 and 2: *Sex and Gender in Southern Europe: Problems and Prospects*, ed. David D. Gilmore and Gretchen Gwynne (Stony Brook, NY, 1985).
42. S. Freud, *The Interpretation of Dreams (First Part)*, The Standard Edition of the Complete Psychological Works of Sigmund Freud, vol. 4, trans. James Strachey (London: Hogarth Press, 1958), Ch. 5: 'The Dream-Work'.
43. 'The Syzygy: Anima and Animus', in H. Read, M. Fordham and G. Adler (eds), *The Collected Works of C. G. Jung*, vol. 9, Part 2, *Aion*, 2nd edition (London: Routledge & Kegan Paul, 1968).
44. Alice Miller, *Banished Knowledge* (London: Virago, 1990).
45. Neville Symington, *The Analytic Experience: Lectures from the Tavistock* (London: Free Association Books, 1986), Chapter 6: 'Freud the Romantic'; H. F. Searles, *Collected Papers on Schizophrenia and Related Subjects* (London: Maresfield Library, 1986) p. 16.
46. R. W. Connell, *Gender and Power*, p. 263; see also R. E. Dobash and R. P. Dobash, *Women, Violence and Social Change* (London and New York: Routledge: 1992) Chapter 7: 'The Therapeutic Society Constructs Battered Women and Violent Men'.
47. A. Miller, *Banished Knowledge*.
48. See Juliet Mitchell, *Psychoanalysis and Feminism* (Harmondsworth: Penguin, 1975); Louise Eichenbaum and Susie Orbach, *Outside In... Inside Out: Women's Psychology: A Feminist Psychoanalytic Approach* (Harmondsworth: Penguin, 1982).

Notes to Chapter 3: Power and Powerlessness

1. J. Hearn, *The Gender of Oppression*, p. 98.
2. L. Segal, *Slow Motion*, p. 82.
3. D. H. Lawrence, *Sons and Lovers* (Harmondsworth: Penguin, 1962) p. 62.
4. Alix Pirani, *The Absent Father: Crisis and Creativity* (London: Penguin Arkana, 1989).
5. Mary Ingham, *Men: The Male Myth Exposed* (London: Century, 1985) p. 2.
6. John Tosh, 'Domesticity and Manliness in the Victorian Middle Class', in M. Roper and J. Tosh (eds), *Manful Assertions*.
7. Ibid., p. 56.
8. Ibid., pp. 66–7.
9. Stanley Brandes, 'Like Wounded Stags: Male Sexual Ideology in an Andalusian Town', in S. B. Ortner and H. Whitehead (eds), *Sexual Meanings*, p. 217; see also the special issue of *Anthropology*, **9**:1 and 2 (1985), *Sex and Gender in Southern Europe: Problems and Prospects*, ed. David D. Gilmore and Gretchen Gwynne.
10. S. Brandes, 'Like Wounded Stags', in *Sexual Meanings*, p. 218.

11. Ibid., p. 234.
12. Ibid., p. 235.
13. See, for example, the essays in S. B. Ortner and H. Whitehead, (eds), *Sexual Meanings*; D. K. Feil, *The Evolution of Highland Papua New Guinea Societies* (Cambridge University Press, 1987); D. Gilmore, *Manhood in the Making*; T. Buckley and A. Gottlieb, *Blood Magic: The Anthropology of Menstruation* (Berkeley: University of California Press, 1988).
14. D. Morgan, *Discovering Men*, Chapter 4; Jeff Hearn, *Men in the Public Eye: The Construction and Deconstruction of Public Men and Public Patriarchies* (London and New York: Routledge, 1992).
15. Francesca M. Cancian, 'The Feminization of Love', *Signs*, **11**:4 (1986).
16. See D. W. Winnicott, *Deprivation and Delinquency* (London: Tavistock, 1984); S. Hall and T. Jefferson (eds), *Resistance through Rituals: Youth Subcultures in Post-war Britain* (London: Hutchinson, 1976).
17. D. W. Winnicott, 'The Anti-social Tendency', in *Deprivation and Delinquency*, p. 124.
18. B. A. Te Paske, *Rape and Ritual: A Psychological Study* (Toronto: Inner City Books, 1982) Chapters 4 and 5; R. E. Dobash and R. P. Dobash, *Women, Violence and Social Change*, p. 245; L. Segal, *Slow Motion*, pp. 246–7 and 252.
19. Michael Roper, 'Yesterday's Model: Product Fetishism and the British Company Man, 1945–85', in M. Roper and J. Tosh, *Manful Assertions*; also Mary Ingham, *Men*, Chapter 1: 'A Man's World'.
20. D. Gilmore, *Manhood in the Making*, pp. 26–9; D. K. Feil, *The Evolution of Highland Papua New Guinea Societies*, p. 189; Karen Horney, 'The Dread of Women', *Feminine Psychology* (New York: W. W. Norton, 1973).
21. D. Haraway, *Primate Visions*, Chapter 14.
22. Kosho Uchiyama Roshi, *Approach to Zen* (San Francisco: Japan Publications, 1973) p. 101.
23. See J. Hearn, *Men in the Public Eye*.
24. D. Morgan, *Discovering Men*, p. 111.
25. Nadine Miller, 'Letter to Her Psychiatrist'. in *The Radical Therapist*, ed. Radical Therapist Rough Times Collective (Harmondsworth: Penguin, 1974) pp. 125–6.
26. R. J. Stoller, 'The Development of Masculinity', in *Presentations of Gender*, p. 182.
27. Jane Flax, 'The Conflict Between Nurturance and Autonomy in Mother–Daughter Relationships and within Feminism', in E. Howell and M. Bayes (eds), *Women and Mental Health* (New York: Basic Books, 1981).
28. J. Hearn, *Men in the Public Eye*, p. 3.
29. Ibid., p. 80.
30. Ibid., pp. 1 and 6.
31. Ibid., p. 6.
32. Andrea Dworkin, *Pornography: Men Possessing Women* (London: Women's Press, 1990).
33. C. G. Jung, 'The Relations Between the Ego and the Unconscious', in *The Collected Works*, volume 7, (ed.) Herbert Read, Michael Fordham and Gerhard Adler (London: Routledge & Kegan Paul, 1977) pp. 187–9.
34. J. Tompkins, *West of Everything: The Inner Life of Westerns*, p. 215.

35. Ibid., p. 44.
36. See the comments in Edward Buscombe, *The BFI Companion to the Western* (London: André Deutsch, 1988) pp. 50–2; Kim Newman, *Wild West Movies* (London: Bloomsbury, 1990) Chapter 10.
37. See Richard Combs, 'Shadowing the Hero', *Sight and Sound*, 2:6 (October, 1992).
38. See Marina Warner, *Alone of All Her Sex: The Myth and Cult of the Virgin Mary* (London: Picador, 1985).
39. All names of clients have been changed.
40. R. J. Stoller, *Sexual Excitement*, p. xiii.
41. Ibid., p. 116.
42. Karen Horney, 'The Distrust Between the Sexes', *Feminine Psychology*, p. 113; see also T. Buckley and A. Gottlieb, *Blood Magic: The Anthropology of Menstruation*; Chris Knight, *Blood Relations: Menstruation and the Origin of Culture*; P. Shuttle and P. Redgrove, *The Wise Wound: Menstruation and Everywoman* (London: Gollancz, 1978).
43. Jacqueline Rose, 'Femininity and its Discontents', in *Sexuality: A Reader*, ed. Feminist Review (London: Virago, 1987) p. 184.
44. R. W. Connell, *Gender and Power*, p. 183.
45. See Salvatore Cucchiari, 'The Gender Revolution and the Transition from the Bisexual Horde to Patrilocal Band: The Origins of Gender Hierarchy', in S. B. Ortner and H. Whitehead, *Sexual Meanings*, pp. 63–6.
46. R. W. Connell, *Gender and Power*, pp. 265–70.
47. Ibid., Chapter 1.
48. J. Rose, 'Femininity and its Discontents', p. 184.

Notes to Chapter 4: Gender and Patriarchy

1. Margot Waddell, 'Gender Identity – 50 Years on from Freud', *British Journal of Psychotherapy*, 5: 3 (1989) p. 383.
2. Michèle Barrett, *Women's Oppression Today: Problems in Marxist Feminist Analysis* (London: Verso, 1980) pp. 12–13; Caroline Ramazanoglu, *Feminism and the Contradictions of Oppression*, p. 35.
3. F. Engels, *The Origin of the Family, Private Property and the State* [1884] (Harmondsworth: Penguin, 1986) p. 217.
4. Michèle Barrett, 'Introduction' to Penguin edition of Engels, *The Origin of the Family*.
5. D. Haraway, *Primate Visions*.
6. Ibid., p. 336.
7. See, for example, M. Esther Harding, *Women's Mysteries Ancient and Modern* (London: Rider, 1982); E. C. Whitmont, *Return of the Goddess* (London: Penguin Arkana, 1987); Alix Pirani (ed.), *The Absent Mother* (London: Mandala, 1991); Erich Neumann, *The Origins and History of Consciousness* (New York: Harper & Row, 1962).
8. E. C. Whitmont, *Return of the Goddess*, Chapter 4: 'The Magical Phase'; also Salvatore Cucchiari, 'The Gender Revolution and the Transition from the

Bisexual Horde to Patrilocal Band: The Origins of Gender Hierarchy', in S. B. Ortner and H. Whitehead, *Sexual Meanings*.

9. See T. Buckley and A. Gottlieb, *Blood Magic*; C. Knight, *Blood Relations: Menstruation and the Origin of Culture*; P. Shuttle and P. Redgrove, *The Wise Wound*.

10. C. Knight, *Blood Relations*, Chapter 11.

11. Ibid., pp. 428–35; also Ian Hogbin, *The Island of Menstruating Men: Religion in Wogeo, New Guinea* (Scranton: Chandler, 1970).

12. F. Engels, *The Origin of the Family*, p. 85.

13. Ibid., p. 85.

14. See Jane F. Collier and Michelle Z. Rosaldo, 'Politics and Gender in Simple Societies', in Sherry B. Ortner and Harriet Whitehead, *Sexual Meanings*; also Salvatore Cucchiari, see note 8; Harriet Whitehead 'The Bow and the Burden Strap: A New Look at Institutionalized Homosexuality in Native America', in Ortner and Whitehead, p. 111.

15. F. Engels, *The Origin of the Family*, p. 96.

16. Alexandra Kollontai, 'Theses on Communist Morality in the Sphere of Marital Relations', *Selected Writings*, ed. Alix Holt (London: Allison & Busby, 1977) p. 225.

17. Ibid., p. 259.

18. Michèle Barrett, 'Introduction', p. 14; V. Mazumdar and K. Sharma, 'Sexual Division of Labour and the Subordination of Women: A Reappraisal from India', in *Persistent Inequalities: Women and World Development*, ed. I. Tinker (New York: Oxford University Press, 1990); D. Haraway, *Primate Visions*, pp. 331–48; Amaury de Riencourt, *Woman and Power in History* (Bath: Honeyglen, 1983) p. 22.

19. J. Hearn, *The Gender of Oppression*, pp. 62 and 65.

20. R. Morgan, *The Demon Lover*, p. 177.

21. R. W. Connell, *Gender and Power* p. 103.

22. F. Engels, *The Origin of the Family* p. 87.

23. 'Women's Suffrage and Class Struggle', in *Selected Political Writings of Rosa Luxemburg*, ed. Dick Howard (New York: Monthly Review Press, 1971) p. 220.

24. A. Dworkin, *Pornography*, p. 13.

25. J. Hearn, *The Gender of Oppression*, p. 165.

26. R. Morgan, *The Demon Lover*, p. 347.

27. A. Dworkin, *Pornography*, p. 68.

28. L. Segal, *Is the Future Female?*, pp. 232–3.

29. See C. Ramazanoglu, *Feminism and the Contradictions of Oppression*, for a full discussion of divisions among women.

30. *The Story of David Gareth Jones by His Father*, (London: New Park, 1985) p. 56.

31. D. Gilmore, *Manhood in the Making*, p. 224.

32. Ibid., p. 120.

33. Ibid., Chapter 9.

34. Ibid., p. 205.

35. Judith Buber Agassi, 'Theories of Gender Equality: Lessons from the Israeli Kibbutz', in J. Lorber and S. A. Farrell (eds), *The Social Construction of Gender*, p. 315; Amaury de Riencourt, *Woman and Power in History*, pp. 44–5;

Simi Afonja, 'Changing Patterns of Gender Stratification in West Africa', in *Persistent Inequalities: Women and World Development*, ed. I. Tinker.

36. D. K. Feil, *The Evolution of Highland Papua New Guinea Societies*, p. 231.
37. See the special issue of *Anthropology*, **9**: 1 and 2 (1985).
38. D. Gilmore, *Manhood in the Making*, p. 204.
39. Thomas Gregor, 'Uneasy Peace: Intertribal Relations in Brazil's Upper Xingu', in J. Haas (ed.), *The Anthropology of War* (Cambridge University Press, 1990); see also Clayton Robarchek, 'Motivation and Material Causes: On the Explanation of Conflict and War' in the same text.
40. D. Gilmore, *Manhood in the Making*, p. 121.
41. L. Segal, *Is the Future Female?* p. 197.
42. 'The Charge of the Light Brigade', *Tennyson's Poems* (London: Collins, n.d.) p. 252.
43. Peter M. Lewis, 'Mummy, Matron and the Maids', in M. Roper and J. Tosh (eds), *Manful Assertions*, pp. 185–6.
44. D. Gilmore, *Manhood in the Making*, Chapter 6.
45. See the essays in Erich Fromm, *The Crisis of Psychoanalysis* (Harmondsworth: Penguin, 1973).
46. Karl Marx, 'Preface to *A Contribution to the Critique of Political Economy*', in *Karl Marx: Early Writings* (Harmondsworth: Penguin, 1975) p. 425.
47. S. Freud, *An Outline of Psycho-analysis*, ed. J. Strachey (London: Hogarth Press, 1973) p. 37.
48. K. Marx, 'Letters from the *Franco-German Yearbooks*', *Early Writings*, p. 209.
49. K. Marx, 'Economic and Philosophical Manuscripts', *Early Writings*, p. 347.

Notes to Chapter 5: The First Woman

1. S. Freud, 'The Tendency to Debasement in Love', *On Sexuality*, Pelican Freud Library, vol. 7 (Harmondsworth: Penguin, 1977) p. 251.
2. S. Freud, *An Outline of Psycho-Analysis*, p. 11; 'Three Essays on the Theory of Sexuality', pp. 141–4; 'The Infantile Genital Organization', p. 308; 'Some Psychical Consequences of the Anatomical Distinction between the Sexes', pp. 334–40, all in *On Sexuality*.
3. J. Mitchell, *Psychoanalysis and Feminism*, p. xv.
4. For further discussion of feminism and psychoanalysis, see Elizabeth Wilson, 'Psychoanalysis: Psychic Law and Order?', and Jacqueline Rose, 'Femininity and its Discontents', in *Sexuality: A Reader*, ed. Feminist Review.
5. Dorothy Dinnerstein, *The Rocking of the Cradle and the Ruling of the World* (London: Souvenir Press, 1976) p. 34.
6. D. W. Winnicott, 'The Foundation of Mental Health', *Deprivation and Delinquency*, p. 169.
7. Ibid., p. 169.
8. Many books deal with these issues. For a historical account see Harry Guntrip, *Psychoanalytic Theory, Therapy and the Self* (London: Maresfield Library, 1977); for a more complex theoretical exegesis see J. R. Greenberg

and S. A. Mitchell, *Object Relations in Psychoanalytic Theory* (Cambridge, Mass.: Harvard University Press, 1983).

9. Margaret Little, *Transference Neurosis and Transference Psychosis: Toward Basic Unity* (London: Free Association Books, 1986) Chapter 6.

10. Margaret Little in fact distinguishes 'undifferentiatedness' from symbiosis. I have conflated them for the purposes of my argument.

11. There is no better introduction to these topics than Freud: S. Freud, *Two Short Accounts of Psycho-Analysis* (Harmondsworth: Penguin, 1963); *An Outline of Psycho-Analysis*; *On Sexuality*.

12. Andrew Samuels, 'A Relation called Father. Part 2: The Father and his Children', *British Journal of Psychotherapy*, **5**: 1 (1988) p. 69.

13. S. Freud, 'Five Lectures on Psycho-Analysis', in *Two Short Accounts of Psycho-Analysis*, p. 77.

14. Richard Green, *The 'Sissy Boy Syndrome' and the Development of Homosexuality* (New Haven and London: Yale University Press, 1987) p. 66.

15. D. K. Feil, *The Evolution of Highland Papua New Guinea Societies*, p. 177.

16. Amaury de Riencourt, *Woman and Power in History*, p. 22.

17. D. Gilmore, *Manhood in the Making*, p. 155, quoted from Ian Buruma, *Behind the Mask: Transvestites, Gangsters, Drifters, and Other Japanese Cultural Heroes* (New York: Pantheon, 1984).

18. See Harriet Whitehead, 'The Bow and the Burden Strap', in S. B. Ortner and H. Whitehead (eds), *Sexual Meanings*.

19. R. J. Stoller, *Presentations of Gender*, Chapters 3, 4 and 11; also R. J. Stoller, *Perversion: The Erotic Form of Hatred* (London: Quartet, 1977) pp. 25–6.

20. R. J. Stoller, *Presentations of Gender*, pp. 57–61.

21. Melanie Klein, 'Inhibitions and Difficulties at Puberty', *Love, Guilt and Reparation*, (London: Virago, 1988) p. 56.

22. R. J. Stoller, *Presentations of Gender*, p. 192.

23. H. F. Searles, 'The Evolution of the Mother Transference in Psychotherapy with the Schizophrenic Patient', *Collected Papers on Schizophrenia and Related Subjects*, p. 349.

24. Janet L. Jacobs, 'Reassessing Mother Blame in Incest', *Signs*, **15**:3 (1990) p. 508.

25. Sherry B. Ortner, 'Gender and Sexuality in Hierarchical Societies: The Case of Polynesia and Some Comparative Implications', in S. B. Ortner and H. Whitehead (eds), *Sexual Meanings*, p. 392.

26. R. Bly, *Iron John*, p. 19.

27. R. J. Stoller, *Presentations of Gender*, p. 195.

28. Edward Tejirian, *Sexuality and the Devil* (New York: Routledge, 1990) p. 129.

29. R. Bly, *Iron John*, pp. 15 and 80.

30. R. J. Stoller, *Presentations of Gender*, p. 14.

31. Elizabeth Grosz, *Jacques Lacan* (London: Routledge, 1990) p. 116.

32. In S. Freud, *On Sexuality*.

33. S. Freud, 'Female Sexuality', *On Sexuality*, p. 374.

34. Maria Torok, 'The Significance of Penis Envy in Women', in Janine Chasseguet-Smirgel (ed.), *Female Sexuality: New Psychoanalytic Views* (London: Maresfield Library, 1988); see also Paula Bennett, 'Critical Clitoridectomy: Female Sexual Imagery and Feminist Psychoanalytic Theory', *Signs* **18**:2 (1993).

35. For a feminist analysis of the mother–daughter relationship, see L. Eichenbaum and S. Orbach, *Outside In ... Inside Out*, Chapter 2: 'Women's Ego Development'.
36. K. Horney, 'The Dread of Woman', *Feminine Psychology*.
37. K. Horney, 'The Flight from Womanhood', *Feminine Psychology*, p. 60; see also Dee Garrison, 'Karen Horney and Feminism', *Signs*, 6:4 (1981).
38. M. Klein, 'Weaning', *Love, Guilt and Reparation*, p. 291.
39. Harold Kelman, 'Introduction' to Horney, *Feminine Psychology*, p. 21.
40. D. K. Feil, *The Evolution of Highland Papua New Guinea Societies*, p. 189.
41. Harriet E. Lerner, 'Early Origins of Envy and Devaluation of Women: Implications for Sex-Role Stereotypes', in *Women and Mental Health*, ed. E. Howell and M. Bayes.
42. M. Klein, 'The Psychotherapy of the Psychoses', *Love, Guilt and Reparation*, p. 233.
43. Andrew Samuels, 'A Relation called Father. Part 2: The Father and his Children', *British Journal of Psychotherapy* 5:1 (1988).
44. L. Segal, *Is the Future Female?*, pp. 134–42; L. Segal, *Slow Motion*, pp. 73–82; L. Eichenbaum and S. Orbach, *Outside In ... Inside Out*, pp. 110–13; C. Ramazanoglu, *Feminism and the Contradictions of Oppression*, pp. 69–75.
45. Erich Fromm, 'The Oedipus Complex: Comments on the Case of Little Hans', *The Crisis of Psychoanalysis*. Freud's original study is 'Analysis of a Phobia in a Five-Year-Old Boy', *The Standard Edition of the Complete Psychological Works of Sigmund Freud*, vol. 10, ed. J. Strachey (London: Hogarth, 1955).
46. D. Dinnerstein, *The Rocking of the Cradle and the Ruling of the World*, pp. 161 and 176.
47. L. Segal, *Slow Motion*, p. 81.
48. One of the terms used in the Little Hans case, see note 45.
49. K. Horney, 'The Dread of Women', *Feminine Psychology*.
50. A phrase borrowed from Barbara Hannah, *Striving Towards Wholeness*, 2nd edition (Boston, Mass.: Sigo Press, 1988).
51. See the essays in J. Chasseguet-Smirgel (ed.), *Female Sexuality: New Psychoanalytic Views*.

Notes to Chapter 6: The Fragile Male

1. See D. Morgan, *Discovering Men*, pp. 190–9 for a fuller discussion of power and difference.
2. R. Green, *The 'Sissy Boy Syndrome' and the Development of Homosexuality*, Chapter 7.
3. Michael Roper, 'Yesterday's Model: Product Fetishism and the British Company Man, 1945–85', in M. Roper and J. Tosh (eds) *Manful Assertions*, p. 195.
4. R. J. Stoller, *Presentations of Gender*, p. 183.
5. D. Gilmore, *Manhood in the Making*, p. 17.
6. Ibid., p. 106.
7. Ibid., pp. 206–8.
8. Ernest Hemingway, *Death in the Afternoon* (Harmondsworth: Penguin, 1966) p. 23.

9. Ernest Hemingway, *The Garden of Eden* (London: Grafton, 1988) p. 25.
10. Kenneth S. Lynn, *Hemingway* (London: Sphere, 1989) p. 110.
11. Ibid., p. 322.
12. Bernice Kert, *The Hemingway Women* (London: W. W. Norton, 1986) p. 231.
13. Letter to Maxwell Perkins, 26 July 1933, in Carlos Baker (ed.), *Ernest Hemingway: Selected Letters 1917–1961* (London: Panther, 1985) pp. 395–6.
14. Male masochism in film is described in Barbara Creed, 'Dark Desires: Male Masochism in the Horror Film', in S. Cohan and I. R. Hark, *Screening the Male: Exploring Masculinities in the Hollywood Cinema.*
15. Mikal Gilmore, 'Family Album', *The Family* (Harmondsworth: Granta, No. 14, 1991).
16. M. Pickering and K. Robins, 'The Making of a Working Class Writer: An Interview with Sid Chaplin', in J. Hawthorn (ed.), *The British Working Class Novel in the Twentieth Century* (London: Edward Arnold, 1984) p. 143.
17. Peter Lewis, 'Mummy, Matron and the Maids', in M. Roper and J. Tosh (eds), *Manful Assertions*, p. 168.
18. Ibid., p. 177.
19. Jane Austen, *Emma* (Harmondsworth: Penguin, 1984) p. 232.
20. Emily Brontë, *Wuthering Heights* (London: Thomas Nelson, n.d.) p. 80.
21. See Camille Paglia, *Sexual Personae: Art and Decadence from Nefertiti to Emily Dickinson* (Harmondsworth: Penguin, 1991) Chapter 17: 'Romantic Shadows: Emily Brontë'.
22. S. Freud, 'Some Psychical Consequences of the Anatomical Distinctions between the Sexes', *On Sexuality*, p. 341.
23. H. Guntrip, *Psychoanalytic Theory, Therapy and the Self.*
24. R. J. Stoller, *Sexual Excitement*, pp. 21 and 158.
25. S. Freud, *An Outline of Psycho-Analysis*, p. 45.
26. Rob Weatherill, 'The Psychical Realities of Modern Culture', *British Journal of Psychotherapy*, 7:3 (1991) p. 273.
27. Juliet Mitchell, 'The Question of Femininity and the Theory of Psychoanalysis', in G. Kohon (ed.), *The British School of Psychoanalysis: The Independent Tradition* (London: Free Association Books, 1986) p. 394.

Notes to Chapter 7: Male Autism

1. John Dean, *Blind Ambition* (London: Star Book, 1977) p. 31.
2. Ibid., p. 98.
3. W. B. Yeats, 'The Second Coming', *Selected Poetry*, ed. A. Norman Jeffares (London: Macmillan, 1962) p. 100.
4. Jean-Paul Sartre, *Being and Nothingness* (London: Methuen, 1974) p. 59.
5. Ibid., p. 59.
6. H. Guntrip, *Psychoanalytic Theory, Therapy and the Self*, p. 148.
7. The factual detail that follows is taken from Brian Masters, *Killing for Company* (London: Hodder & Stoughton, 1991).
8. Ibid., p. 119.
9. Ibid., p. 151

10. Ibid., p. 130.
11. Ibid., p. 238.
12. Ibid., p. 243.
13. Ibid., p. 256.
14. Ibid., p. 189.
15. H. Guntrip, *Psychoanalytic Theory, Therapy and the Self*, p. 93.
16. J. Weeks, *Sexuality and its Discontents*, p. 130.
17. Elizabeth Cowie, 'Pornography and Fantasy: Psychoanalytic Perspectives', in L. Segal and M. McIntosh (eds), *Sex Exposed: Sexuality and the Pornography Debate* (London: Virago, 1992), p. 136.
18. Lynne Segal, 'Sweet Sorrows, Painful Pleasures', in *Sex Exposed*, p. 81.
19. H. Guntrip, *Psychoanalytic Theory, Therapy and the Self*, p. 120.
20. J. R. Greenberg and S. A. Mitchell (eds), *Object Relations in Psychoanalytic Theory*, p. 3.
21. L. Segal, *Slow Motion*, p. 80.
22. J. R. Greenberg and S. A. Mitchell (eds), *Object Relations in Psychoanalytic Theory*, p. 405.
23. Karen V. Hansen, ' "Helped Put in a Quilt": Men's Work and Male Intimacy in Nineteenth-Century New England', in J. Lorber and S. A. Farrell (eds), *The Social Construction of Gender*.
24. Ibid., pp. 99–101.

Notes to Chapter 8: Rippers, Muggers, Soldiers

1. Joan Smith, 'There's Only One Yorkshire Ripper', in *Misogynies*, p. 204.
2. Nicole Ward Jouve, *'The Street Cleaner': The Yorkshire Ripper Case on Trial* (London: Marion Boyars, 1988) p. 35. Much of the following detail is taken from this book, from Joan Smith, 'There's Only One Yorkshire Ripper' in *Misogynies*, and from Gordon Burn, *'Somebody's Husband, Somebody's Son': The Story of Peter Sutcliffe* (London: Heinemann, 1984).
3. N. W. Jouve, *'The Street-Cleaner'*, p. 144.
4. Ibid., p. 66.
5. Ibid., pp. 74–8.
6. J. Smith, 'There's Only One Yorkshire Ripper', in *Misogynies*, p. 193.
7. Marie Bonaparte, *Female Sexuality* (New York: Grove Press, 1965), quoted in Kate Millett, *Sexual Politics* (London: Abacus, 1972) p. 204.
8. M. Klein, 'Criminal Tendencies in Normal Children', *Love, Guilt and Reparation*, p. 170.
9. B. A. Te Paske, *Rape and Ritual*, p. 120.
10. Ibid., p. 116.
11. Diana Birkett, 'Psychoanalysis and War', *British Journal of Psychotherapy*, **8**:3 (1992) pp. 300–7; Roger Horrocks, 'More about War', Correspondence, *British Journal of Psychotherapy*, **9**:1 (1992) pp. 113–15.
12. C. G. Jung, 'Diagnosing the Dictators', in W. McGuire and W. F. C. Hull (eds), *C. G. Jung Speaking* (London: Picador, 1980) p. 126.
13. N. W. Jouve, *'The Street Cleaner'*, p. 106.

14. Ibid., p. 106.
15. Ibid., p. 121.
16. E. Fromm, 'The Oedipus Complex: Comments on the Case of Little Hans', *The Crisis of Psychoanalysis*, pp. 102–3.
17. N. W. Jouve, *'The Street Cleaner'*, p. 137.
18. Ibid., p. 109.
19. M. Klein, 'The Oedipus Complex in the Light of Early Anxieties', *Love, Guilt and Reparation*, p. 408.
20. N. W. Jouve, *'The Street Cleaner'*, p. 143.
21. M. Klein, 'The Oedipus Complex in the Light of Early Anxieties', *Love, Guilt and Reparation*, p. 417.
22. Valerie Solanas, *SCUM Manifesto* (London: Phoenix, 1991) p. 28.
23. L. Segal, *Slow Motion*, pp. 262–3.
24. *Guardian*, 9 February 1993, p. 8.
25. L. Segal, *Is the Future Female?*, p. 59.
26. Peter Lehman, ' "Don't Blame This on a Girl": Female rape-revenge films', in S. Cohan and I. R. Hark (eds), *Screening the Male: Exploring Masculinities in the Hollywood Cinema.*
27. See Amy Taubin, 'Invading Bodies: *Alien³* and the Trilogy', *Sight and Sound*, 2:3 (July 1992).
28. R. E. Dobash and R. P. Dobash, *Women, Violence and Social Change*, pp. 9–10.
29. Pat Mayhew, David Elliott and Lizanne Dowds, *The 1988 British Crime Survey* (London: HMSO, 1989) p. 77; N. A. Weiner amd M. E. Wolfgang, 'The Extent and Character of Violent Crime in America, 1969–1982', in Lynn A. Curtis (ed.), *American Violence and Public Policy* (New Haven and London: Yale University Press, 1985) p. 21.
30. T. Jones, B. MacLean and J. Young, *The Islington Crime Survey* (Aldershot: Gower, 1986) pp. 60 and 65.
31. Ibid., p. 211.
32. Ibid., p. 19.
33. R. Morgan, *The Demon Lover*, p. 152.
34. *Guardian*, 11 February 1993, p. 8.
35. C. G. Jung, 'The Post-War Psychic Problems of the Germans', in *C. G. Jung Speaking*, p. 157.
36. Andrea Dworkin, *Right-wing Women* (London: Women's Press, 1988) p. 87.
37. Lynn S. Chancer, 'New Bedford Massachusetts, March 6 1983–March 22 1984: The "Before and After" of a Group Rape', in J. Lorber and S. A. Farrell (eds), *The Social Construction of Gender*, p. 289.
38. B. A. Te Paske, *Rape and Ritual*, p. 126.
39. Ibid., p. 76.
40. David Lisak, 'Sexual Aggression, Masculinity and Fathers', *Signs*, 16:2 (1991) p. 248.
41. Segal, *Slow Motion*, p. 186; N. A. Weiner and M. E. Wolfgang, 'The Extent and Character of Violent Crime in America, 1969–1982', in L. A. Curtis (ed.), *American Violence and Public Policy*, p. 28.
42. J. Smith, 'Crawling from the Wreckage', in *Misogynies*, p. 155.
43. Brian Keenan, *An Evil Cradling* (London: Hutchinson, 1992) p. 208.
44. V. I. Lenin, *State and Revolution* (Peking: Foreign Languages Press, 1965) p. 10.

45. I. M. Lewis, *Social Anthropology in Perspective* (Cambridge University Press, 1985) p. 321.
46. Robert L. Carneiro, 'Chiefdom-level Warfare as Exemplified in Fiji and the Cauca Valley', in J. Haas (ed.), *The Anthropology of War*, p. 190.
47. See the essays in J. Haas.
48. A paraphrase of K. Marx, 'Preface to *A Contribution to the Critique of Political Economy*', in *Early Writings*, p. 425: 'It is not the consciousness of men that determines their existence.'

Notes to Chapter 9: Male Images and Stereotypes

1. Sara David, 'Emotional Self-defense Groups for Women', in D. E. Smith and S. J. David (eds), *Women Look at Psychiatry* (Vancouver: Press Gang, 1975) p. 176.
2. See articles in *Women and Mental Health*, ed. Elizabeth Howell and Marjorie Bayes (New Nork: Basic Books, 1981); M. M. Weissman and G. L. Klerman, 'Sex Differences and the Epidemiology of Depression'; W. R. Cusky, L. H. Berger and J. Densen-Gerber, 'Issues in the Treatment of Female Addiction: A Review and Critique of the Literature'; Judy Fraser, 'The Female Alcoholic'.
3. See Steve Neale, 'Masculinity as Spectacle: Reflections on Men and Mainstream Cinema', in S. Cohan and I. R. Hark, *Screening the Male*.
4. See Susan Jeffords, 'Can Masculinity be Terminated?', in S. Cohan and I. R. Hark, *Screening the Male*; Chris Holmlund 'Masculinity as Multiple Masquerade: The "Mature" Stallone and the Stallone Clone' in the above.
5. J. Tompkins, *West of Everything*, Chapter 1.
6. See Martin Pumphrey, 'Masculinity' in E. Buscombe, *The BFI Companion to the Western*, pp. 182–3; S. Neale, 'Masculinity as Spectacle'.
7. Evangeline Kane, *Recovering from Incest: Imagination and the Healing Process* (Boston: Sigo Press, 1989) p. 15.
8. See Graham McCann, *Rebel Males* (London: Hamish Hamilton, 1991).
9. Ibid., facing p. 118.
10. D. Rees and L. Crampton, *Book of Rock Stars* (Enfield: Guinness, 1991) p. 64.
11. J. Weeks, *Sexuality and its Discontents*, p. 47.
12. Rock Hudson and Sara Davidson, *Rock Hudson: His Story* (London: Weidenfeld & Nicolson, 1985) pp. 13 and 221.
13. R. von Krafft-Ebbing, *Aberrations of Sexual Life: The Psychopathia Sexualis* (London: Panther, 1965).
14. J. Weeks, 'Pretended Family Relationships', *Against Nature*, p. 137.
15. Alexander Lowen, *The Language of the Body* (New York: Macmillan, 1979) Chapter 14.
16. Ibid., p. 299.
17. Philip Roth, *Portnoy's Complaint* (London: Corgi, 1969) p. 19.
18. Ibid., pp. 54–5.

Notes to Chapter 10: Growing Up

1. D. H. Lawrence, *Lady Chatterley's Lover* (Penguin: Harmondsworth, 1961) p. 56.
2. Ibid., p. 258.
3. Ibid., p. 210.
4. Ibid., p. 212.
5. Ibid., p. 182.
6. Ibid., p. 219.
7. Joan Smith, 'There's Only One Yorkshire Ripper', *Misogynies*, p. 204.

Index